Please return
on or before
the last date
stamped below

'RA(
CAF

21.

'RACE', HEALTH AND SOCIAL CARE

Series editors:

Dr Waqar I.U. Ahmad, Head of Research Unit on Ethnicity and Social Policy, Department of Social and Economic Studies, University of Bradford.

Professor Charles Husband, Professor of Social Analysis and Associate Head, Research Unit on Ethnicity and Social Policy, Department of Social and Economic Studies, University of Bradford.

Minority ethnic groups now constitute over 5 per cent of the UK population. While research literature has mushroomed on the one hand in race and ethnic relations generally, and on the other in clinical and epidemiological studies of differences in conditions and use of health and social services, there remains a dearth of credible social scientific literature on the health and social care of minority ethnic communities. Social researchers have hitherto largely neglected issues of 'race' and ethnicity, while acknowledging the importance of gender, class and, more recently, (dis)ability in both the construction of and provision for health and social care needs. Consequently the available social science texts on health and social care largely reflect the experiences of the white population and have been criticized for marginalizing black people.

This series aims to provide an authoritative source of policy-relevant texts which specifically address issues of health and social care in contemporary multi-ethnic Britain. Given the rate of change in the structure of health and social care services, demography and the political context of state welfare, there is a need for a critical appraisal of the health and social care needs of, and provision for, the minority ethnic communities in Britain. By the nature of the issues we will address, this series will draw upon a wide range of professional and academic expertise, thus enabling a deliberate and necessary integration of theory and practice in these fields. The books will be interdisciplinary and written in clear, non-technical language which will appeal to a broad range of students, academics and professionals with a common interest in 'race', health and social care.

Current and forthcoming titles
Waqar I.U. Ahmad and Karl Atkin: *'Race' and Community Care*
Elizabeth N. Anionwu and Karl Atkin: *The Politics of Sickle Cell and
    Thalassaemia – 20 Years on*
Kate Gerrish, Charles Husband and Jennifer Mackenzie: *Nursing for a
    Multi-ethnic Society*
Lena Robinson: *Interracial Communication and Social Work Practice*

'RACE', COMMUNICATION AND THE CARING PROFESSIONS

Lena Robinson

Open University Press
Buckingham · Philadelphia

Open University Press
Celtic Court
22 Ballmoor
Buckingham
MK18 1XW

email: enquiries@openup.co.uk
world wide web: http://www.openup.co.uk

and
325 Chestnut Street
Philadelphia, PA 19106, USA

First Published 1998

A catalogue record of this book is available from the British Library

ISBN   0 335 19550 4 (pb)   0 335 19551 2 (hb)

Library of Congress Cataloging-in-Publication Data
Robinson, Lena. 1957–
    'Race', communication, and the caring professions / Lena Robinson.
        p.   cm. – ('Race', health, and social care)
    Includes bibliographical references and index.
    ISBN 0-335-19560-4 (pbk.). – ISBN 0-335-19551-2
1. Communication in human services–Great Britain. 2. Communication in social
work–Great Britain. 3. Communication in medicine–Great Britain. 4. Social service
and race relations–Great Britain. 5. Social work with minorities–Great Britain. 6.
Blacks–Services for–Great Britain. 7. Black–Great Britain–Race identity. 8. Race
awareness–Great Britain. I. Title. II. Series.
HV245. R448   1998
361–dc21   97-47446
                                                                                                            CIP

Copy-edited and typeset by The Running Head Limited, London and Cambridge
Printed in Great Britain by Biddles Ltd, Guildford and King's Lynn

Contents

Acknowledgements   vii
Introduction   1

1   Influences of racial identity states on interethnic communication   8

2   Beliefs, attitudes, values and interethnic communication   34

3   Culture and interethnic communication   54

4   The role of language in interethnic communication   77

5   Nonverbal communication in interethnic settings   101

6   Interpersonal perception and interethnic communication   121

7   Conclusion   141

References   144
Index   164

Acknowledgements

I am grateful to both Waqar Ahmad and Charles Husband for their constructive remarks and suggestions on earlier versions of the text. Needless to say I am responsible for any weakness or inaccuracies in the text.

At a family level, I wish to register my sincere thanks to Gerald and Andrew for their continued support and patience, during this period of writing.

Introduction

Little of the current social work and health care literature in Britain has addressed the issue of interethnic communication. A recent text written for social workers – Joyce Lishman's (1994) *Communication in Social Work* – states that 'Effective communication is an essential component of traditional social work activities, e.g. providing basic care, giving advice, making assessments, counselling . . . and acting as clients' advocates' (p. 1) but takes little account of interethnic communication. However, Lishman does acknowledge that 'the analysis of communication and culture is limited' (p. 144). Articles and books written for social and health care workers on communications are Eurocentric in nature and as a result require considerable adaptation before they can be responsive to some of the needs of black groups.

Understanding minority communication styles and patterns is indispensable for social and health care workers working with ethnic minority groups. Euro-American cultural values have dominated the social sciences and have been accepted as universal. In turn, these values have been imposed on non-Western cultures. Most studies of interethnic communication are binary, invoking comparisons between European Americans and one other group, with the European-American group as the assumed norm or point of comparison. Most of the research is Eurocentric in theory, method and focus. Eurocentric theories are derived from European-American theories, conducted by whites about whites, and the results are assumed to be culture-general rather than culture-specific. Fairchild and Edwards-Evans (1990: 76) argue that 'Because of the omnipresence of white racism . . . much of the social sciences . . . has revealed clear white racial biases concerning studies of African Americans [and other black groups].' One of the major problems confronting the analysis of communicative behaviours among people is the Eurocentric manner in which all behaviour is assessed. We need to recognize that the Eurocentric view is only one way of looking at the world.

Downs (1971: xiii) highlighted one of the premises of this book when he said that 'one of the greatest stumbling blocks to understanding other peoples within or without a particular culture is the tendency to judge others' behavior by our own standards'. According to Borden (1991: xvi), 'for effective intercultural [(interethnic)] communication one's attitude is more important than one's knowledge and/or understanding [of other cultures]'. Social work and health care students of interethnic communication need to learn that there is no such thing as a 'deprived culture' – rather, there are only different cultures, and no culture is better than the other. This is a hard lesson to learn when brought up with the Eurocentric perspective (Asante 1983).

Black people living in the West are nearly always familiar with white culture since it is conveyed as a 'norm' and is widely disseminated in school, the media and literature. As a result, black people are usually able to understand the communication of whites. However, black cultures are less widely disseminated, with the consequence that whites may know little about black people and have difficulty understanding their communication (Davis and Proctor 1989).

Interethnic communication comprises both verbal and nonverbal interaction, and individuals may convey messages through a variety of communication 'channels'. According to Davis and Proctor (1989: 27), 'communication channels include the verbal, the visual, the facial, the paralinguistic (voice tone, pauses, rate of speech) and the kinetic'. In communicating with another person we rely principally on the nonverbal channel for denotative/representational communication. Davis and Proctor (1989: 27) note that 'a person who is uncomfortable about racial dissimilarity but chooses not to express that discomfort verbally may reveal or "leak" their true feelings through nonverbal channels'.

This book examines interethnic communication from a black perspective. This perspective is committed to replacing the white distortion of black reality with black writings of black experience. It values differences and recognizes strengths. The black psychological perspective, 'embodied in the qualities of emotional vitality, realness, resilience, interrelatedness, the value of direct experience, and distrust and deception, determines how events are experienced, interpreted, and expressed in the phenomenal field' (White 1984: 83). White (p. 83) suggests that:

> Communication between blacks and whites about complex social realities is problematic because they may not be looking at issues, such as racial progress, police brutality, and control of the decision-making apparatus, from a common psychological perspective. In order to move toward resolving the conflicts associated with differences in cultural and psychological perspectives between blacks and whites, it is essential that the black perspective be taken into consideration by social services planning, education [and social work and health care services].

The framework for developing a black perspective is based on the notion of common experiences that black people in Britain share (for example racism, discrimination, and the history of colonialism and imperialism). This book attempts to articulate, from a black perspective, a framework for understanding interethnic communication. However, the book does acknowledge cultural diversity and ethnic differences. It examines the critical differences between Asians, African Caribbeans and African Americans, and the implications for interethnic communication.

This book aims to provide a basic introduction to interethnic communication for social work and health care students and practitioners. It is written from a psychological perspective and provides a broad overview of variables that are central to the topic of interethnic communication. The book is written primarily for social work and health care carers – including counsellors, doctors and nurses – who deal with black clients. There are several commonalities in these groups. The 'commonalities include (a) the necessity of establishing good interpersonal relations with [black] people and (b) communicating effectively in the presence of cultural differences that can interfere with good relations' (Brislin and Yoshida 1994: 5). These commonalities form the basis of the present book, which aims to provide social and health care workers with a precise framework in which to view and define the diverse factors at work during interethnic communication. It is my hope that this book is a starting point that will inspire discussion and debate in the social work and health care fields, and will generate theoretical and research questions.

Definition of key concepts

It is important to clarify and define some concepts used in this book. These terms are: black, 'race', ethnicity, intercultural and interethnic communication.

Black

The term 'black' has direct relevance to the discussion throughout this book, and has been used to describe people from South Asian, African and Caribbean backgrounds. While it is necessary to emphasize the heterogeneity of black people, of equal importance is the consideration of how black people in Britain differ from the white group. In Britain, 'Asian groups claim they are not "black" as part of their struggle to assert their own particularity in historical, cultural, ethical and linguistic terms' (Dominelli 1997: 7–8). This book does not, however, use the term 'black' to deny the uniqueness of different ethnic groups. It is used 'as an inclusive political term to counter the divisive aspects of racism' (p. 7).

The three main areas in which the experience of black people in this country has been unique from the white group are: racism and discrimination;

the history of colonialism and imperialism; and the 'existence of immigration and nationality legislation that has historically been instituted to keep out [black people]' (Singh 1992: 31). As Hall (1994: 252) comments:

'black' was coined as a way of referencing the common experience of racism and marginalisation in Britain and came to provide the organising category of a new politics of resistance, amongst groups and communities with, in fact, very different histories, traditions and ethnic identities.

The Social Services Committee of Lambeth Borough Council in 1981 defined 'black' as 'a description of any person whose skin colour renders them liable to the application of racism, irrespective of ethnic background, linguistic or academic ability, country of origin, or length of stay in this country' (Dominelli 1997: 10).

Other significant ethnic minority groups found in British society include the Jews and the Irish – making racism more than a matter of black and white. They constitute the 'non-Anglo-Saxon ethnic minorities [which] include all those people, black and white, who are not considered "indigenous" British of white English and Nordic European origins settled in Britain' (Dominelli 1997: 9). However, this book will focus on the black–white division, because 'the groups currently being subjected to the most vicious and intractable expressions of racism are black people, of Asian, African and Caribbean descent' (Dominelli 1997: 9).

According to Boyd-Franklin (1989: 10), 'skin colour is a badge of difference'. Black people 'are aware from a very early age that their blackness [(colour)] makes them different from mainstream White America [and Britain]' (p. 34). Racism and discrimination based on skin colour is evident at all levels of US and British society.

'Race'

Popular definitions of 'race' have conceptualized the term within a biological classification system. Krogman's (1945: 49) definition is a good example: 'A sub-group of people possessing a definite combination of physical characters, of genetic origin, the combination of which to varying degrees distinguishes the sub-group from other sub-groups of mankind [and womankind].' However, the validity of 'race' as a purely biological variable has been hotly debated and rejected, and 'race' has come to have a social and political meaning that, in part, is related to its original assumed biological roots (Yee *et al.* 1993). Distinctions based on 'race' tend to categorize people into distinctly different groups, and yet there are more differences *within* racial groups than between them. Atkinson *et al.* (1989) highlight that the term 'race' has no biological consequences, but what people believe about 'race' has profound social consequences. The concern here is that through subtle socializing influences, people come to accept as 'fact' the numerous stereotypes about a group of people based solely on their skin colour, facial features, and so forth. Pedersen (1992) notes that the 'race' construct has been discredited as a scientific and biological term, but that it remains an important political and psychological concept. The concept of 'race' has been used as a political pawn by the power-dominant group in maintaining the oppression of minority groups (Philips and Rathwell 1986; d'Ardenne and Mahtani 1990; Fernando 1991). When 'race', in Britain and the US, is used as a social classification system, physical characteristics of different human groups are believed to reflect emotional, cognitive, psychological, intellectual and moral qualities (Smedley 1993). Fernando (1995: 5) notes that 'reference to "race" does . . . imply that people are treated differently because of skin colour – that the concept of 'race' is asocial. Thus, the reader should be careful not to confuse genetics or biology with 'race', as noted by Smedley (1993: 22):

> It [('race')] was the cultural invention of arbitrary meaning applied to what appeared to be natural divisions within the human species. The meaning has social value but no intrinsic relationship to the biological diversity itself. Race has a reality created in the human mind, not a reflection of objective truths . . . The physical differences were a major tool by which the dominant whites constructed and maintained social barriers and economic inequalities; that is they consciously sought to create social stratification based on visible differences.

Ethnicity

A great deal of confusion surrounds the meaning of the term 'ethnic' or 'ethnicity'. Many uses and definitions of the terms can be found in the literature. A controversy exists regarding the interchangeable use of the terms 'race' and 'ethnicity'. Both terms, however, seem to label two different processes (Betancourt and Lopez 1993; Wilkinson 1993). According to Wilkinson (1993: 19), ethnicity refers to 'a shared culture and lifestyle'. My usage of the term 'ethnic group' parallels Yinger's (1976: 200) definition:

> A segment of a larger society whose members are thought, by themselves and/or others, to have a common origin and to share important segments of a common culture and who, in addition, participate in shared activities in which the common origin and culture are significant ingredients.

However, in the United States, ethnicity has been used as a euphemism for 'race' when referring to people of colour (that is, those persons whose ostensible ancestry is at least in part African, Asian, Latin American, and/or combinations of these groups and/or white or European ancestry) and as a nonracial designation for whites (Betancourt and Lopez 1993). Similar usages of the term 'ethnicity' can be found in Britain.

Intercultural communication

Blubaugh and Pennington (1976: 12) define intercultural communication as 'a special case of interpersonal communication where the backgrounds, experiences, customs, beliefs, values, associations . . . are sufficiently distinct between the two communicators that they interfere with rather than facilitate communication'. According to Porter and Samovar (1994: 7), intercultural communication 'occurs whenever a message produced in one culture must be processed in another culture'. Intercultural communication, therefore, 'entails the investigation of those elements of culture that most influence interaction when members of two different cultures come together in an interpersonal setting' (p. 7). My usage of the term 'intercultural communication' parallels that of Porter and Samovar's definition. The term 'culture' will be defined in Chapter 3.

Interethnic communication

Blubaugh and Pennington (1976: 13) define 'interpersonal communication between members of groups [who] have a visible, perceptible "racial identity" as interracial or interethnic communication [(terms are used interchangeably)]'. The authors do not define 'race' but 'rely upon perceived racial identity or skin color distinctions made by either communicator as the critical feature for identifying an interethnic communication situation' (p. 13). As will be apparent below, in this text we shall seek to problematize the use of 'interracial communication' as a synonym of interethnic communication since the former may all too easily apparently legitimate 'race' as real.

Interethnic communication describes 'differences in communication between members of [ethnic] groups who are all members of the same nation-state' (Lustig and Koester 1993: 60). Similarly, in this book, communication between African Caribbeans/Asians and white British people is referred to as interethnic communication. Lustig and Koester categorize interethnic communication as a 'subset of intercultural communication . . . as ethnicity contributes to the perceived effects of cultural differences on communication' (p. 60).

In this book, interethnic communication refers to the differential power-influenced communication between whites and blacks in a white-dominated society with blacks (i.e. African Caribbeans, Africans, Asians and African Americans) occupying a marginal position in the society. Interethnic communication does not take place in a vacuum isolated from larger sociopolitical influences. It mirrors the state of interethnic relationships in the wider society.

Structure of the book

Chapter 1 discusses the relationship between ethnic identity development and interethnic communication. It describes Cross's model of psychological nigrescence for black people and identity development models for other minority groups. It discusses white identity development and its implication for interethnic communication. Chapter 2 explores the concepts of belief, attitude and values, and their impact on interethnic communication. It argues that the lack of trust so prevalent in interethnic communication is in great measure based on the realization of the incongruity between expressed beliefs, attitudes and values, and actual behaviour. Chapter 3 examines the culture-bound values of black people and their relationship to interethnic communication. The chapter notes the cultural differences that may exist within any single racial/ethnic group. Notwithstanding this caution, it is important for white practitioners to have a knowledge of black people's culture-bound values. Within groups, variables such as acculturation level and racial identity development are essential components for accurately understanding and assisting clients from respective racial and ethnic minority groups.

Chapter 4 examines the role of language in interethnic communications. It examines the role of Black English in interethnic communication. It discusses the implications of interacting with black (Asian) clients who may have English as a second language, or who may not speak English at all. It explores the effects of racist language in interethnic settings. Chapter 5 discusses the importance of nonverbal communication in interethnic settings. Much communication that takes place between members of different ethnic groups is nonverbal. It addresses the impact of racism and discrimination on black people's presentation of self to others and impression management. It discusses the implications for social work and health care workers.

Finally, Chapter 6 focuses on the relationship between perception and interethnic communication. It examines the relationship between the white communicator's stereotypes, perceptions, prejudice and interethnic communication. Many problems erupting in interethnic communication settings can be attributed to our tendency to perceive selectively and perpetuate stereotypes.

I

Influences of racial identity states on interethnic communication

Introduction

This chapter discusses the relationship between black people's stages of racial identity development and interethnic communication. Lee (1994: 3) has described racial and ethnic identity development as 'being at the leading edge of thinking on multicultural counselling [and interethnic communication] in the United States at the present time'.

Racial identity theories do not suppose that racial groups in the United States [and Britain] are biologically distinct, but rather suppose that they have endured different conditions of domination or oppression' (Helms 1995: 181). Membership of these groups is determined by 'socially defined inclusion criteria (e.g. skin colour) that are commonly (mistakenly) considered to be "racial" in nature' (p. 181). Racial identities arise from the process of racialization (Miles 1989: 73). Racialization occurs whenever 'race' is used to categorize individuals or explain behaviour. Since 'race' is not a biologically defensible phenomenon, racialization always involves an ideological process in which 'race' is given a status as an apparent truth. Thus in this text racial identity does not imply acceptance of 'race' as real, but acknowledges the social and political reality that people live in societies in which 'race' identities are attributed to them, and that these attributions have real consequences for their experience of life. It is only appropriate to speak of racial identities because the processes of racialization have such potent power to shape people's perception of their shared world.

A variety of models of identity development have been proposed in the United States. This chapter describes Cross's model of psychological nigrescence, Parham's (1989) elaboration of the model, Atkinson *et al.*'s (1989, 1993) minority identity development model and Helms's people of colour racial identity development model. Cross's (1971, 1978) model delineates a four-stage process in which black people move from a white frame of reference to a positive black frame of reference. It is argued that black people go through several stages of racial identity development and that one's stage of racial identity may have a stronger impact on the communication process than 'race' per se. That is, cognitions resulting from one's racial world-view may influence how participants perceive and interact with each other. Different combinations of stages should, therefore, result in different styles of interactions. Although these identity development models pertain specifically to the black experience, various other minority groups have proposed similar processes. Other models developed in this area include Phinney's (1990) model of adolescent ethnic identity development, Kim's (1981) model of Asian American identity development and Arce's (1981) model of Chicano development. However, all the research work has been carried out in the United States. Similar work needs to be carried out in the British context.

In addition, this chapter will discuss the different models of white identity development. Helms (1984) proposed a five-stage process of white identity development – in which she describes how whites go through the process of defining themselves as racial beings. In their revised white identity development theory, Helms (1990b, 1992, 1994) and Helms and Piper (1994) proposed a six-stage process. Since the majority of social workers and health care workers are white, it is argued that white identity development and its implication for interethnic communication are important to consider. White workers need to deal with their concepts of whiteness and to examine their own racism. This chapter will explore the relationship between racial identity attitudes and interethnic communication patterns. It examines Helms's (1984) interactional model and the manner in which an individual's stage of racial identity affects the individual's communication style and the manner in which individuals (black and white) interact.

Models of black racial identity development

A perspective that has largely been ignored by traditional Eurocentric psychology is the research on the psychology of nigrescence (a Latin word that means the 'process of becoming black'). The study of nigrescence developed in the late 1960s as black American psychologists tried to outline the identity transformation that accompanied an individual's participation in the black power phase (1968–75) of the Black Social Movement. Nigrescence models tend to have four or five stages – and the common point of departure is not the change process per se but an analysis of the identity to be changed. These models are useful as they enable us to understand the problems of black identity confusion and to examine, at a detailed level, what happens to a person during identity change. If a black person, as Baldwin (1985) asserts, is exposed to an environment which is unsupportive, denigrating, oppressive and even hostile, and affirmation and validation for one's existence is lacking or nonexistent, then a negative sense of self is a likely outcome, with the models of nigrescence serving as an appropriate explanation of the resolution process that an individual will be likely to experience. The nigrescence approach studies black identity in adolescents and adults. However, it is important to remember that nigrescence models 'speak to the phenomenon of identity metamorphosis within the context of a social movement and not the evolution of identity from childhood through adult life' (Cross 1980: 97).

In the discussion which follows the reader should recognize that identity development is a life-time process which takes place within specific social and political contexts. We shall see below how theories have been modified to incorporate a life-time developmental dynamic. And as we note in Chapter 3, identities are not rigid, fixed nor unidimensional. The concept of racialization indicates the social construction of 'race' as a significant dimension in contemporary identities. But it is not, and cannot be, an inclusive personal identity. It may predominate and be exclusively salient on occasions, but racial identity takes meaning for individuals in its interaction with numerous other variables; of which gender, age, class, sexual preference and nationality are merely some of the more politically significant. Nor in a text written from a 'black perspective' can we neglect the contemporary debates and social dynamics in which black consciousness as a political recognition of shared oppression is challenged by powerful ethnic social movements. As Taylor (1992) has argued, 'the politics of recognition' has moved toward a 'politics of difference' in which universalist claims for the recognition of a common humanity are being challenged by collectivist claims for the recognition of, and respect for, group difference (see Kymlicka 1995). Thus, for example, in contemporary Britain, Modood (1997) has been an eloquent and persistent critic of universalist anti-racism because of its failure to recognize and address the particular ethnic and religious agendas of South Asians. And consequently in the text below, as we explore racial identity and interethnic communication it must remain a perpetual empirical question in any client–professional interaction as to how a particular individual has come to focus their response to racism. Some may respond to racism through a reciprocal racial identity as black; some may have come to experience their ethnicity in a racialized world as the vehicle through which they orchestrate their identity and resistance to oppression; and some experiencing the racial assault upon their ethnic identity being most pointedly experienced as Islamophobia may mobilize around a predominantly religious identity.

In seeking to employ the predominantly North American literature presented in this chapter the reader should not fail to recognize that the nigrescence model has a specific history (Mama 1995) and that it outlines a specific case of what we would argue are generic psychological processes. The analysis developed below reveals psychological strategies which may characterize individuals' attempts to negotiate ubiquitous personal denigration and oppression. This literature has developed in North America in relation to racist oppression, but the dynamics revealed may equally offer insight into individuals' negotiation of sexism or homophobia. In this text the reader is invited to explore the relevance of this theoretical tool for illuminating their understanding of the potential dynamics of identity negotiation which may underlie interethnic communication in a contemporary context where racism and racialized identities are part of a shared societal context.

Several models of black identity development and transformation were introduced in the early 1970s. Each hypothesized that identity development was characterized by movement across a series of sequential stages and was influenced by an individual's reaction to social and environmental pressures and circumstances (Cross 1971, 1978; Thomas 1971; Jackson 1975). For example, Thomas described a five-step process that he proposed as a necessary condition for black people to destroy 'Negromachy'. This term is defined by Thomas as that which is dominated by a confusion of self-worth and dependence on white society for definition of self:

> Inherent in this concept of approval is the need to be accepted as something other than what one is. Gratification is based upon denial of self and a rejection of group goals and activities. The driving force behind this need requires Afro-Americans to seek approval from whites in all activities, to use white expectations as the yard stick for determining what is good, desirable or necessary.
>
> (Thomas and Thomas 1971: 104)

Cross's model of black identity development

Perhaps the best known and most widely researched model of black identity development is Cross's (1971, 1978, 1980) model of the conversion from 'Negro' to 'black'. Cross's (1971) initial conceptualization of racial identity development was developed in the context of consequences and adjustments to interethnic interaction (Ponterotto 1988).

Cross suggests that the development of a black person's racial identity is often characterized by his/her movement through a five-stage process, the transformation from pre-encounter to internalization-commitment.

1 *Pre-encounter*. In the first stage the person is likely to view the world from a white frame of reference (Eurocentric). The black person accepts a 'white' view of self, other blacks and the world. The person has accepted a deracinated frame of reference, and because their reference point is usually a white normative standard, they develop attitudes that are pro-white and anti-black. The person will also deny that racism exists. Pre-encounter attitudes have been found to be related to high levels of anxiety and low self-esteem (Parham and Helms 1985a). Cross *et al.* stress that this stage 'is in evidence across social class' (Cross *et al.* 1991: 323). They state (pp. 322–3) that:

> At the core of the Stage 1 description is an aggressive assimilation-integration agenda, an agenda linked not only to the search for a secure place in the socio-economic mainstream, but motivated as

well by a desperate attempt to escape from the implications of being a 'Negro'. In this light, the Stage 1 Negro is depicted as a deracinated person who views being black as an obstacle, problem or stigma and seldom a symbol of culture, tradition or struggle. The Negro is thus preoccupied with the thoughts of how to overcome his stigma, or how he can assist whites in discovering that he is 'just another human being' who wants to assimilate.

2 *Encounter.* In the second stage some shocking personal or social event makes the person receptive to new views of being black and of the world. The person's Eurocentric thinking is upset by an encounter with racial prejudice and precipitates an intense search for black identity. The encounter stage involves two steps: first, experiencing and personalizing the event – the person realizes that his or her old frame of reference is inappropriate, and he or she begins to explore aspects of a new identity; the second part is portrayed by Cross *et al.* (1991: 324) 'as a testing phase during which the individual [first] cautiously tries to validate his/her new perceptions', then definitively decides to develop a black identity.

Consequently, when the person absorbs enough information and receives enough social support to conclude that: (1) the old identity seems inappropriate and (2) the proposed new identity is highly attractive, the person starts an obsessive and extremely motivated search for black identity. At the end of the second stage the person is not depicted as having obtained the new identity, but as having made the decision to start the journey towards the new identity. The person feels less internally secure and seeks authentication through external validation.

The encounter phase is marked by confusion about the meaning and significance of 'race' and an increasing desire to become more aligned with one's black identity. The individual experiences 'inner-directed guilt, rage at White people, and anxiety about becoming the right kind of Black person' (Cross 1995: 106). Pyant and Yanico (1991) found that encounter attitudes were predictive of low psychological well-being, low self-esteem, and high depression scale scores. Munford (1994) also found encounter attitudes to be related to high depression and low self-esteem. In other studies, encounter attitudes for black college students were associated with low anxiety, high self-actualization, and high self-regard (Parham and Helms 1981, 1985b). Mitchell and Dell (1992) found that black students with a predominance of encounter attitudes were more likely to be involved in black-oriented campus activities.

Interethnic interaction is one important means of stimulating negotiation of and movement between stages. For example, a 'pre-encounter's' negative (e.g. racist) interaction with the power-dominant white culture may be the mechanism for inciting 'encounter' attitudes and perspectives (Cross 1995).

3 *Immersion–emersion.* 'This stage encompasses the most sensational aspects of black identity development' (Cross 1971: 20). This is the

period of transition in which the person struggles to destroy all vestiges of the 'old' perspective. This occurs simultaneously with an intense concern to clarify the personal implications of the new-found black identity (Cross 1978). An emotional period ensues where the person glorifies anything black and attempts to purge him or herself of their former worldview and old behaviour. The old self is regarded in pejorative terms, but the person is unfamiliar with the new self, for that is what he/she hopes to become: 'thus the person is forced to erect simplistic, glorified, highly romantic and speculative images of what he or she assumes the new self will be like' (Cross *et al.* 1991: 325). The person begins to immerse him- or herself into total blackness. He/she attaches him/herself to black culture and at the same time withdraws from interactions with white people. The person tends to denigrate white people and white culture, thus exhibiting anti-white attitudes. Cross *et al.* (p. 325) state: 'Since the new black identity is something yet to be achieved, the Stage 3 person is generally anxious about how to demonstrate to others that he/she is becoming the right kind of black person.' Hence, the demonstration of one's blackness is prominent – for example, black clothes and hairstyles, linguistic style, attending all-black functions, reading black literature. The person does not feel secure about their blackness. They can be vicious in attacks on aspects of the old self that appear in others or themselves, and may even appear bizarre in their affirmation of the new self. The potential personal chaos of this stage is generally tempered by the social support a person gains through group activities. The groups joined during this period are 'counterculture institutions', which have rituals, obligations and reward systems that nurture and reward the developing identity, while inhibiting the efficacy of the 'old identity'. Although the initial part of Stage 3 involves total immersion and personal withdrawal into blackness, the latter part of this stage represents emergence from the reactionary, 'either–or' and racist aspects of the immersion experience. The person's emotions begin to level off, and psychological defensiveness is replaced by affective and cognitive openness. This allows the person to be more critical in his/her analysis of what it means to be black. The strengths, weaknesses, and oversimplifications of blackness can now be sorted out as the person's degree of ego-involvement diminishes and her/his sense of perspective expands. The person begins to feel in greater control and the most difficult period of nigrescence comes to an end.

4 *Internalization.* In this stage, the person focuses on things other than themselves and their ethnic or racial group. They achieve an inner security and self-confidence with their blackness. They feel more relaxed, more at ease with self. The person's thinking reflects a shift from how friends see them (Am I black enough?) towards confidence in personal standards of blackness. The person also exhibits a psychological openness and a decline in strong anti-white feelings. The person still uses 'blacks as a primary reference group, [but] moves towards a pluralistic and nonracist perspective' (Cross 1991: 326). Thus: 'As internalization

and incorporation increase, attitudes toward White people become less hostile, or at least realistically contained, and pro-Black attitudes become more expansive, open and less defensive' (Cross 1971: 24).

This stage and the fifth stage, *internalization-commitment*, are characterized by positive self-esteem, ideological flexibility, and openness about one's blackness. In the fifth stage the person finds activities and commitments to express his/her new identity. Cross (1985: 86) contends that:

Implicit in the distinction between 'internalization' and 'internalization-commitment' is the proposition that in order for Black identity change to have 'lasting political significance', the 'self' (me or 'I') must become or continue to be involved in the resolution of problems shared by the 'group' (we).

There is an extensive empirical literature that confirms Cross's model of black identity development (see Cross 1971; 1991; 1995; Hall *et al.* 1972; Williams 1975). However, readers need to be aware of some possible limitations of Cross's model. Thus, 'while the theory of nigrescence may provide a useful description of the development of black identity' (Mama 1995: 162), the model does not adequately address issues of class, age and gender. Thus, 'the black individual is still assumed to be a unitary subject (albeit a black one) devoid of gender, [and] class' (p. 162).

Cross sees the person in stage five – internalization-commitment – as the 'ideal', that is, psychologically healthy black person. They have made their new pro-black identity and values their own. They have a 'calm, secure demeanor' characterized by 'ideological flexibility, psychological openness and self-confidence about one's blackness' (Cross 1980: 86). Blacks are a primary reference group, but the person has lost his/her prejudices about 'race', sex, age and social class. He/she also struggles to translate his/her values into behaviour that will benefit the black community. According to Cross *et al.* (1991: 328):

For the person who has reached Stage 4 and beyond, the internalized black identity tends to perform three dynamic functions: to defend and protect a person from psychological insults, and where possible to warn of impending psychological attacks that stem from having to live in a racist society; to provide social anchorage and meaning to one's existence by establishing black people as a primary reference group; to serve as a point of departure for gaining awareness about, and completing transactions with, the broader world of which blackness is but a part.

Cross (1995: 113) maintains that 'the successful resolution of one's racial identity conflicts makes it possible for the person to shift attention to other identity concerns such as religion, gender and sexual preference, career development [and] social class'.

In summary, the research suggests that:

1 Many blacks have a predominantly positive racial identity, with perhaps a minority having a negative identity.

2 Black identity has links to behaviour.
3 Black identity can have links to other attitudes and personality characteristics.

More recently, Cross (1991, 1995) has proposed revisions in the conceptualizations of nigrescence. His recent descriptions of the stages depict
a more diverse set of attitudes and behaviours associated with the different
stages than he originally described (see Cross 1995 for detailed discussion).
For example,

> the pre-encounter stage covers a broad range of attitudes toward 'race'
> that range from 'low salience' or 'race' neutrality, to anti-Black. Per-
> sons who hold low salience views do not deny being physically Black,
> but consider this 'physical' fact to play an insignificant role in their
> everyday life.
>
> (Cross 1995: 98).

Pre-encounter persons have a Eurocentric cultural frame of reference and
value things 'other than their Blackness, such as their religion, their
lifestyle, their social status, or their profession' (p. 98).

The five stages of black identity development, however, remain the same.
He notes that the immersion–emersion stage can result in regression, fixation or stagnation instead of continued identity development. Regression
refers to those people 'whose overall experience is negative and thus non-
reinforcing of growth toward the new identity [and therefore] may become
disappointed and choose to reject Blackness' (Cross 1991: 208). Some
people can become fixated at this stage due to extreme and negative
encounters with white racists. Thus: 'Individuals who experience painful
perceptions and confrontations will be overwhelmed with hate for white
people and fixated at stage 3' (p. 208). Finally, dropping out of any involvement with black issues is another response to the immersion–emersion
stage. Some people might drop out because they wish to 'move on to what
they perceive as more important issues in life' (p. 209). These people tend to
label their experience as their 'ethnicity phase'. Cross has noted that this
often occurs with black American college students.

Although Cross's identity development model has been developed with
African American samples in the USA, it is argued by various authors (for
example, Maxime 1986, 1993; Sue and Sue 1990) that other minority
groups share similar processes of development. For instance, Sue and Sue
(1990: 95) indicate that:

> Earlier writers (Berry 1965; Stonequist 1937) have observed that
> minority groups share similar patterns of adjustment to cultural
> oppression. In the past several decades, [in the USA] Asian Americans,
> Hispanics, and American Indians have experienced sociopolitical
> identity transformations so that a 'Third World consciousness'
> has emerged with a cultural oppression as the common unifying
> force.

Parham's lifespan nigrescence model

Perhaps the most important theoretical advance in the field of nigrescence is Parham's application of a lifespan perspective to the study of nigrescence. In Cross's model nigrescence was regarded as a 'one-time event' in the person's life cycle.

Parham (1989) proposed that identity development may recycle throughout adulthood. Some people might have completed the nigrescence cycle at an early stage in the life cycle – for example, in adolescence or adulthood – but they may find that the challenges unique to a later phase in the life cycle – for example, middle age or late adulthood – may bring about a recycling through some of the stages.

Parham presents a life-cycle nigrescence model based on a modification of the Cross model. Parham is concerned to identify the earliest phase of the life cycle at which a person is capable of experiencing nigrescence. He argues that the 'manifestations of Black identity [during childhood] may be a reflection of externalized parental attitudes or societal stereotypes that a youngster has incorporated rather than a crystallized personal identity' (Parham 1989: 95). Accordingly, he proposes that it is during adolescence and early adulthood that a person might first experience nigrescence, and after this first experience, the likelihood of experiencing nigrescence is present for the rest of a person's life. Parham's model assumes that there is a qualitative difference between the nigrescence experience at adolescence or in early adulthood than in, say, middle or late adulthood, because:

> A Black person's frame of reference is potentially influenced by his or her life stage and the developmental tasks associated with that period of life . . . [and] within the context of normal development, racial identity is a phenomenon which is subject to continuous change during the life cycle.
>
> (Parham 1989: 196)

A person's racial identity development does not have to begin with a pro-white/anti-black viewpoint (pre-encounter stage). For instance, 'if an adolescent is raised in a home environment in which the parents have strong Immersion–Emersion attitudes, then [Parham] . . . speculates that [the adolescent's] attitudes are likely to be Immersion–Emersion as well' (p. 213).

Parham proposes three different ways in which people deal with their racial identity as they advance through life: stagnation, stage-wise linear progression and recycling. Stagnation is defined 'as maintaining one type of race-related attitude throughout most of one's lifetime' (p. 211). The stage-wise linear progression refers to the 'movement from one stage to another in a stage-to-stage fashion (i.e., pre-encounter to internalization) over a period of time in one's life' (p. 213). Recycling is defined as:

> The reinitiation into the 'racial' identity struggle and resolution process after having gone through the identity process at an earlier stage in one's life. In essence, a person could theoretically achieve

identity resolution by completing one cycle through the nigrescence process (internalization) and, as a result of . . . identity confusion, recycle through the stages again.

(p. 213)

According to Mama (1995: 62), 'the most important advance Parham makes is that he puts forward a theory of the black person as a dynamic subject . . . it is a theory of subjectivity that moves some way beyond the linear stage models of black identity development'. However, Parham does not address the 'possibility that multiple stages (or positions) may coexist within (or be available to) a given individual at any given moment' (Mama 1995: 62).

Atkinson, Morten and Sue's minority identity development model

Atkinson, Morten and Sue (1989, 1993) proposed the minority identity development (MID) model, which is intended to describe the issues of identity development common to members of all groups in the United States and Britain who are politically and/or socially oppressed. The MID model is anchored in the belief that all minority groups experience the common force of oppression (Atkinson *et al.* 1989). In their model, Atkinson *et al.* (1989, 1993) proposed that the search for a positive racial-cultural identity involves progression through five stages: conformity, dissonance, resistance and immersion, introspection, and synergetic articulation and awareness. In content, the stages are similar to those of racial identity development, as addressed above. The dimensions described by Atkinson *et al.* (1989, 1993) are: (a) attitudes toward oneself, (b) attitudes toward other members of one's own racial/cultural group, (c) feelings and attitudes toward other minorities, and (d) attitudes toward members of the majority culture. The five stages are described below.

1 *Conformity*. In this stage minority individuals have an unequivocal preference for the values of the dominant culture and have a strong desire to assimilate and acculturate into the dominant culture. They have negative, self-deprecating attitudes toward themselves as racial beings, as well as toward others of the same minority. They have a discriminatory attitude toward others of different minorities, and positive attitudes toward the dominant (white) group.
2 *Dissonance*. In this stage minority individuals 'experience frequent conflict with respect to depreciating and appreciating attitudes toward the self, others of the same minority, others of different minorities, and the dominant group' (Atkinson *et al.* 1993: 40). Movement into this stage is often caused by a personal 'race'-related experience – for example, a personal experience with racism.
3 *Resistance and immersion*. Minority individuals in this stage endorse the values of their own group and reject the values of the dominant group. They accept racism and oppression as a reality and have 'a group-

appreciating attitude toward their own group . . . and group-depreciating attitudes toward the dominant group' (Atkinson *et al.* 1993: 42).
4 *Introspection*. Minority individuals in this stage 'experience uncertainty with the rigidly held group views of Stage 3 and attend more to notions of individual autonomy' (Atkinson *et al.* 1993: 44).
5 *Synergetic articulation and awareness*. In this final stage, the minority individual has a confident and secure racial identity, and there is a desire to eliminate all forms of oppression. This stage is characterized by a high level of positive regard toward self and toward one's group. Individuals have a 'selective appreciation of the dominant group' (Atkinson *et al.* 1993: 47).

Helms's people of colour racial identity development

Helms and Cook (1996) contend that the central racial identity develop-mental theme of all people of colour (e.g. Africans, Asians) is to recognize and overcome the psychological manifestations of internalized racism. Their model which explains the process by which this adaptation poten-tially occurs is a derivative of Cross's (1971) model and Atkinson *et al.*'s (1989) minority identity development model.

Helms (1994), Helms and Piper (1994) and Helms and Cook (1996) viewed racial identity as ego identity statuses rather than developmental stages. At any one point, an individual has many levels of identity but only one dominant level. According to Helms (1994), the predominant racial identity level operates psychologically as a world-view or ego state, and each level has its own constellation of emotions, beliefs, motives and behav-iours, which influence its expression.

The model consists of five ego statuses and information processing strat-egies (IPS):

1 *Conformity* status: individuals adapt and internalize white society's def-initions of one's group either by conforming to the existing stereotypes of one's group or by attempting to become white. It implies devaluing of one's own group and allegiance to white standards of behaviour (Helms and Piper 1994: 130).
2 *Dissonance* status: individuals are confused and ambivalent about their commitment to their socioracial group; they have an 'ambivalent socio-racial self-definition'. IPS: 'Repression of anxiety-provoking "racial" information' (Helms and Piper 1994: 131). Example: 'I talked "White", moved "White", most of my friends were White . . . But I never really felt accepted by or truly identified with the White kids. I was never comfort-able enough in my "Blackness" to associate with [blacks]. That left me in sort of a grey area' (Wenger 1993: 4).
3 *Immersion–emersion* status: individuals idealize one's own group and denigrate that which is perceived as white. Individuals 'use own group external standards to self-define, and own-group commitment and

loyalty is valued'. IPS: 'Hypervigilance toward "racial" stimuli and dichotomous thinking' (Helms and Piper 1994: 132).

4 *Internalization* status: individuals are positively committed to their own group and are able to 'assess and respond objectively to members of the dominant group'. IPS: 'Flexibility and analytic thinking' (Helms and Piper 1994: 133).

5 *Integrative awareness* status: individuals express a positive racial self and also 'empathize and collaborate with members of other oppressed groups'. IPS: 'Flexibility and complexity' (Helms and Piper 1994: 134).

White racial identity development

A subject that has not been adequately researched is white racial identity development and its effects on interethnic communication. A number of authors have emphasized the need for white people to deal with their concepts of whiteness and to examine their own racism (Helms 1984; Ponterotto 1988). Helms (1984: 155) observes that '[study] of prejudice provides no information about how Whites feel about themselves as "racial" beings'. However, earlier studies – for example, Katz and Ivey (1977: 486) – found that 'when a White person [is asked] what he or she is "racially", you may get the answer "Italian", "English", "Catholic", or "Jewish". White people do not see themselves as White'. Katz and Ivey argue that whites deny that they belong to a 'race' and that certain prescribed attitudes and values are associated with belonging to the white 'race'. Since the majority of social and health care workers are white individuals this is an important area of study. Sabnani *et al.* (1991) recognize the importance of the counsellor's racial identity development to the cross-cultural counselling process.

Hardiman (1982) and Helms (1984) independently proposed a white racial identity development model. But, Helms's model (1984, 1990a) is the only one to date to have received any empirical substantiation (Helms 1990a). Prior to these models, no theory existed to 'explain how Whites developed attitudes toward their racial-group membership (White) rather than their "ethnic" group (e.g., Greek, Italian, German, etc.)' (Carter and Helms 1990: 105). Models of white racial identity appear to share some basic assumptions. These include the following:

1. Racism is an integral part of US [and British] life and permeates all aspects of [US and British] culture and institutions; 2. Whites are socialized into US [and British] society and, therefore inherit the biases, stereotypes, and racist attitudes, beliefs, and behaviors of [those societies].

(Sue and Sue 1990: 113)

Helms (1990a: 49) states that 'the development of White identity in the United States [and Britain] is closely intertwined with the development and progress of racism . . . The greater the extent that racism exists and is denied, the less possible it is to develop a positive White identity.' Thus, according to Helms (1990a: 49), the development of 'a positive racial identity consists of two processes, the abandonment of racism and the development of a nonracist White identity'.

Helms's (1984) stages are: contact (characterized by a naive lack of awareness of racial differences); disintegration (the person is forced to acknowledge that he/she is white); reintegration (the person becomes hostile toward blacks and more positively biased toward his or her own racial group); pseudo-independence (characterized by an intellectual acceptance of white responsibility for racism); and autonomy (acceptance of racial differences and similarities). At the autonomy stage, the person 'actively seeks opportunities to involve herself or himself in cross-racial interactions because he or she values cultural diversity and is secure in his or her own racial identity' (Helms 1984: 156). Helms (p. 155) maintains that:

> Because Whites are the dominant race in [the USA and Britain], they can choose environments that permit them to remain fixated at a particular stage of racial consciousness . . . Since Whites usually do have greater freedom to leave arenas in which their racial attitudes might be challenged, it is possible that each stage can culminate in either a positive or negative resolution. Positive resolutions should be associated with greater personal adjustment and better interpersonal relationships with people of other races.

In 1990, Helms revised the above (Helms 1984) model. There are two basic assumptions which underlie Helms's (1990a) revised white racial identity development theory. The first assumption is that whites are socialized to feel superior to visible racial/ethnic people by virtue of their white skin alone. This sense of white superiority operates on an individual, institutional and cultural level. The second assumption is that whites can avoid, deny or ignore dealing with their whiteness. Most whites do not recognize their 'race' until, or unless, they have to confront the 'idea' or the physical reality of blacks and other visible/ethnic groups in their life space (Helms 1990a).

Helms's (1990a) revised model hypothesized that white racial identity evolves through a six-status process of: contact, disintegration, reintegration, pseudo-independence, immersion–emersion and autonomy. This process is similar in its developmental outline and some of its stages to Cross's (1971, 1978) model of black racial identity development. The statuses are divided into two phases: the abandonment of a racist identity, which incorporates the first three stages; and the establishment of a nonracist white identity, which incorporates the last three stages. This model has been subjected to empirical scrutiny (e.g. Carter and Helms 1990; Helms and Carter 1990). Helms's (1990a) statuses are considered in detail below.

Contact

This status is characterized by a lack of racial awareness about the self and others. An individual is unaware of racism and one's participation in it. Individuals in this stage evaluate blacks according to white criteria (e.g. white cultural values, standardized tests). Hence, normality is established on a model of the middle class, Caucasian male of European descent. The more one approximates to this model in appearance, values and behaviour, the more 'normal' one is considered to be (Robinson 1995).

The individual is unaware that he or she might be judged according to other racial/cultural group criteria (e.g. communication styles). For instance, white practitioners evaluate black (Asian) clients' indirect forms of communication according to direct forms of verbal communication based on Western standards of communication in which both the speaker (e.g. the social worker) and the listener (e.g. the client) must look expressive and be active. When Asians are exposed to verbal communication, they often look quiet, act passive, and make a great deal of effort to avoid offending others (Chung 1992). This indirect form of verbal communication is very appropriate among Asians but may create problems during the assessment of Asian clients by white social work and mental health practitioners.

Statements such as 'I don't notice what "race" a person is'; 'I just treat people as people'; 'You don't act like a black person' and 'I don't view you as a black person, I see you as a human being' illustrate attitudes associated with people in the contact status. Thomas and Sillen (1974) noted that, for some therapists, it is easier and more comfortable to deny that racial differences exist and see problems only in class or economic terms. Such a belief is unfounded and thus counterproductive, leading to what Thomas and Sillen (1974) have referred to as the 'illusion of colour blindness'. This phrase refers to the tendency for many members of the mental health field to deny the impact of colour differences in therapy. Various authors (Block 1980; Dominelli 1988) caution service providers about being influenced by, and promoting the illusion of, colour blindness.

A person at the contact stage is 'likely to continue to engage in minimal cross-racial interaction, is unlikely to be forced to rethink her or his racial perspective, [and his or her behaviour and views are] . . . tolerated by his or her racial peers' (Helms 1990a: 57). There is limited accurate knowledge of black people, but a great deal of adherence to social stereotypes.

Disintegration

An individual acknowledges his or her whiteness and understands the benefits of being white in a racist society. This stage is characterized by conflicts arising from wanting to be accepted by the norm (white) group, while at the same time experiencing a moral dilemma over treating (or considering) blacks inferior to whites. For example, an individual's belief that all 'people should be treated equally regardless of "race"' is in direct contrast to in-group expectations. To resolve his or her confusion and conflict, a white person may (a) avoid contact with black people, (b) try to convince white people that black people are not inferior, (c) support the view that racism does not exist, or if it does, that it is not the white person's fault. Helms (1990c: 59) notes that 'It seems likely that the person who can remove herself or himself from interethnic environments or can remove Blacks from White environments will do so. Given the racial differences in social and economic power, most Whites can choose this option.'

Pope-Davis and Ottavi (1994) found disintegration attitudes to be associated with racism. Block *et al.* (1995) found that individuals characterized by high disintegration attitudes are likely to 'react negatively toward interethnic situations at work such that they do not endorse principles of equality' (p. 79). They also do not think discrimination against blacks is real, and are not comfortable with blacks in work-related social situations or as colleagues (Block *et al.* 1995).

Reintegration

This phase is characterized by 'idealization of one's socio"racial" group, denigration and intolerance for other groups' (Helms 1990a: 60). The reintegration identity is essentially a racist identity. An individual believes that white privilege should be protected and preserved because he or she earned the privilege. He or she assumes that 'negative race-related conditions result from Black people's inferior social, moral, and intellectual qualities' (p. 60). According to Block *et al.* (1995: 84) this stage of racial identity resembles 'old-fashioned racism . . . the tendency to endorse negative racial stereotypes about blacks and to be opposed to all aspects of integration'. British and American society's racial and cultural norms enable many whites to remain in the reintegration status indefinitely. Often, a personally significant event is needed for the individual to begin questioning and to abandon his or her racist identity. When this occurs, the individual is ready to move into the pseudo-independent phase.

Block *et al.* (1995) found that individuals characterized by high reintegration attitudes were also strongly negative about interethnic situations at work. As noted above, during this stage a person is angry and hostile toward blacks. He or she develops anti-black and pro-white attitudes and sees blacks stereotypically. However, 'if the individual uses these feelings to become more aware of [his or her] Whiteness and attempts to understand the socio-political implications of being White in a racist society, then it is possible that feelings of anger and fear will dissipate' (Helms 1984: 11).

Pseudo-independence

This is the first stage of Phase 2 – 'defining a Nonracist White Identity'. Individuals begin to question the assumption that blacks are innately inferior to white people and to realize that white people have a responsibility for racism. These changes, however, are primarily intellectual. Helms (1990c: 62) notes that individuals in this phase may still 'behave in ways that unknowingly perpetuate racism'. For example, cultural differences are still interpreted from a white perspective and interactions with blacks may take the form of helping them to meet current white standards. These attitudes have been found to be related to comfortableness with blacks in various situations (Claney and Parker 1988). Block *et al.* (1995) found that pseudo-independent attitudes were associated with support of management and institutional efforts toward equity in the organization.

During this phase, individuals begin to feel marginal regarding 'race' and racial issues. However, 'if they have incentives to persevere, these people will continue their quest for positive aspects of being White that are unrelated to racism and a better understanding of one's Whiteness' (Helms 1990c: 62).

Immersion–emersion

During this phase white people ask questions such as 'Who am I racially?', 'Who do I want to be?' and 'How can I feel proud of my "race" without being a racist?' (Helms 1990c: 62). Whites attempt to educate and change other whites. Helms (1990c: 62) notes that:

> Successful completion of this stage apparently requires emotional catharsis in which the person re-experiences previous emotions that were denied or distorted . . . Once these negative feelings are expressed, the person may begin to feel euphoria perhaps akin to a religious rebirth.

Autonomy

This is the final stage of the white identity model. The person abandons personal, cultural and institutional racist practices and has a more flexible world-view. These individuals value cross-racial experience. They also acknowledge and work to eliminate other forms of oppression (e.g. sexism, ageism).

Taub and McEwen (1992) found that autonomy attitudes were positively related to mature interpersonal relationships. Tokar and Swanson (1991: 299) found that 'a secure appreciation and acceptance of oneself and others (autonomy) appears to be associated with a liberation from rigid adherence to social pressures and with a strong inner reliance (inner directedness)'. When seeking mental health services, Helms and Carter (1991) found that individuals with high autonomy attitudes indicated no preference for a white counsellor, unlike prospective clients with pseudo-independence attitudes.

Most commentators agree that more research is needed on white racial identity development (Sabnani *et al.* 1991). Most of the work has been done in the US, with little comparable work in Britain.

Racial identity attitudes and communication patterns

This section discusses the relationship between racial identity attitudes and interethnic communication. The theories of black racial identity (for example, Thomas 1971; Cross 1978, 1980; Parham 1989) are relevant to issues related to interethnic communication. As noted above, these stage theories are progressive, characterized by early confusion and a poor sense of identity and by later ethnic acceptance and identity integration. Black self-identity issues are likely to affect the response of black people to white social workers, counsellors and health workers. Those lower in black consciousness (pre-encounter stage) may devalue a social/health worker who is black, while those very immersed (immersion–emersion stage) in exploring their blackness may question the legitimacy of any white workers and may contribute to anxiety-provoking interactions with whites (Helms 1990a). The manner in which people express their racial identity resolutions, therefore, influences the quality of their interactions with one another, especially in situations in which 'race' is salient.

Social and health care workers need to have an understanding of identity development and its effects on interethnic communication. Parham (1989) asserts that recognizing the within-group variability among black clients may assist a counsellor in understanding how the racial identity attitudes of a client may influence the ability to establish a workable relationship with that client. For example, pro-black and anti-white attitudes of a black client could be interpreted by the social worker as a stage in black identity development and not as a personalized attack. It is important to recognize the dangers in this situation of the insight obtained by the use of identity theory becoming corrupted into lazy psychological reductionism. The social worker's acknowledgement of the client's racial identity attitudes must not replace their sensitivity to and knowledge of the client's experience of exclusion and discrimination on the grounds of 'race'. To replace an empathic understanding of a client's existential experience of racism by a simplistic psychological labelling would be a perverse misuse of racial identity theory; this must be continuously borne in mind as we continue this discussion.

In the pre-encounter stage the black client is most likely to prefer a white worker over a black worker. Consequently, a white service provider may have little difficulty breaking down the social distance and establishing a working alliance between him or herself and the client where ethnicity is concerned. The black client at this stage believes that white workers are more competent and capable than black workers. If a black worker is matched with a client with strong pre-encounter attitudes, the client might believe that the black worker is less qualified than a white counterpart and therefore less capable of providing effective care. Black workers may encounter negative reactions, resistance or open hostility. Maxime (1986: 105) notes that 'Many black social workers have experienced comments such as "I don't want a black social worker", "don't come near me", or verbal and sometimes physical abuse.' Maxime (1993) (a black clinical psychologist) encountered negative reactions when she attempted to do clinical work with a black girl at the pre-encounter stage. On meeting Maxime for the first time the girl 'snarled, "Go away, I'm not talking to you, I have nothing to say to you". In this stage, the child usually makes a request for a white psychologist/therapist' (Maxime 1993: 106). Parham and Helms (1981: 253) found support for the 'idea that possession of certain racial identity attitudes influences black people's acceptance of black counsellors [and other professionals]'. Thus, pre-encounter attitudes 'tended to be associated with pro-white, anti-black counsellor preferences' (p. 254).

The black client may be over-eager to identify with the white worker in order to seek approval. Most individuals at the pre-encounter stage will find attempts to explore racial identity or to focus upon feelings very threatening. Social workers and counsellors (black or white) need to help the client to sort out conflicts related to racial/cultural identity. The black social and health care worker can take a nonjudgemental stance toward the client and provide a positive black role model. The white worker, on the other hand, needs to communicate positive attitudes about black people and culture. Helms (1984) has suggested that a white practitioner might experience some difficulty in working with a black client with pre-encounter attitudes. The difficulty Helms cites seems to be related to the worker's lack of understanding about the client's identity issues, which can cause the 'therapy [and communication] process to become "bogged down" (p. 160). Both black and white service providers need to guard against unknowingly reinforcing the black client's self-deprecating attitude toward him/herself and other black people.

Black clients at the encounter stage are more racially aware than pre-encounter clients and are likely to prefer to work with social/health care workers who possess a good knowledge of the client's cultural group. Parham and Helms (1981: 255) found that 'encounter and immersion –emersion attitudes were associated with pro-black, anti-white counsellor [and service provider] preferences'. Richardson and Helms (1994) found that encounter attitudes were predictive of black males' reactions to white counsellor/black client counselling simulations; high encounter attitudes were negatively associated with a willingness to self-disclose to a white counsellor. Clients at the encounter stage are preoccupied by questions concerning their concept of self, identity and self-esteem. White social workers and counsellors should capitalize on the black client's motivation toward self-exploration and help the client deal with his or her identity conflicts.

Black clients at the immersion–emersion stage are usually suspicious and hostile towards white professionals. They are likely to regard their psychological problems as products of oppression and racism. In this stage black clients are likely to believe that 'openness or self-disclosure to [white workers] other than one's own [black] group is dangerous because white [professionals] are enemies and members of the oppressing group' (Sue and Sue

1990: 110). A white worker will be viewed by the black client as a 'symbol of the oppressive Establishment. If the worker becomes defensive and personalize the "attacks", he or she will lose his or her effectiveness in [communicating] with the client' (p. 110). Black clients in the immersion–emersion stage will constantly test the sincerity and openness of the white worker. White guilt and defensiveness can only serve to hinder effective interethnic communication.

A black client in the immersion stage is likely to share his or her problems only with a black worker. However, an immersion client may be anxious that the black worker will not meet his or her standards of blackness. Since the black worker's education, training, authority and status require participation in the white world, the client might believe that these achievements are an indication that the worker is 'psychologically invested' in the world that he or she is rejecting. Parham and Helms (1985a) point out that positive therapeutic work can result if the 'client's perception of the therapist are worked through in the initial stages of therapy' (Parham and Helms 1981: 256). This also applies to the social worker–client relationship.

Some authors have noted an unwillingness by blacks with high levels of immersion–emersion attitudes to use mental health services. For instance, Austin *et al.* (1990) suggest that people with high levels of immersion–emersion attitudes may believe that seeing a counsellor is stigmatizing and reflects personal weakness.

At the internalization stage, black clients may prefer a black social worker but they are also receptive to white social workers as long as the white workers can share, understand and accept their world-views. Parham and Helms (1981: 255) found that 'internalization attitudes were not strongly related to preferences for a counsellor of either race [(black or white)]'. It appears that as the black client becomes more comfortable with his or her racial identity, the 'race' of the service provider becomes less important. Thus, in order to understand black people's behaviour, white practitioners need 'to search beyond black people's racial self-designation' (p. 255).

We need also to examine the ability of a black worker to work with black clients at various racial attitudinal stages. This issue is particularly important because many service providers often assume that a black staff member is a better therapeutic match for a black client than a white staff member. Such an assumption seems questionable if, for example as noted above, the black service provider is paired with a client with strong pre-encounter attitudes. One consequence of such an interaction might be premature termination by the client who believes that a black therapist is less qualified than his or her white counterpart and, thus, less capable of delivering effective treatment.

On the other hand, a black worker at the encounter stage may have confused feelings when working with a black client. Pinderhughes (1989: 109) gives the following example of an Asian therapist in a training workshop.

I have always rejected my 'race'. It seemed that people held negative views of Asians so to fit in I rejected being Asian. Now I realize how that might have been harmful to me and my view of other Asians and people of color. I am not sure anymore what being Asian means but I think I need to understand and accept that part of myself. Because I am uncomfortable around other Asians and people of color. I am not sure how I would respond to an Asian client.

The racial identity development model serves as a useful assessment tool for white and black service providers to gain a greater understanding of their black clients (Helms 1986) and themselves, and to communicate in an effective manner.

Helms's interaction theory

Helms's (1984) interactional model attempts to provide a framework that guides professionals (for example, social workers, mental health workers) in their effort to understand how 'race' and racial identity influences the communication process. Her framework considers within-group variation in interethnic dyads through the use of the racial identity construct. Helms outlines the interactional dynamics that may occur in dyads as a result of the various combinations of racial identity attitudes held by the participants.

Helms's original rationale for offering a framework was to enable counsellors to diagnose tensions in the environment and to intervene to resolve them in a manner compatible with the racial identity dynamics of the participants. Originally, 'environment' referred to dyadic counselling or psychotherapy relationships (Helms 1984). Subsequently, the concept of environmental context was extended to refer to other dyadic interactions in which 'the participants differ in social power and/or status due to role expectations [(for example, social worker–client, health care worker–patient)] . . . In addition, "relationship dynamics" should be substituted for "counseling process"' (Helms 1990a: 177). Social power is defined according to social roles, numerical presence, and/or sociopolitical histories of the racial groups within the environment (Helms 1990a). Thus, whites generally have more power than blacks in a white-dominated society; and authority figures (for example social workers, doctors, nurses) have more social power than clients (Helms 1990a).

Helms's (1984) interaction theory, which builds on her racial identity theory, proposes that a person's stage of racial identity, rather than racial group membership per se determines the quality of the communication process. Helms argues that different combinations of stages should result in different styles of interactions. Racial identity affects a client's and worker's style, and the manner in which they interact. Implicit in Helms's (1984) interaction model is the idea that a social/health care worker's actions are a result of his or her racial identity status attitudes, which influence a client's reactions, and that a client's racial identity status attitudes might influence a worker's behaviours (i.e. intentions). According to Helms (1984, 1990a) there are four communication patterns: parallel, crossed, progressive and regressive. The following section discusses which combinations of social/health care worker–client racial identity attitudes lead to which of the four types of interactions.

Parallel

Parallel relationships are perhaps 'the least contentious of dyadic interactions because [the social/health care worker and client] share a racial world view' (Helms 1990a: 180). Hence, in a parallel relationship a social/health care worker and client share the same stages of identity. For example, a parallel relationship is formed when the black client is at the pre-encounter stage and the worker is at the contact stage; or when the black client exhibits predominantly encounter attitudes and the white professional is at the disintegration stage. In the latter type of dyad, both participants may try to raise the topic of 'race' but because both the worker and the client are confused, their efforts may be half-hearted. On the other hand, when the client is at the pre-encounter stage and the worker is at the contact stage, the client and the worker might coexist by denying the significance of 'race' in their daily interaction. In a parallel relationship where the client is at the immersion–emersion stage and the white worker is in the reintegration stage, the salience of 'race' might be exaggerated.

In parallel relationships, there are less communication problems because the participants have similar styles of handling racial issues and 'affectively are rather placid'. However, the more advanced each participant's level of racial identity development, the less ineffectual is a parallel relationship. Thus, a relationship that is parallel with respect to autonomy or internalization ought to be more beneficial to both participants than one that is parallel with respect to contact or pre-encounter because in the first type of relationship both participants are more likely than those in the latter type to have moved toward resolving their own racial issues. However, it is important to note that even when the client and the worker are in similar racial identity stages, the power differential between the two can influence the communication process and outcome. Because of the social and health care worker's powerful role in the interaction, his or her racial identity has the potential to exert more influence on the communication process than the client's. If problems do occur in these type of relationships, they are 'in response to one member's (usually the least powerful) communications being perceived by the other member as challenges to her or his world view' (Helms 1990a: 180). Helms contends that 'the impetus for such communications would have to come from outside the [practitioner–client] relationship' (p. 180). Thus, others might supply the racial viewpoints that are potentially disruptive of the parallel interaction.

Crossed

In a crossed relationship, the world-views of the client and the worker are totally opposite. Helms (1990a: 181) argues that these individuals will have 'difficulty in communicating with each other because they do not share any part of a common frame of reference where the racial parts of themselves are concerned'. There is a greater risk of a prolonged conflict with these types of relationships. For example, in a cross-racial dyad, a black client may have a predominantly immersion status, and the white worker may have a predominantly reintegration status. Neither the client or the worker empathizes with the other's racial attitudes. This may result in the relationship breaking down. Thus, 'crossed relationships are at greatest risk for long-lasting conflict' (Helms 1990a: 181). The following case study involves a cross-racial dyad (a white social worker and a black client) and illustrates characteristics of a crossed type of relationship.

Tina is a 12-year-old black girl, who from the age of 6 lived with white foster parents. She was referred to a white social worker when she exhibited behavioural problems. Tina experienced a situation that brought her face to face with racism. The experience was so shattering that it forced her to reinterpret her world (encounter stage). (Previously, Tina was at the pre-encounter stage and exhibited anti-black and pro-white attitudes.) The white social worker is in the contact stage of racial identity development. A social worker with a high level of contact attitudes will, therefore, be less likely to attend to 'race'-related material.

The social worker has difficulty in communicating with Tina because they do not share the same stages of racial identity development. According to Maxime (1993: 106), 'an understanding of [the client's] experience is vital . . . because the focus at this stage must be on the internal turmoil that the [client] is experiencing'.

Thus, in an interethnic situation, where the white worker is at the contact stage and the black client exhibits encounter attitudes, the black participant might try to raise the topic of 'race', but because the worker does not think 'race' issues are important he or she will make statements such as 'I don't notice what "race" a person is' and 'I just treat people as people.' Social workers adopting such an approach take the view that black people are like white people. For example, Dominelli (1988: 36) noted that social workers made the following remarks to her about black people: '"race" is unimportant. Knowing them as people is'; 'I treat black people and white people the same.' Thus, a social worker's stage of white identity development can either enhance or retard effective communication.

Progressive

A progressive relationship exists when the social/health care worker's racial identity status is at least one level above the client's. The worker may be empathic and accepting, while the client is self-exploring. In this type of relationship, one would expect low levels of anger and anxiety, and the sessions should be evaluated as positive and beneficial by both members of the dyad. These interactions are likely to be 'most growthful and harmonious when the [worker's] stage of racial identity does not exceed [the client's] stage by more than one stage' (Helms 1990a: 181). Ideally, in a progressive relationship, the worker will be able gradually to move the client toward a healthier stage. Yet if the worker remains at the same stage, then the relationship becomes parallel.

Regressive

A regressive relationship exists when the client's racial identity status is at least one level more advanced than the worker's. For example, a black client may have predominantly encounter status attitudes, and the white social worker may have predominantly contact attitudes.

In this type of relationship, the process may resemble a power struggle; both participants may have strong affective reactions to each other, and conflict may characterize the relationship's dynamics. Helms (1990a: 180) suggests that 'The affective style of regressive relationships can vary from testy to conflictual, depending upon how much more advanced the [client's] racial identity development is than the [worker's].' If the client 'advances more than one stage beyond the worker, then one can expect increasing levels of tension as the participants' world views become more disparate' (p. 181). These differences in racial identity attitudes generate miscommunication in interethnic communication. For example, a social or health care worker who is less comfortable facing racial issues than the client may attempt to change the client's thinking and behaviour in directions that feel wrong to the client. As a consequence, regressive relationships are often characterized by varying degrees of disharmony, conflict, tension and rebellion. Since the client has less direct control over the quality of the interaction, he or she may engage in acting out and/or passive-aggressive behaviours to express her or his discomfort with the quality of the relationship. For their part, social and health care workers may engage in punitive (both overt and covert) activities, whose perhaps unconscious purpose is to coerce the client to think as the practitioner does.

In a regressive relationship, one would expect the black client to have more negative reactions to the worker's statements and intentions than in a progressive relationship. Certain client reactions, including hostility, anxiety and anger, are likely to be present in a regressive dyadic interaction.

The following illustrates an example of a form of regressive dyadic interaction that can occur in a social work interview with a black adolescent. The black adolescent may want to talk about racism in his/her school and the attitudes of teachers to black students. The social worker, however, may insist that such issues should not be important to the young person. The black adolescent can feel disrespected and devalued in this situation. The social worker risks miscommunication if he or she cannot allow the client to develop the racial aspects of self.

Racial identity theory and the group process

Helms (1990a) extended racial identity theory to the group process by describing types of communication patterns that might exist in the group. Helms suggested that a group member's role as a majority or minority group member acts interactively with racial ideas to influence the group communication process.

Parallel relationship

In a parallel group, both the leader and members share the same stages of identity. When the leader and group are racially heterogeneous, then parallel relationships involve pre-encounter/reintegration, internalization/autonomy, and perhaps encounter or disintegration stages. 'The common theme in parallel relationships is inertia . . . [but] this inertia is less problematic the more advanced the participants' stages of identity are' (Helms 1990a: 200–1). Thus, group members or leaders in the internalization or autonomy stages might be inclined to respect each other as 'racially' different, and this respect could encourage growth and an eagerness to understand others' world-views.

Crossed relationship

A crossed pattern exists when the stages of identity between the group leader and subgroups (within the larger group) represent opposite world-views. Group participants are unwilling to look outside their own world-view in order to gain an understanding of others' perspectives. Helms (1990a) asserts that crossed relationships tend to be contentious and combative:

> For instance, the Internalized/Disintegration crossed relationship . . . might be one in which the leader (or coalition) is attempting to avoid discomfort by ignoring racial issues or turning them into something else, while the other party is attempting to accentuate discomfort for the purpose of better self-understanding.
>
> (Helms 1990a: 201)

Progressive relationship

As noted above, a progressive pattern exists when the group leader's stage of racial identity development is at least one stage more advanced than the group participants' stage. The leader who runs this type of group may be the most successful at challenging as well as supporting group members' views and identities. This pattern is considered to be the most effective in 'promoting the longevity and functionality of groups' (Helms 1990a: 203).

Regressive relationship

In a regressive pattern, group participants' stage of racial identity is more advanced than that of the group leader. Thus, group members might be at the internalization stage of development while the group leader might be at the pre-encounter stage. Consequently, high levels of conflict with the leader may develop, and the development of the group may stagnate. It appears that the crossed and regressive patterns are the most damaging to the group process.

White group leaders need to become aware of their racial identity development, as well as how these identity issues affect group members and group work. An awareness of a black identity continuum will compel the group leader to acknowledge, rather than deny, 'race' and colour.

Conclusions

Currently little is known about how white people in Britain come to view and accept their identity as white, and how this impacts interethnic communication. Helms (1984: 185) concluded that 'much is to be gained by understanding how race operates in social interactions if social work and health care practitioners as well as researchers will exhibit more adventurousness in studying issues of racial identity development'.

The racial identity models provide a context in which social and mental health workers can gain an appreciation for, and empathic understanding of, a black client's frame of reference (how he or she interprets the world). If workers can acquire such knowledge – it might enable them to communicate more effectively with black clients. A white service provider's stage of racial identity development can also affect the process and outcome of interethnic communication. However, studies on racial identity development have not yet been incorporated into the majority of social work and health care training courses.

The value of studying interethnic communication using racial identity development models is 'that such situations may be rendered less mysterious and thus, more manageable' (Helms 1995: 196). If, for example, the 'potential participants [(white social worker and black client)] are crossed with respect to "racial" identity, then it is foolhardy to expect them to make peace without a peacemaker who can acknowledge the "racial" identity concerns underlying their various perspectives' (p. 196).

Racial identity development models will allow social workers and health care practitioners not only to mediate racial problems once they have occurred, but to anticipate and resolve tensions before they become problems. Racial /ethnic identity development models will become increasingly influential in the study of interethnic communication in social work and health care settings.

Annotated bibliography

Cross, W.E. (1991) *Shades of Black: Diversity in African American Identity.*
Philadelphia, PA: Temple University Press.
This book introduces the reader to models of psychological nigrescence. It provides a clear introduction to racial identity theory.
Helms, J.E. (ed.) (1990a) *Black and White Racial Identity: Theory, Research, and Practice.* Westport, CT: Greenwood Press.
This book provides an overview of black and white racial identity models.
Mama, A. (1995) *Beyond the Masks: Race, Gender and Subjectivity.* London: Routledge.
It examines the history of psychology and the way in which the discipline has propagated racism. It also offers an important theoretical perspective on ethnicity, gender and identity.

2

Beliefs, attitudes, values and interethnic communication

Introduction

This chapter provides an overview of the concepts of belief, attitude and value and the impact they have on the communicator's behaviour in interethnic communication. These concepts will be discussed in greater detail in subsequent chapters. I will argue that the lack of trust so prevalent in interethnic interaction is in great measure based on the realization of the incongruity between expressed beliefs, attitudes and values, and actual behaviour.

In this chapter I will examine the values that underlie all cultures. It draws on Kluckhohn and Strodtbeck's (1961) value-orientations model. In the next chapter I will focus on specific conceptual dimensions that are useful for understanding cultural differences.

This chapter discusses Bennett's developmental model, which describes people's attitudes to different cultural values. However, Bennett's (1986) model does not discuss the relationship between an individual's cultural identity attitudes and his/her attitude to cultural values. In this chapter I will examine the relationship between racial/cultural identity models and cultural values and within-group cultural differences. I will argue that a black client's stage of racial identity can influence his/her attitude to white Euro-American values.

Definitions

Beliefs

According to Rokeach (1973: 2), 'Beliefs are inferences made by an observer about underlying states of expectancy.' A belief 'is any simple proposition, conscious or unconscious, inferred from what a person says or does, capable of being preceded by the phrase "I believe that"' (p. 113). Rokeach has classified five types of beliefs. His classification is relevant to the understanding of belief because it functions as part of the interethnic communication structure. Rokeach's classification is based on the assumption that an individual's beliefs are not all equally important, but vary in intensity; the most central beliefs are more resistant to change and have a greater impact on the belief system if they are changed. Rokeach describes five types of belief: type A beliefs are the most central and are therefore those on which there is unanimous agreement. These beliefs are learned through an individual's direct encounter with his or her environment; type B beliefs are those which are based upon individual experience and perceptions of reality; type C and type D beliefs are based on authoritative sources and reference groups. These beliefs are less central and are more susceptible to change than types A and B. Type E beliefs are of relatively little consequence and relate primarily to personal preference and taste.

The content of a belief cannot be directly observed by others but must be inferred by an observer on the basis of the overt behaviour of the believer. What the believer says or does becomes the clue to his or her belief system. A white man who publicly states that he believes black people are equal to him but who resists black people moving into his neighbourhood demonstrates that expressed beliefs are very poor predictors of behaviour (Fishbein and Ajzen 1975).

Beliefs among black groups and the white majority can differ. For instance, a black person and a white person may share the same value of equality. The white person who has never been refused employment or promotion may believe that equality of opportunity exists – after all he/she never had any trouble. However, the black person who has always been relegated to menial tasks with no possibility for advancement perceives the situation differently. He or she believes that he or she has been discriminated against, and that equality of opportunity in employment does not exist.

Attitudes

In the social psychological literature, more than 100 definitions of the term 'attitude' can be found. Porter and Samovar (1994: 15) suggest that attitude 'may be defined as a learned tendency to respond in a consistent manner to a given object or orientation'.

There appears to be a general consensus that an attitude is a learned predisposition to respond in an evaluative (from extremely favourable to extremely unfavourable) manner toward some attitude object (Davidson and Thompson 1980). Attitudes are generally conceptualized as having three components: cognitive, affective and conative (Baron and Byrne 1991). The cognitive component involves our beliefs about the attitude object. The affective component involves our emotional or evaluative reaction to the attitude object. Finally, the conative component of an attitude involves our behavioural intentions toward the attitude object – for example, an intention to avoid black people.

One of the most disruptive attitudes that can emerge in interethnic interaction is racial prejudice. Prejudice is an attitudinal response that expresses unfavourable feelings and behavioural intentions toward a group or its individual members (Davis 1978).

Although the term 'attitude' has been well defined, difficulty arises when attempts are made to measure attitudes and to correlate them with behaviour. For example, in one study, La Piere (1934) concludes that attitudes of whites expressed toward a certain racial group in written response situations are not always the same attitudes seemingly demonstrated by whites in the behavioural situations. Put differently, in majority–minority communication, it is difficult to determine how participants best communicate their true attitudes or whether certain behaviours can be attributed to the existence of certain attitudes.

In his classic study, La Piere (1934) toured the United States with a Chinese couple, stopping at more than 250 hotels, motels and restaurants. In all that time, he and his friends were refused service only once. When La Piere wrote to the same businesses several months later and asked whether they would serve Chinese patrons, 92 per cent reported they would not. This study points to an incongruity between peoples' personally held and publicly expressed attitudes. It is likely that some white practitioners will express one ethnic attitude in a face-to-face interethnic setting and a contrary one in an impersonal situation. In a face-to-face interethnic situation the white practitioner will be more likely to inhibit the overt expression of prejudice. This tendency may explain the black stereotype of whites as 'evasive' and 'concealing' as suggested in Chapter 5. The outright expression of racism in the United States has declined in recent years (Katz and Taylor 1988), due in part to the social stigma attached to racism.

Values

Values are influential in dictating the behaviour of a communicator in interethnic settings. Rokeach (1979) defines a value 'as a type of belief – centrally located within one's total belief system'. Rokeach (p. 2) notes that 'values are core conceptions of the desirable within every individual and society. They serve as standards or criteria to guide not only action but also judgment, choice, attitude, evaluation, argument, exhortation, rationalization and one might add attribution of causality.'

According to Kluckhohn and Strodtbeck (1961: 21), 'a value is a conception, explicit or distinctive of an individual or characteristic of a group, of the desirable which influences the selection from available modes, means, and ends of action'. Values tell us how we should behave. Values may be explicit (stated overtly in a value judgement) or implicit (inferred from nonverbal behaviour), and they may be individually held or seen as part of a cultural pattern or system. Porter and Samovar (1994: 15) suggest that values are the 'valuative aspect of our belief/value/attitude systems. Valuative dimensions include qualities such as usefulness, goodness, aesthetics, need satisfaction, and pleasure.' The authors also point out that in addition to our unique set of personal values, individuals hold cultural values. These values are 'a set of organized rules for making choices, reducing uncertainty, and reducing conflicts within a given society. They are usually derived from the larger philosophical issues inherent in a culture' (p. 15). The authors define normative values as 'values [which] express themselves within a culture as rules that prescribe the behaviours that members of the culture are expected to perform' (p. 15).

Beliefs and interethnic communication

Conflict arising from differences in core beliefs among communicators can result in the disruption of interethnic communication. Core beliefs are based on an individual's direct personal experience with reality. They are held firmly and are resistant to change. White practitioners and black clients experience different realities. Such a divergence in experience will consequently result in a different set of core beliefs. Understanding this variation in core beliefs between white and black people points to the enormous distance between interethnic communicators and the problems they must overcome in order to engage in effective interaction. For example, a white middle class person who left school at 18 after completing A levels, and a black person who dropped out of school at 16, might encounter core belief conflicts. For the white person, school provided a career and the opportunity to succeed, whereas for the black person, the school system was oppressive and discriminatory. Consequently, the white person may believe that the school system is fair whereas the black person may hold negative views about the school. Thus, different life experiences result in different core beliefs and lead towards conflict when individuals of different backgrounds interact. Given the different realities of majority and minority people living in Britain, conflicts in beliefs serve as a persistent obstacle to interethnic communication. Brislin and Yoshida (1994: 14) argue that 'cross-cultural [and interethnic] encounters can be extremely stressful in that our beliefs of what is right or wrong are often challenged'. When practitioners meet clients with different beliefs 'it is much easier for [them] to dismiss [the clients] as being wrong or primitive rather than having to think carefully about them' (p. 41). White practitioners need to develop the attitude of wanting to learn about the reality of others. Only when practitioners are willing to take the step toward acknowledgement of multiple realities will they be able to overcome conflicts in core beliefs in an interethnic setting.

In interethnic communication, there are no rights or wrongs as far as beliefs are concerned. White social and health care workers must be able to recognize and to deal with their black clients' beliefs if they wish to obtain satisfactory and successful communication.

Attitudes and interethnic communication

An individual's attitudes play an important role in interethnic communication. An individual's attitudes are, however, as difficult to detect as his or her beliefs, because, like beliefs, they can only be inferred from the verbal and nonverbal reactions of individuals. When a communicator repeatedly reacts positively or negatively in relation to a certain object or person, we infer that he or she has established a specific attitude towards that object or person. In order to identify an individual's attitude, we observe his or her behaviour. Nonverbal behaviour is more reliable than verbal behaviour in accurately predicting an individual's attitudes (see Chapter 5). As discussed in Chapter 5, nonverbal behaviours are more difficult to control than verbal responses. Thus, a white practitioner may want to express a friendly attitude overtly, but his or her nonverbal behaviour (for example, pulling away from the black client) might contradict his or her verbal greeting. These issues will be discussed in more depth in the chapter on nonverbal communication. Most of the tension and hostility observed in interethnic communication is based on the attitudes of the communicators and the verbal and nonverbal manner in which those attitudes are expressed and interpreted. Facial expressions (resentment, boredom, dismissal, distrust, mockery, condescension, arrogance) and physical postures (tension, retraction, attempts to make physical contact such as handshaking, touching or patting) reveal a multitude of attitudes in the interethnic setting. Such actions may constitute a clear communication of an attitude, particularly when the physical expression and the verbal expression are inconsistent or the communication of interethnic attitudes is ambiguous (see Chapter 5).

Racism and interethnic communication

One of the most destructive attitudes that may be held and expressed by white people (in power – who control the major institutions of the society) in the interethnic setting is that of racism. Jones (1981: 28) defines racism as follows: '[Racism] results from the transformation of "race" prejudice and/or ethnocentrism through the exercise of power against a "racial" group defined as inferior, by individuals and institutions with the intentional or unintentional support of the entire culture.' Power is a key issue in interethnic communication. Power is linked to racism in the sense that power provides those elevated to the 'superior' position with the ability to carry out their perceptions and role definitions. Lago and Thompson (1994: 21) argue that 'if one views things from a prejudiced perspective and has the power to act out those views, the outcome is going to be racist'. Power is the force that drives racism, and the white – particularly male – majority clearly holds the balance of power in Britain.

Jones (1972, 1981) specifies three main forms of racism. *Individual* racism is conceptualized as a person's 'race' prejudice based on biological considerations and involving actual behaviour that is discriminatory in nature. Without institutional backing, individual racism remains at the level of prejudice (Dominelli 1992). *Institutional* racism includes the intentional or unintentional manipulation or toleration of institutional policies that unfairly restrict the opportunities of targeted groups. Institutional racist practices relate to the exclusion of black groups from having access to employment, housing, education, health and social services. The third type of racism disruptive to the interethnic communication process is *cultural* racism (discussed in Chapter 3). Cultural racism refers to the beliefs, feelings and behaviours of members of a cultural group that assert the superiority of the group's accomplishments, achievements and creativity, and attribute this claimed cultural superiority to inherent racial differences. In cultural racism the 'in-group/out-group' division is based on the supposed superiority of culture and racial background of one group over another (Axelson 1985). These three forms of racism are in dynamic interaction with one another (Dominelli 1997).

Dominelli (1992: 165) states that 'It is the subtle presence of racism in our normal activities, coupled with our failure to make the connections between the personal, institutional and cultural levels of racism, which make it so hard for white people to recognize its existence in their particular behaviour and combat it effectively.'

The impact of cultural, institutional and individual racism is felt by all ethnic minority groups. Social work and health care workers need to be aware that racism consists of the dynamic interaction between individual, cultural and institutional racism.

In an interethnic setting, communication that promotes or condones institutional racism produces responses which are destructive to the outcome of the interaction. According to Dominelli (1992: 165), 'racism permeates social work [and health care] interactions unless we take specific steps to counter it'. Racism in social work operates 'through two channels which shape client–worker interactions: the exclusive channel and the inclusive one' (pp. 165–6). The exclusive channel refers to the exclusion of black people from service provisions or employment opportunities; and the inclusive channel refers to the overrepresentation of some black people in the mental health and criminal justice systems. Thus, black people

> are consistently underrepresented as consumers of beneficial and supportive social care services, while they are over-represented as recipients of the more controlling aspects of social care, such as compulsory admission to psychiatric hospital.
>
> (Braye and Preston-Shoot 1995: 41)

Social workers may, for example, use stereotypes such as black families do not need services because 'they look after each other' to justify the bias and inequality in service provision.

Several studies have found that individual, cultural and institutional racism permeates health care interactions (for example Littlewood and

Lipsedge 1989; Baxter 1993; Fernando 1995). In a study of the communication needs of black and ethnic minority pregnant women in Salford, Baxter (1993: 11) noted that the participants 'felt they were treated with disrespect and unfavourably to other women on the wards'. Baxter (p. 12) quotes one woman: 'My sister came to visit me. The nurse stopped her because it was outside visiting hours. Yet she allowed another English couple to go inside to visit their daughter. They were also ridiculed because they were wearing traditional clothes.'

Many scholars have outlined ways that individual, cultural and institutional racism continue to influence counselling practice, research and training (D'Andrea 1992; Atkinson *et al.* 1993; Ponterotto and Pedersen 1993; D'Andrea *et al.* 1994). White counsellors and social workers must initiate and encourage open discussions about the manifestations of individual and cultural racism in social work and health care practice. Lago and Thompson (1994: 208) argue that 'the issue of racism has to be addressed and worked with by counsellors [and social and health care workers] in training who plan to work in today's multi"racial" society'. Although white counsellors may deny that they are racists,

> this view does not take into account a whole range of mechanisms, perceptions, and experiences to which white people have been exposed throughout their lives. Such phenomena, if they remain unconscious, may affect the counsellor's behaviour and responses in ways that prove negative in cross-'race' counselling.
>
> (Lago and Thompson 1994: 209)

Racist attitudes (when expressed even in the most subtle or unconscious fashion in the interethnic setting) disrupt the communication process. Ridley (1989) breaks down the varieties of racism encountered in counselling. Individual and institutional racism are broken down into smaller units of analysis based on whether the behaviour is overt or covert, and whether it is intentional or unintentional. Overt racism, which may be either individual or institutional, is easy to identify and is always intentional (Ridley 1995). However, covert racism is more subtle and may be either intentional or unintentional. Justice and Justice (1990: 13) argue that 'covert racism is found throughout [the counselling profession] and [that we] have to try and understand each other's cultures in order to avoid this. By just teaching [minority groups] our own culture [(Euro-American)] and patronising theirs is certainly not the answer.'

Of the various forms of racism, unintentional racist acts are the most insidious. Unintentional racism may be either individual, institutional or cultural. Unintentional racists are unaware of the harmful consequences of their behaviour. They are more likely to deny their racism. However, 'unintentional racists, cloaked in their sincerity and desire to do good, often do some of the greatest harm' (Ridley 1995: 39). According to Ridley (p. 39), 'counsellors [and social workers], in many ways, are socialized and trained to behave as racists without even knowing it'. There is no reason to believe that counsellors, therapists and social workers are any less vulnerable to manifesting various types of intentional and unintentional racism than other members of society (Locke 1992).

The existence of racism has produced a variety of defence and survival mechanisms among black people. Jones (1985) feels that it is important for the worker to acknowledge the existence of these factors and to help the client identify maladaptive means of dealing with racism. For example, an individual may have only a limited or reflexive response in dealing with these situations. In working with a client, in which racism plays a part, the worker must assist the client in developing a wider range of options and encourage the development of a more conscious, problem-solving mode.

Although all people need to be involved in the fight against prejudice (see also Miles 1989), white people, particularly, must acknowledge their past and present racism and take a proactive lead in combating all forms of racism (see, particularly, Bowser and Hunt 1981; Helms 1992).

Distrust and deception

The experiences of slavery, colonization and institutional racism have taught black people to distrust white people. In view of the distrust black people have developed in their dealings with white people, it should come as no surprise that black people have been reluctant to share what is really on their minds with white people (see Chapter 5). Probably the most frequently mentioned barrier in interethnic helping situations is distrust and suspiciousness (Siegel 1970). Thompson *et al.* (1994) note that Terrell and Terrell (1981, 1984) have defined cultural mistrust as a 'survivalistic posture assumed by blacks to endure generations of "racial" oppression [and linked it] to premature termination with white counselors [and social workers]' (Thompson *et al.* 1994: 155). Among black people, distrust of whites has been well documented for its survival function and has been viewed as a 'healthy cultural paranoia' by Grier and Cobbs (1968) (see Chapter 5). Indeed, black people use different roles in an attempt to survive in a white-dominated society. Black people are not willing to disclose their problems and feelings until significant rapport and trust have been established.

Watkins and Terrell (1988) found that highly mistrustful blacks who were assigned to white rather than to black counsellors tended to have diminished expectations for counselling. They regarded the white counsellor as less credible and less able to help them with anxiety, shyness, and inferiority feelings – in comparison to black counsellors (Terrell *et al.* 1989). Thus, for white counsellors that see highly mistrustful blacks, the establishment of an effective counselling relationship may be particularly difficult to achieve. Terrell *et al.* (1989) note that their study emphasizes the need for counsellors to be sensitive to the mistrust issue and its potential effects on black client–white counsellor relationships.

Family therapy that takes place between black families and white practitioners can also be hindered by mistrust (Gwyn and Kilpatrick 1981).

Gwyn and Kilpatrick (p. 265) believe that this barrier, albeit significant, can be bridged if therapists 'explore and recognize their own prejudices, clarify this influence on their practice, and overtly allow the "racial" issue to be part of the therapeutic process'.

The results of a study carried out by Grant-Thompson and Atkinson (1997) indicate that mentor ethnicity, mentor cultural sensitivity and student level of cultural mistrust all play a role in how black (African American) male students perceive a university faculty mentor. A faculty mentor who was described as an African American was rated as a more credible source of help and more cross-culturally competent than a faculty mentor described as a European American. However, the ethnicity of the faculty mentor is most important for African American students who are highly mistrustful of whites. Those African American men who were low in cultural mistrust rated the credibility of a European American faculty about the same as they did the credibility of an African American faculty mentor. These findings may be generalized to other white–black relationships – for example white social worker–black client or white doctor–black patient.

White practitioners who experience distrust from black clients need to have an understanding of the historical and cultural reasons for black clients' distrust of whites and should recognize the adaptive and survival role that distrust often serves for black people. According to Davis and Proctor (1989: 27), 'the underlying "healthy paranoia" should be recognized and respected'. White social work and health care workers must be alert to themes of concealment, suspicion and disguise.

If effective interethnic communication is to take place, the establishment of trust is imperative. Overcoming the black client's mistrust is the greatest contribution practitioners can make to the 'working alliance' (Gelso and Fretz 1992). But trusting a white counsellor or social worker is often difficult for black clients. Toward this end, practitioners must demonstrate their goodwill; that is, they must convey that they are well-meaning individuals who have elected to work with people whom they value. In particular they must be as free as possible of racism. Trust is also enhanced by the worker's demonstration of the skills necessary to address the black client's problems (Davis and Proctor 1989).

Values and interethnic communication

Sitaram and Haapanen (1979: 159) note that:

> The first rule of intercultural communication is that each participant should understand the other's values. That understanding should precede any attempts to communicate interculturally. Because communicative techniques are manifestations of one's own values, the participants communicate differently. The second rule is that each should adapt his/her communication to the other's values. Adaptation

implies respect for the other value system. Without such respect one cannot adapt his/her communicative behaviour to the other system. Adaptation should be an on-going act. A person should know the art of constant adaptation to other cultures.

Values, therefore, play an important role in interethnic communication. Sue and Sue (1990: 215) suggest that 'Black values have been shaped by cultural factors, social class variables, and experience with racism.' In order to communicate effectively with a black client the practitioner must first be very aware of his or her own value biases; second, he or she must be knowledgeable, sensitive and appreciative of the client's value system, and finally, he or she must be careful not to impose his or her value system onto the client.

Many social work and health care practitioners are not aware of their own value biases (Sue 1981; Katz 1985; Pedersen 1988). Katz (1985: 616) points out that 'because White culture is the dominant cultural norm in the United States [and Britain], it acts as an invisible veil that limits many people from seeing it as a cultural system'. As discussed in Chapter 3, there is an identifiable 'dominant' value system in Britain that is associated with the majority (white middle class) group, and which pervades most social work courses (Dominelli 1988). Practitioners need to understand the value bases of the power-dominant cultural system that forms the basis of training and practice. White people in Britain are raised to believe that their value system is the most appropriate, 'the best', and that people possessing non-middle class white values should try their best to assimilate and adapt to the majority culture system. This ethnocentric bias serves as a barrier to effective interethnic communication. Social and health care workers who have little understanding of black (Asian and African Caribbean) culture tend to look upon the black client's values and culture as inherently inferior to their own. For example, as noted in Chapter 3, black people come from cultures that value group affiliation and collectivism. Practitioners from a Eurocentric perspective – where individualism is valued – may misinterpret the behaviour of these clients as codependency. This is reflected in 'white social workers' scepticism about black families' child-rearing practices; contempt for the close relationships between black parents and their children; and disdain in judging women's position within black families' (Dominelli 1988: 51).

The white middle class culture is very competitive; and having a highly competitive nature is considered a valued trait. Compared to the white middle class culture, some cultural/ethnic groups feel less comfortable, or even uncomfortable with competition. The concept of achievement is highly interrelated with those of individualism and competition. White culture is highly achievement oriented. In contrast, in some ethnic groups, the concept of individual achievement is not so highly valued, and in fact may be devalued. As a group, black people tend to be more group centred, to be sensitive to interpersonal matters, and to value cooperation (Jackson

1983). Nobles (1976) feels that some of these values are due to some black people's African heritage, which stresses groupness, community, cooperation and interdependence, and being one with nature.

As noted in Chapter 3, most major theories of social work, counselling and psychotherapy originated in Eurocentric ideology. To use traditional counselling theories beneficially with black people, counsellors need to evaluate them for cultural bias. Some assumptions identified by Pedersen (1988) reflecting cultural bias in counselling are: a common measure of 'normal behaviour'; emphasis on individualism; overemphasis on independence; and cultural encapsulation (defined in Chapter 3).

When counselling cross-culturally, the chances that the client and the counsellor enter the counselling relationship with differing values are heightened. A counsellor's value system affects his or her beliefs and attitudes which in turn influence his or her perception of the counselling process. The black client, too, enters counselling with a certain, culturally established value system, which affects his or her view of the appropriateness of counselling. Counsellors need to examine counselling theories for cultural bias.

Katz (1985: 619) suggests that white American cultural values form the basis of psychotherapeutic theory and practice:

> The similarities between White culture and the cultural values that form the formulations of traditional counseling theory and practice are interchangeable. Because counseling theory and practice developed out of the experience of White therapists and researchers working almost exclusively with White client systems, it comes as no surprise that the profession reflects white cultural values. [This] affects [practitioners'] abilities to be effective cross-culturally.

Traditionally trained counsellors and social workers are so caught up in their own belief system that they are unaware of their specific values, and they neglect to realize that there are alternative, equally justifiable cultural value systems.

I will examine the cultural values that underlie all cultures. I will be drawing on the work of Kluckhohn and Strodtbeck (1961) and their theory of value orientations. Kluckhohn and Strodtbeck proposed a value-orientations model that is useful in comparing cultural values and attitudes. Kluckhohn and Strodtbeck put forward three conclusions that apply to all cultures: people in all cultures face common human problems for which they must find a solution; the range of alternative solutions to a culture's problems is not limitless; within a given culture, there will be preferred solutions, which most people within the culture will select, but there will also be people who will choose other solutions. In the model, participants are asked to solve five common problems with three possible solutions. The five problems are:

1 What is the innate character of human nature (evil, mixed or good)?

2 What is the relationship between people and nature (subjugation, harmony or mastery)?
3 What is the temporal focus of the culture (past, present or future)?
4 What is the appropriate form of self-expression (being, being-in-becoming or doing)?
5 What are the proper social relations (lineal, collateral or individual)?

According to Kluckhohn and Strodtbeck, cultures must select their solutions from a range of available alternatives. A culture's available alternatives to the problem 'What is the nature of human beings?' can range from 'people are born with evil inclinations' through 'humans are born both good and evil' to 'humans are good'. A culture's response to problems in the relationship of humans to nature can range from a belief that 'nature guides one's life' through 'nature is one's partner in life' to 'nature is used for one's own purpose'. A culture's preferred time orientation can emphasize events and experiences from the past (traditional customs are paramount), the present (here-and-now events are most important, or the future (planning for events that are to occur receives primary attention). A culture's activity orientation can involve 'being' (values nonaction; activity is spontaneous self-expression), 'being-in-becoming' (activity is integrated in the personality), or 'doing' (external goals are the source of action-oriented self-expression). Finally, interpersonal relationships can vary along a continuum from 'lineal' (lines of authority are clearly established, based on kinship or heredity), 'collateral' (group-oriented goals are most important), or 'individual' (individual goals are most important).

Black cultural values are more likely to be characterized by beliefs in collateral group relations, or sharing, present time, and harmony with nature or spirituality (Carter and Helms 1987). For instance, an African worldview operationalizes the individual's link with nature and all mankind. Akbar (1976: 175) writes:'African people throughout the world have a world view which is conceived as a universal oneness . . . There is an interaction of all things which compose the universe.' Similarly, it may be argued that within Asian cultures there is a recurrent belief that individuals should live in harmony with nature.

By contrast, Euro-American cultural values have a 'doing' orientation, an orientation for the future, a belief in control over nature, a preference for individualism, and a belief that people are basically good and changeable. There are differences between blacks (African Americans, Africans and Asians) in Kluckhohn and Strodtbeck's 'activity' orientation. Black cultures are usually regarded as 'being' cultures. For example, Indians often believe that all events are determined by fate and are therefore inevitable or fatalistic. This is another characteristic of a 'being' orientation. 'Doing' is the dominant characteristic of Euro-Americans, who rarely question the assumption that it is important to get things done. The 'doing' culture is often the striving culture, in which people seek to change and control what is happening to them. A culture's activity orientation also influences the pace of life. The pace of life in Euro-American culture is dictated by clocks, appointments and schedules (see Chapter 5). This contrasts with the more relaxed pace of life in cultures such as India and among Africans and African Americans. According to Daniel and Smitherman (1976: 32),

> Being on time has to do with participating in the fulfillment of an activity that is vital to the sustenance of a basic rhythm, rather than with appearing on the scene at, say 'twelve o'clock sharp'. The key is not to be 'on time' but 'in time'.

Thus, in African American cultures, orientations to time are driven less by a need to 'get things done' and conform to external demands than by a sense of participation in events that create their own rhythm.

These different orientations to 'activity mode' influence interpersonal communication patterns in every culture. As discussed above, in 'doing' cultures, interpersonal communication is characterized by concerns about what people do and how they solve problems. In 'being' cultures, interpersonal communication is characterized by being together rather than by accomplishing specific tasks.

Thus, Kluckhohn and Strodtbeck's (1961) model assumes there is a set of core dimensions that are pertinent to all peoples of all cultures. However, the authors argue that not all people from a culture will make exactly the same set of choices, and in fact some people from a culture may select other alternatives – the model is a framework which predicts actions in specific contexts.

Kluckhohn and Strodtbeck's work has been very influential in intercultural communication research. It forms the foundation for Hall's (1966) high and low context cultural dimension and Hofstede's (1980) cultural dimensions discussed in Chapter 3. White American and British values – described in Kluckhohn and Strodtbeck's (1961) model – influence the way white people live and develop. For example the 'future time sense mode' is expressed in the way whites plan their families, education and occupations. The dominant white American and British choices in each cultural value dimension fit together well. Spiegel (1982: 42) notes that:

> If the personal achievement implied by Doing is to be facilitated, then it is good to be able for the Future, as an Individual not too constrained by family or group ties, with optimism supplied by the Mastery-over-Nature orientation, and the pragmatic morality, with which self-interest is justified, afforded by the Neutral [mixed alternative] view of the Basic Nature of Man.

The five value orientations outlined by Kluckhohn and Strodtbeck (1961) are interconnected and play an important role in how white people behave in interethnic communication settings.

Racial/cultural identity models and cultural values

As discussed in Chapter 1, racial/cultural identity models describe an individual's psychological orientation to membership in both the dominant and nondominant cultures in the US and Britain. Given the context of racism and oppression that permeates British society, the models describe how an individual experiences membership in either the dominant or the nondominant group.

Thomas (1995: 175) argues that the culture of young (second generation) black people in Britain is

> formed by [their] day-to-day struggle to exist in a society which denies them certain rights, provides them with some opportunities but often does not give them the chance to contribute fully to the society they see as their own.

Thus, young black people are confronted with a set of dualities defined by being part of, yet apart from, British society; in it but not of it, included at some level and excluded at others. This duality dilemma is reflected in the writings of Semaj (1981), who presented three phases of black extended identity. According to Semaj, the apparent struggle many black people (African and African Americans) engage in between Eurocentric and Afrocentric polarities is reflected in different identities – alien, diffused and collective. The aliens have a Eurocentric world-view and denigrate their Africanity. The diffused try to balance the black and alien world-views, believing that black is beautiful while understanding that white is power. Finally, the collective demonstrate an Afro-centric world-view. In the struggle to sustain personal worth in a multi-ethnic and racist context, negotiating the politics of racial exclusion and cultural denigration must also deal with the competing cultural orientations of in-group and out-group identified by Kluckhohn and Strodtbeck (1961).

There are some parallels between the model described above and Gushue's model. Gushue (1993) proposed a model of nondominant culture identity – based on Helms and Carter's (1986) racial identity model, to explain within-group cultural differences. Although Gushue describes cultural as opposed to racial identity, he stresses that the distinction should not obscure 'the fundamental affinity between these two constructs'. Thus, both constructs discuss a 'psychological "coming to terms" with one's membership in a group that is oppressed and devalued by the cultural ideology of the larger society of which an individual's group forms a part' (Gushue 1993: 496).

Gushue's model has four stages: the first stage, conformity, refers to 'naive acceptance of the dominant culture's values. Tendency to denigrate one's own culture and idealize the dominant culture': At the second stage, dissonance/introspection, an individual begins to 'question uncritical assimilation to dominant culture in self and others. [There is] growing interest in one's own cultural heritage.' The third stage, resistance, refers to 'exclusive interest and pride in one's own culture, outright rejection of the dominant culture's values'. The final stage, awareness, refers to 'a critical interest and pride in one's own culture. [There is] a critical acceptance of certain aspects of the dominant culture, combined with continued efforts to resist cultural assimilation to "the mainstream"' (Gushue 1993: 497).

Gushue proposed the above model to explain within-group cultural differences in families. The ethnic/cultural paradigm considers how some of the same differences in world-view are expressed in differing psychological orientations to ethnic/cultural membership in the context of social power and oppression (Gushue 1993).

Gushue has also put forward a dominant culture-identity development model based on Helms's (1984) model for white ethnic identity development (see Chapter 1). Reframing Helms's discussion of white identity, Gushue (1993) described the process from the perspective of dominant culture identity. The model depicts six stages. An individual in the first stage (contact) has a monocultural perspective, is unaware of other cultural points of view and believes that the values, beliefs and behaviours of the dominant culture are normative. The second stage, disintegration, is characterized by an individual 'discovering' other cultures and 'naive enthusiasm for the "exotic" combined with initial consciousness of membership in dominant (oppressive) culture'. The third stage, reintegration, refers to 'denigration of and hostility toward nondominant cultures'; the fourth stage, pseudo-independence, describes an individual's 'intellectual awareness of the validity of differing cultural perspectives'; in the fifth stage, immersion–emersion, the individual 'attempts to work out a nonoppressive dominant-culture identity'. And in the sixth stage, autonomy, the individual has a multicultural perspective and 'values (rather than tolerates) diversity' (Gushue 1993: 498).

Gushue, however, notes that there are two potential moderating variables in the cultural identity models – 'race' and degree of social power. The patterns of the cultural-identity development model are intensified for 'people of color' as 'the individual is exposed to the combination of racial [(i.e. colour)] and cultural prejudice' (p. 506). However, for white people of a nondominant cultural group, the 'experience of prejudice may be mitigated somewhat because they belong to the socially powerful "race"' (p. 506). Secondly:

> A person's relative position of social power (via socioeconomic status or cultural acceptability) may moderate the intensity with which he or she experiences the xenophobia of the dominant [white] society and, consequently, the intensity with which he or she experiences the various attitudes associated with stages of the nondominant culture identity development model.
>
> (p. 507)

Gushue extended Helms's interaction theory (see Chapter 1) to multicultural family counselling. Gushue's model enables practitioners to 'identify an individual's psychological orientation toward the dominant and nondominant cultures, predict the types of relationships . . . and develop a treatment [communication] strategy . . . [which are] indispensable steps toward a successful counseling [and communication] outcome' (pp. 509–10).

Bennett's (1986) developmental model

This section briefly explores Bennett's (1986) developmental model. This model outlines people's attitudes to different cultural values and describes the various stages people go through when placed in an unfamiliar culture where they must function according to different rules. Bennett (1986) presents six stages: denial, defense, minimization, acceptance, adaptation and integration. He labels the first three stages – denial, defense and minimization – the 'ethnocentric stages' and the next three stages the 'ethnorelative stages'. People who have lived most of their lives in a relatively homogeneous community tend to be in the denial stage. It is difficult for these people 'to conceptualize the possibility that others may operate on a completely different value system from themselves. They impose their own value system of what is good or bad on other people' (Brislin and Yoshida 1996: 61). During the defense stage, people are

> more or less conscious of the fact that other value systems may exist. However, because they are afraid to acknowledge that fact because of its ramifications for their self-esteem, they resort to defensive behaviours such as negative stereotyping of others.
> (Brislin and Yoshida 1996: 61)

During the minimization stage people admit that although there are differences between cultures, they are insignificant compared to the similarities between human beings in general. This attitude is similar to the colour blind approach (see Dominelli 1988). In the acceptance stage, 'people have accepted that their values and norms are not necessarily "right" and that other cultures have their own values and norms that are just as responsible' (Brislin and Yoshida 1996: 62). The adaptation stage 'is marked by behavioural changes. People not only accept cultural differences but are able to empathise with individuals from other cultures and change their behaviours when interacting with them . . . they have become bicultural' (p. 63). Finally, the integration stage refers to the stage where 'people must learn to integrate multiple sets of values into their identities even when some of the values may clash with one another' (p. 65).

However, Bennett (1991) argues that people (for example black people) who have been oppressed by the dominant white culture go through the developmental stages in a different way. Thus, black people spend a considerable amount of time in the defense stage and skip the denial and minimization stages. Bennett (p. 71) argues that black people:

are often in situations where they see and feel differences between themselves and the dominant [white] group. Therefore, denial or minimization of differences is less likely to occur in their minds. Instead, defending their own cultural identities through negative stereotyping of others' is more likely to occur since, as a repressed group, the need to solidify their identities has historically been extremely strong.

Individuals in Cross's (1971, 1978) encounter and immersion–emersion stage of black identity development are more likely to spend more time in Bennett's defense stage of development. Social work and health care workers need to familiarize themselves with the Bennett model, in order to assess their developmental stage before communicating with black clients and to utilize the most appropriate methods of intervention.

A knowledge and understanding of how individuals may vary with respect to their level of racial and cultural identity is an essential aspect of cultural knowledge. The models described above provide a paradigm that is both practically and conceptually useful for social and health care workers in understanding within-group cultural differences. The stage of racial identity could influence a black client's attitudes to white values. A black person at the pre-encounter phase of Cross's model (see Chapter 1) sees white values as positive. At an encounter phase, during which the individual becomes aware of their 'blackness', they suffer an identity conflict, and begin to seek a new identity. They see black values as positive. An immersion–emersion phase describes a stage during which the individual actively identifies with black values and rejects white middle class values. Finally, an internalization phase refers to a stage during which self-identity is strong and the individual becomes comfortable interacting with other cultures.

Carter and Helms (1987) used the Kluckhohn and Strodtbeck (1961) model of value orientations described above. Carter and Helms (1987), in a study of the relationship between black (African American) students' value orientations and their racial identity attitudes, found that only those stages of racial identity that were associated with identification with black culture predicted value-orientations preferences for blacks. The value preferences predicted by higher levels of racial identity were harmony with nature (i.e. people and nature coexist in harmony), collateral social relations (consulting friends/families when problems arise), and being-in-becoming (i.e. activity is integrated in the personality). Carter and Helms (1987) concluded that the results supported black psychologists' and theorists' belief that black cultural values consist of a combination of African elements as well as values developed as mechanisms by which to cope with the racism and discrimination that blacks have experienced in America. In a similar study of the relationship between white racial identity and cultural values, Carter and Helms (1990) found that white racial identity attitudes were predictive of cultural values. Thus, it seems that in studying both blacks and whites, racial identity attitudes may be an important factor that influences cultural values.

The following tables provide a summary of the main models discussed in this chapter.

Table 2.1   Kluckhohn and Strodtbeck's (1961) value orientations model

Orientation	Alternatives		
Model of human nature	evil	mixed	good
Mode of person/nature	subjugation to nature	harmony with nature	mastery over nature
Time sense mode	past	present	future
Activity mode	being	being-in-becoming	doing
Social relations mode	lineal	collateral	individual

Table 2.2   Bennett's (1986) model

Ethnocentric stages

1	Denial	Individuals impose own value system on other people
2	Defense	Individuals are conscious that other value systems exist – but there is negative stereotyping of other cultures
3	Minimization	Individuals admit that there are differences between cultures – but these differences are insignificant

Ethnorelative stages

4	Acceptance	Individuals accept that their values and norms are not necessarily 'right'
5	Adaptation	Individuals accept cultural differences and empathize with individuals from other cultures
6	Integration	Individuals integrate numerous sets of values – even when some values may clash

Table 2.3   Gushue's (1993) identity development models

Nondominant culture identity model	
Conformity	Tendency to denigrate one's own culture and idealize the dominant culture
Dissonance/introspection	Growing interest in one's own culture
Resistance	Exclusive interest in one's own culture and rejection of the dominant culture's values
Awareness	A critical interest and pride in one's own culture
Dominant culture-identity development model	
Contact	Monocultural perspective
Disintegration	Curious about other cultures
Reintegration	Denigration of and hostility toward nondominant cultures
Pseudo-independence	Intellectual awareness of the validity of differing cultural perspectives
Immersion–emersion	Attempt to work out a nonoppressive dominant culture identity
Autonomy	Multicultural perspective

Conclusion

Some disparity does exist in beliefs, attitudes and values between communicators of different racial and cultural backgrounds. There is no simple effective solution to the problem of interethnic belief, attitude and value conflict. However, social and health care workers must try in interethnic settings to step outside themselves in order to gain an understanding of the reality of others.

Social and health care workers should be aware both of their own attitudes and behaviour and those communication situations in which they are likely to display negative behaviours. Such an awareness is at least a first step in mitigating problems in black and white verbal and nonverbal communication. Practitioners need to be conscious that racist attitudes, even when expressed in a subtle or unconscious fashion, can disrupt the interethnic communication process.

An understanding of Bennett's developmental model will enable practitioners to assess their developmental stage before communicating with black clients. For instance, a white social worker at the denial stage is likely to interpret a black client's nonverbal behaviour from a Eurocentric perspective. This will lead to miscommunication and a failure to meet the black client's needs.

Practitioners should have an understanding of Kluckhohn and Strodt-beck's value orientations model, as these values may influence the manner in which practitioners communicate in interethnic communication settings. The practitioner's values will lead them to communicate in certain ways, because values will determine which ways of communicating are deemed more desirable than others. Conflict in value systems is a major cause of communication breakdown in interethnic settings. As noted earlier, the problem that arises with the difference in values is that we tend to use our own values as the standard when judging others. We tend to assume that our value system is best, an assumption that causes us to make value judgements of others. White practitioners need to become more aware of their own values and beliefs and should be encouraged to share these in interethnic communication. Practitioners should consciously examine the bases of their values and beliefs and the actual role served by them in their own life as well as in their culture. Workers can then determine whether any of their values and beliefs are serving as deterrents to good interethnic communication.

White social and health care workers need to explore and discover their racial identity attitudes because white racial identity attitudes are predictive of racist attitudes. Black people's racial identity attitudes and value orientations may also have an impact on interethnic communication. A knowledge of the relationship between black people's value orientations and their racial identity attitudes will enable social and health care workers to communicate more effectively with black clients. Finally, the literature that addresses some of the issues (for example, the relationship between white racial identity attitudes and racist attitudes; the relationship between black people's value orientations and their racial identity attitudes) discussed in this chapter is limited at best. Much more research is needed in the areas noted above, in both the United States and Britain.

Annotated bibliography

Dominelli, L. (1997) (2nd edn) *Anti-Racist Social Work*. London: Macmillan.
  This book explores the complex and dynamic processes whereby racism is reinforced in social work. It uses case studies, good practice guidelines and exercises to assist the reader in understanding racism in social work practice.
Lago, C. and Thompson, J. (1996) *Race, Culture and Counselling*. Buckingham: Open University Press.
  This book explores some of the major dimensions and subtleties underlying the issues of 'race' and culture and how these might impact upon counselling relationships.
Porter, L.A. and Samovar, R.E. (1994) *Intercultural Communication*. Belmont, CA: Wadsworth.
  This book provides an overview of some of the main issues addressed in intercultural communication.

3

Culture and interethnic communication

Introduction

This chapter discusses the impact of cultural racism and the deficit/deficiency model on interethnic communication. It examines the impact of the multicultural and black perspective on interethnic communication.

I will examine some of the culture-bound values of black people identified in the cross-cultural communication literature and their relationship to interethnic communication. A cultural framework will enable us to understand black people's communication style. The values discussed are: power–distance; uncertainty avoidance; individualism versus collectivism; masculinity; low and high context communication; immediacy and expressiveness; emotional and behavioural expressiveness; and self-disclosure. While the intent of this chapter is to discuss the cultural values of black people it must be kept in mind that social class and gender can also influence black people's cultural values. In this chapter I will also examine the impact of intracultural differences within black groups on interethnic communication.

Finally, implications for social work and health care practice are explored in the conclusion.

Definitions

The word '"culture" denotes a way of life (family life, patterns of behaviour and belief, language, etc.) but it is important to note that cultures are not static, especially in a community where there are people from several cultures living side by side' (Fernando 1995: 5). Culture refers to 'child rearing habits, family systems, and ethical values or attitudes common to a group' (Fernando 1991: 10).

According to Fernando (1991), culture is characterized by behaviour and attitudes; it is determined by upbringing and choice, and perceived as changeable (assimilation and acculturation). Acculturation is a variable that must be considered in discussions of interethnic/intercultural communication (Danna 1993). In general, acculturation may be defined in terms of the degree of integration of new cultural patterns into the original cultural patterns (Moyerman and Forman 1992; Danna 1993). In contrast to the usual perception of relatively fixed 'cultures', Fernando argues that 'culture' needs to be considered as something that is subject to a fluidity of movement (Fernando 1991). Indeed over the last decade and more the concept of culture has become a subject of critical debate in anthropology; and the idea of a stable, bounded and territorially specific culture has been transformed into a conception of culture as fluid, complex and transnational (Hannerz 1996; Olwig and Hastrup 1997). Debates flourish on globalization and its impact on ethnic identities; and consequently the linkages between culture, shared histories and current identities are increasingly being seen as complex and specific. Human geographers, for example, are pointing out how the common status of 'immigrant' may obscure very different histories of social upheaval, geographic mobility and cultural dislocation between different ethnic minority communities (Keith and Pile 1993). Gilroy (1993) is but one of the many analysts examining the implications of the diasporic experience of minority ethnic communities in Britain for an understanding of their current culture and identity. Notions of cultural hybridity and complexly fluid ethnic identities must necessarily be held in mind when interpreting and employing the psychological models outlined in this text (see for example Rattansi and Westwood 1994; Werbner and Modood 1997).

Cultural racism

Cultural racism is a relatively new form of racism and has been called 'modern racism' (McConahay and Hough 1976; McConahay 1986), 'aversive racism' (Gaertner and Dovidio 1986) and 'symbolic racism' (Sears 1988). The root of 'modern racism' is in a continuing Eurocentric philosophy that values mainstream (dominant culture) beliefs and attitudes more highly than culturally diverse belief systems. Modern racism is subtle and often beyond conscious awareness whereas overt racism – known as 'old-fashioned racism' (Greeley and Sheatsley 1971) or 'dominative racism' (Gaertner and Dovidio 1986) – is evident in individuals who act out bigoted beliefs (Gaertner and Dovidio 1986).

According to Fernando (1991: 18), 'racism affects our perceptions of culture and these assumptions are incorporated into the training of professionals'. In British society 'there is a hierarchy of cultures and those of "racial" minority groups are ranked very low indeed' (Ahmed 1996: 123). White Western European religion, music, philosophy, law, politics, economics, morality, science and medicine are all considered to be the best in the world. Thus, 'references to black clients' cultures frequently reflect negative valuations rather than sensitivity' (Ahmed 1996: 123). Gushue (1993) also notes that certain cultures (for example Northern European) are judged as more acceptable by the dominant culture than are others (e.g. African, Asian). Cultural racism includes the individual and institutional expression of the superiority of one 'race''s cultural heritage (and concomitant value system) over that of other 'race's. Therefore, the white majority value system summarized by Katz (1985) and elaborated upon in more recent texts (Pedersen 1988; Ponterotto *et al.* 1990; Ponterotto and Casas 1991) serves as a foundation for cultural racism when it is perceived as the 'model' system, and when those individuals who possess alternative value systems are thought of by the white majority as being deficient in some way. White communication styles and patterns (verbal and non-verbal) are considered to be superior to black communication styles.

Deficit/deficiency model

The deficit/deficiency model – which can be traced in Western Eurocentric social science research of black and minority groups – contends that black people are deficient with respect to intelligence, cognitive styles and family structure due to lack of proper environmental stimulation, racism and oppressive conditions. From this deficit model came such hypotheses as 'cultural deprivation' (Valentine 1971), which presumed that, due to inadequate exposure to Eurocentric values, norms, customs and lifestyles, blacks were 'culturally deprived' and required cultural enrichment. Implicit in the concept of cultural deprivation, however, is the notion that the dominant white middle class culture established the normative standard. Thus, any behaviours, values, and lifestyles that differed from the Euro-American norm were seen as deficient. Some psychologists express little interest in trying to understand any culture other than their own. Wheeler and Reis (1988: 36) argue that 'It takes more intellectual resources than we have just to understand our own current culture . . . We just don't have time to read about [other cultures].' Such sentiments are widespread among European American psychologists who represent the dominant white majority (Lonner 1994).

For many white social scientists the word 'different', when applied to black people, became synonymous with 'deficient'. A main feature of Eurocentric psychology is the assumption among psychologists that people are alike in all important respects. In order to explain 'universal human phenomena', white psychologists established a normative standard of behaviour against which all other cultural groups were to be measured. What appeared as normal or abnormal was always in comparison to how closely a specific thought or behaviour corresponded to that of white people. Hence, normality is established on a model of the middle class Caucasian male of European descent. The more one approximates this model in appearance, values and behaviour, the more 'normal' one is considered to be. The obvious advantage for Europeans (whites) is that such norms confirm their reality as *the* reality. But, the major problem with such normative assumptions for non-European people is the inevitable categorization of anyone unlike this model 'as deviant'. In fact, the more distinct or distant you are from this model, the more pathological you are considered to be (Robinson 1995).

It appears, therefore, that when two people meet from different cultures, they judge each other's behaviour in terms of their own cultural criteria which they do not share and do not verbalize. This inherent tendency to judge (most often negatively) rather than striving to understand can form the basis of breakdowns in communication between culturally different people. Wrenn (1985) introduced the concept of 'cultural encapsulation' for counselling. A feature of this perspective is that 'we define reality according to one set of cultural assumptions and stereotypes . . . [also] we become insensitive to cultural variations among individuals and assume that our view is the only real or legitimate one' (Pedersen 1991: 10). Thus, the 'encapsulated counselor [and social/health care worker] is trapped in one way of thinking that resists adaptation and rejects alternatives' (p. 11). In Britain, some black people assert that methods of psychotherapy are 'culturally encapsulated within a white western view of the world and are consequently insensitive and totally inappropriate in their unthinking application to all counselling situations' (Lago and Thompson 1994: 208). For example, Eurocentric counselling practices emphasize individualism, independence, and an aggressive and assertive orientation. These values are predominantly found in individualistic cultures, like Britain and the United States. Whereas, in collective cultures (for example Asian and African), subordination to the family and (generally) to the collective, is encouraged; autonomy is discouraged and perceived as an obstacle to good relations. Another example can be found in the field of mental health. Eurocentric standards of mental health are often inappropriate for black people because they are based on the philosophies, values and mores of Euro-American culture, and these variables are used to develop normative standards of mental health. What constitutes sane or insane behaviour, mental health or mental illness, or normal or abnormal behaviour is, therefore, always in relation to a white normative standard. These standards are applied to black people by mental health workers who usually have little or no understanding of the black community's cultural requirements (Baughman 1971). For instance, generally speaking, in Eastern thinking integration, balance and harmony, both within oneself and within the family or community, are important aspects of mental health. In the West, self-sufficiency, efficiency and individual autonomy seem to be important. Thus, 'professionals trained in Western schools of thought will see ideals of self-sufficiency, personal autonomy, efficiency and self-esteem as the correct basis for discussions about mental health' (Fernando 1991: 18).

Social and health care workers who have little understanding of Asian and African Caribbean cultures tend to look upon the black client's values and cultures as inherently inferior to their own. In Britain it is often assumed that distinctive racial, cultural and linguistic features are deviant, inferior or embarassing. Triseliotis argues that:

> expression of emotions and feelings, the display of moods, the tone of voice, physical contact, posture, facial expression and gestures, the management of conflict and the observance of personal and physical boundaries are all shaped and bound by culture and by cultural norms, rules and experiences. As a result, people from ethnic minority groups who handle their day to day interactions in ways that are familiar to them but may not always confirm with ethnocentric expectations may be negatively discriminated.
>
> (in Brearley 1995: 69)

Black people are under strong pressures to adopt the ways of the dominant culture. Their own cultural heritage is seen as a handicap to be overcome, something to be ashamed of, and to be avoided. Thus, they may be taught that to be different is to be deviant, pathological or sick. According to Dominelli (1988), the dominant culture would much prefer that black clients conformed as closely as possible to the white ideal. Implicit in this position is the ideology of assimilation, which maintains that 'ethnic' problems (for example, communication problems) would disappear if black people relinquished their own cultures and embraced the dominant one. It has been argued by Bauman (1990) that assimilation is a characteristic rationale and practice of the modern nation state and that 'within the policy of assimilation, tolerance aimed at individuals was inextricably linked with intolerance aimed at the collectivities' (p. 160). In other words the nation state extends individual recognition to 'strangers' to the extent that they dissociate themselves from alternative, ethnic-minority generated, value-generating and value-legitimating authorities. The pressure to assimilate may be felt throughout the range of personal experience, and is orchestrated through different political ideologies in different countries (see, for example, Wrench and Solomos 1993; Heckmann and Bosswick 1995). The blunt, and subtle, expressions of the politics of assimilation operating in conjunction with racist ideologies represent one of the most insidious forms of assault upon minority ethnic identities in multi-ethnic societies.

Multicultural perspective

Minority groups took the initiative in defining themselves rather than being defined by the deficit/deficiency models of the white culture. The multicultural model contends that all culturally distinct groups have strengths and limitations. The differences between ethnic groups are viewed as simply different, rather than being viewed as deficient. Thus, black people's behaviour, lifestyles, communication patterns (verbal and nonverbal), and so forth, can only be judged as appropriate or inappropriate within a specific cultural context (Grier and Cobbs 1968; White 1972). The multicultural perspective has certain pitfalls. It 'lacks a power analysis. It sees other cultures as valua le and interesting but the central reality of racism is either ignored, or racis is ascribed to the personal prejudices of a small number of intolerant peo le' (Ahmed 1996: 124). It also 'reflects a white view of black cultures as aditional, homogeneous, static and exotic' (p. 124).

Another probl e relates to the issue of stereotyping. Although cultural knowledge is imp ortant in helping the social and health care worker identify potential con flic areas, he or she must be careful not to apply cultural information in a ste otypic way. White practitioners need to identify possible gender differences within black groups. According to Ahmed (1996: 124), 'black women negotiate between a number of cultures . . . the culture of "traditionalists" within black communities . . . [and] the culture of resistance to "traditionalism". . . . [However], above all, there is the culture of racism of the dominant society.' Thus, white practitioners also need to examine the impact of racism and discrimination on black people's communication styles.

Black perspective

In order to move toward resolving the conflicts associated with differences in cultural perspectives between blacks and whites, it is essential that the black perspective be taken into consideration. The training black and white social and health care workers receive is first 'in white middle class institutions, and second theoretically and culturally Eurocentric and American (i.e. US) in origin' (Lago and Thompson 1994: 210). Therefore, 'many white people are quite unable to cope with radical black perspectives and black people's pain and anger, specifically in relation to racism' (p. 211).

A black perspective in the study of cultural differences is concerned with combating racist and stereotypic, weakness-dominated and inferiority-oriented conclusions about black people. This perspective is interested in the psychological well-being of black people and is critical of oppressive research paradigms and theoretical formulations. Much of the work and research involved in developing a black perspective in psychology was initiated in the USA by black psychologists (see for example, White 1972; Akbar 1981). The black perspective in Britain has referred to the knowledge base of black research in the US and adapted it to fit in with the British experience. An understanding of the black frame of reference will enable social and health care workers to come up with more accurate and comprehensive explanations of black behaviour – including black communication patterns.

Culture-bound values

This section will focus on some culture-bound values that are especially relevant for intercultural communication. These include power–distance, uncertainty avoidance, individualism versus collectivism, and masculinity

(Hofstede 1980); low and high context communicatio d, immediacy and expressiveness (Hall 1966); emotional and behavioural e pressiveness, and self-disclosure.

According to Hecht *et al.* (1989: 385) 'cultural dis nctiveness, and its attendant differences, may be most notably expresse in communication rules and style'. An understanding of black people' s ultural values will, therefore, enable social and health care workers to communicate effect- ively with black clients. Although it is essential for s ocial and health care workers to have a basic understanding of black pec ple's cultural values, there is the ever-present danger of overgeneralizing and stereotyping. For example, the listing of black values does not indicate that all persons coming from a specific group will share all or even some of the traits. Information about Asian and African Caribbean cultural values should act as guidelines rather than absolutes. Belonging to a particular group may mean sharing common values and experiences; but, as noted above, indi- vidual members of a culture may vary greatly from the pattern that is typ- ical within that culture.

There are several different conceptualizations of how cultures differ. Hofstede's (1980) studies of cultural differences in work-related value orientations offer one approach to understanding the range of cultural dif- ferences. Hofstede's work represents the best available attempt to measure empirically the nature and strength of value differences among cultures. He published the results of his study of over 100,000 employees of a large multinational in 40 countries (Hofstede 1980, 1983) and identified four dimensions that he labelled power–distance, uncertainty avoidance, indi- vidualism and masculinity. By comparing the position of two cultures on these four dimensions, one can get an idea of the relative importance of these values to these cultures and, perhaps, enhance the effectiveness of the communication between them. Hofstede's dimensions have been fre- quently used to contrast cultures.

Hofstede's work provides 'a unique and readily accessible mechanism for hypothesizing the potential value differences that lie between the [white practitioner] and [his or her] client' (Lago and Thompson 1996: 50). How- ever, Hofstede's findings must be applied cautiously to interethnic commu- nication settings. As Lago points out, Hofstede's 'ideas cannot be attributed unthinkingly, to every particular client' (p. 50).

Power–distance

Each culture, and all people within cultures, develop ways of interacting with different people according to the status differential that exists between the individual and the person with whom he or she is interacting. Power–distance (PD) refers to the degree to which different cultures en- courage or maintain power and status differences between interactants. Cultures high on PD develop rules, mechanisms and rituals that serve to maintain and strengthen the status relationships among their members.

Cultures low on PD, however, minimize those rules and customs, eliminating if not ignoring the status differences that exist between people.

In Hofstede's (1980) study, the Philippines, Mexico, Venezuela and India had the highest score on the power–distance dimension. These findings suggest that the cultures underlying these countries maintained strong status differences. The countries which had the lowest marks on PD were New Zealand, Denmark and Austria. The cultures underlying these countries did the most to minimize status and power differentials. Britain had a relatively low score, reflecting some degree of minimizing of power differences (see Hofstede 1980 for a detailed review).

Lago and Thompson (1996: 46) note that power–distance 'is reflected in the values of the less powerful members of society as well as in those of the more powerful ones'.

Uncertainty avoidance

Uncertainty avoidance (UA) is a dimension observed in Hofstede's (1984) study that described the degree to which different cultures develop ways to deal with the anxiety and stress of uncertainty. It refers to 'how well people in a particular culture tolerate ambiguity and uncertainty' (p. 65). Sex differences in 'uncertainty avoidance are negligible . . . [and] the most important correlations are with national anxiety level' (p. 110).

In Hofstede's survey, Sweden and Denmark had the lowest scores on uncertainty avoidance. Low uncertainty avoidance cultures have a high tolerance for ambiguity, are more willing to take risks, have less rigid rules and accept a certain amount of deviance and dissent. Britain had a moderately low level of uncertainty avoidance (Hofstede 1984). Weak uncertainty avoidance means that 'the uncertainty inherent in life is more easily accepted and each day is taken as it comes' (Lago and Thompson 1996: 47). Different degrees of uncertainty avoidance exist in every culture, but one tends to predominate. In Hofstede's survey, Greece, Portugal, Belgium and Japan were the four countries with the highest scores on this dimension. Pakistan had a higher score on uncertainty avoidance than Britain and India.

Cultures with a strong uncertainty avoidance are typified as active, aggressive, emotional, compulsive, security-seeking and intolerant; while cultures with a weak uncertainty avoidance are likely to be contemplative, less aggressive, unemotional, relaxed, accepting personal risks, and relatively tolerant. Differences in the level of uncertainty avoidance can result in unexpected problems in intercultural communication. For instance, when white British social workers communicate with a client from Pakistan, they are likely to be perceived as too nonconforming and unconventional by the client, and the social workers may view their client as rigid and overly controlled. Social and health care workers need to have an understanding of the consequences of uncertainty avoidance for intercultural communication.

Individualism versus collectivism

Individualism and collectivism have been two of the most extensively studied concepts in the field of intercultural communication (e.g. Hofstede 1980; Triandis *et al.* 1988) and is the major dimension of cultural variability used to explain intercultural differences in behaviour. Indeed, Triandis (1986) believes that the individualism–collectivism dimension is the most important attribute that distinguishes one culture from another. The definitions of the two cultural types are extreme in that they only broadly describe cultural patterns. However, it is useful to examine the dimension of individualism–collectivism in terms of the different behaviour patterns their members present.

Individualism refers to 'the subordination of the goals of the collectivities to individual goals, and a sense of independence and lack of concern for others', and collectivism refers to' the subordination of individual goals to the goals of a collective and a sense of harmony, interdependence, and concern for others' (Hui and Triandis 1986: 244–5). These constructs reflect individual societal values regarding self, others, family and community, and thus are related to attitudes and social behaviour. Individualist societies value autonomy, independence, achievement, identity, self-reliance, solitude and creativity. Collectivistic societies value loyalty to the group, dependence, tradition, harmony, respect for authority, and cooperation (Triandis 1990).

In individualistic cultures, 'people are supposed to look after themselves and their immediate family only', while in collectivistic cultures, 'people belong to ingroups or collectivities which are supposed to look after them in exchange for loyalty' (Hofstede and Bond 1984: 419). In individualistic cultures the development of the individual is foremost, even when this is at the expense of the group, whereas in collectivistic cultures the needs of the group are more important, with individuals expected to conform to the group (Gudykunst and Ting-Toomey 1988). Conformity is valued in collectivistic cultures, but diversity and dissent are more esteemed in individualistic cultures. The 'I' identity has precedence in individualistic cultures over the 'we' identity, which takes precedence in collectivistic cultures. The emphasis in individualistic societies is on individuals' initiative and achievement, while emphasis is placed on belonging to groups in collectivistic societies. Because people from collectivist cultures view 'interdependence as important [they] foster it through children's socialization processes' (Brislin and Yoshida 1994: 93).

While cultures tend to be predominantly either individualistic or collectivistic, both exist in all cultures. Individualism has been central to the life of Western industrialized societies such as the US and Britain (Hofstede 1984). Collectivism is particularly high among Asian and African societies. However, diversity within each country is very possible. In the US, for instance, Hispanics and Asians tend to be more collectivist than other ethnic groups (Triandis 1990), and in Britain, Asians and African

Caribbeans tend to be more collectivist than white people. According to Hecht *et al.* (1989: 170), the 'extreme individualism in the US makes it difficult for its citizens to interact with those from less individualistic cultures'. For instance, in individualistic countries, 'affiliativeness, small talk, and initial acquaintance are more important than in collectivist countries, where the social network is more fixed and less reliant on individual initiative' (p. 171).

Western psychology and its associated views of human nature, maturity and mental health are based on individualistic values and are thus one-sided. Sue and Sue (1990: 35) note that 'most forms of counselling and psychotherapy [and social casework] tend to be individual-centred that is, they emphasize the "I-though" relationship'. In therapy and counselling, Asian clients are described as being dependent, unable to make decisions on their own, and lacking in maturity. Many of these analyses are based on the fact that many Asian clients do not see a decision-making process as an individual one. When an Asian client states to a worker: 'I can't make that decision on my own; I need to consult with my parents or family' – he or she is seen as being quite immature. White practitioners dealing with clients from an Asian cultural background need 'to be sensitive to the difference between Western individualist counselling [and communication style] and the client's collectivist culture' (d'Ardenne and Mahtani 1990: 4). Counsellors and social workers 'do not have a prominent niche in [collectivist cultures] because friends and family provide the support that individuals need' (Brislin and Yoshida 1994: 94).

Practitioners need to understand the importance of family responsibility and respect for elders within this framework. An Asian social worker working mainly with Asian elders discussed the clash between the 'European' theoretical framework and working with Asians. She points out that 'if you're even dealing with one person – you expect that the whole family will be sitting there. So there is no individualism' (in Butt 1994: 37). Thus, Asian social workers

> are prepared mentally to deal with the whole [Asian] family, rather than dealing with the individual – even if the person is elderly, or woman or children – any age, any group, any difficulties. The whole family is involved – that's not the concept with other white clients.
>
> (Butt 1994: 38)

Asians are allocentric, not idiocentric, and the individual is expected to make sacrifices for the good of the group – more specifically, the family (Hofstede 1980; Segal 1988; Triandis *et al.* 1988). Asians typically place great emphasis upon the individual–family relationship (Sue and Sue 1990) and upon the extended family. Segal (1991: 239) points out that 'traditionally, Indians have retained their own culture and religious values, regardless of the country to which they have migrated'. However, in the US, Segal notes that these traditional Asian values are 'eroded to a large degree as a result of living in the US . . . [which] is especially apparent in the individualistic behaviour of the children and grandchildren of Indian immigrants' (p. 235). It is possible that similar findings can be found among second generation Asians living in Britain. Modood *et al.* (1994) found that among second generation Asians there was a strong commitment to the immediate family which was not translated into a strong commitment to the extended family. Whereas for first generation Asians, 'it was extremely important to be in contact with the family' (Modood *et al.* 1994: 24).

Afshar (1994) studied the values of three generations of Pakistani women. Her hypothesis that the 'youngest generation in these households would show the greatest resistance to old norms and values and would be most likely to rebel against traditional notions of Islam and the kinds of identities that it would have imposed on the family' (Ahmad 1996: 69) was not supported. Many women 'chose an Islamic identity for struggles both within families and outside' (Ahmad 1996: 69). In another study, Drury (1991) found that there was 'little evidence of wholesale rejection of cultural values or intergenerational conflict' among Sikh girls.

The African view of the world encompasses the concept of 'groupness' (Nobles 1976). In the theoretical model of black psychology presented by Nobles (1976), interrelatedness, connectedness and interdependence are viewed as the unifying philosophic concepts in the African American experience base. The African philosophical tradition recognizes that 'only in terms of other people does the individual become conscious of his [or her] own being' (Mbiti 1970: 5). Only through others does one learn his or her duties and responsibilities toward himself or herself and others. An essential point in understanding the traditional African's view of oneself is that one believes 'I am because we are; and because we are, therefore, I am' (Mbiti 1970: 10).

Harmony plays a critical role in influencing Asian behaviour in various human interactions. Self-limits, shame, cooperation with the group and embarrassment are natural products under this value system. Ho (1976) warns that the conflict or confrontation approach, rather than helping Asian clients, may violate their cultural rules. Harmony is what Asians – consciously or unconsciously – seek and is evidenced by their behaviour.

To summarize, the individualism–collectivism dimension allows for similarities and differences in communication to be identified and explained across cultures.

Masculinity

The masculinity dimension refers to the degree to which cultures foster or maintain differences between the sexes in work-related values. Cultures high on masculinity – such as Japan, Austria and Italy – were found to be associated with the greatest degree of sex differences in work-related values. Cultures low on masculinity – such as Denmark, Netherlands,

Norway and Sweden – had the fewest differences between the sexes. Managers in cultures high on masculinity valued leadership, independence and self-realization; cultures low on masculinity placed less importance on these constructs. Employees in high masculinity cultures regarded earnings, recognition, advancement and challenge as relatively more important than did employees in low masculinity cultures.

Low and high context communication

As noted above, individualism–collectivism provides a powerful explanatory framework for understanding cultural similarities and differences in interethnic communication. While individualism–collectivism defines broad differences between cultures, Hall's (1976) low and high context scheme focuses upon cultural differences in communication processes. A high context communication or message is one in which 'most of the information is either in the physical context or internalized in the person, while very little is in the coded, explicit, transmitted part of the message' (p. 79). High context cultures pay great attention to the surrounding circumstances or context of an event; thus, a high context communication relies heavily on nonverbals and the group identification/understanding shared by those communicating. It therefore follows that in interethnic communication the elements of phrasing, tone, gestures, posture, social status, history and social setting are all crucial to the meaning of the message.

A low context communication or message, in contrast, is one in which 'the mass of information is vested in the explicit code' (Hall 1976: 70). Low context cultures therefore place a greater reliance on the verbal part of the message. In addition, low context cultures have been associated with being more opportunistic, more individual rather than group oriented (Smith 1981). While no culture exists at either end of the continuum, the culture of the US and Britain is placed toward the lower end. Most Asian and African cultures fall toward the high context end of the continuum. Many black people require fewer words than their white counterparts to communicate the same content (Jenkins 1982). In the United States, more-verbal people were perceived as more attractive, whereas in Korea, a high context culture, less-verbal people were perceived as more attractive (Elliott *et al.* 1982). People from low context cultures are often perceived as excessively talkative by those from high context culture, while people from high context cultures may be perceived as nondisclosing, sneaky and mysterious by those from low context cultures (Andersen 1990).

The level of context influences all other aspects of communication:

High-context cultures make greater distinction between insiders and outsiders than low-context cultures do. People raised in high-context systems expect more of others than do the participants in low-context systems. When talking about something that they have on their minds, a high-context individual will expect his [or her] interlocutor to know what's bothering him [or her], so that he [or she] doesn't have to be specific. The result is that he [or she] will talk around and around the point, in effect putting all the pieces in place except the crucial one. Placing it properly – this keystone – is the role of his [or her] interlocutor.

(Hall 1976: 98)

Members of low context, individualistic cultures tend to communicate in a direct fashion, while members of high context, collectivistic cultures tend to communicate in an indirect fashion. Levin (1985: 28) describes communication in the US (a low context culture) in this way: 'The [North] American way of life, by contrast, affords little room for the cultivation of ambiguity . . . It expresses itself in such common injunctions as "Say what you mean", "Don't beat around the bush" and "Get to the point".'

When white social and health care workers (from low context cultures) interview black clients from high context cultures, they are liable to have difficulty in communicating because the high context messages do not contain sufficient information for practitioners to gain true or complete meaning. White practitioners may interpret a high context culture's message according to their low context disposition and reach entirely the wrong meaning. In a high context culture, much more is taken for granted and assumed to be shared, and consequently nearly all messages are coded in such a way that they do not need to be explicitly and verbally transmitted. Instead, the demands of the situation and the shared meanings among the interactants mean that the preferred interpretation of the messages is already known. Clients from high context cultures are more likely to be adept at reading nonverbal behaviour (see Chapter 5). They have an expectation that white practitioners are also able to understand the unarticulated communication; hence they do not speak as much as people from low context cultures.

Asians may assess the feelings of the social worker and tend to give their opinions in an indirect manner (Servaes 1988) in order to avoid offending the social worker. Unlike the Western ideal of self-expression, the Eastern cultures aim to express feelings in such a way that it is not harmful either to oneself or to others. This, therefore, influences the style of communication, placing more value on indirect and metaphorical communication rather than direct and clear communication as emphasized in the Western culture. According to Lau (1988: 194), 'The Western trained therapist's expectation of clear, direct verbal communication is often at variance with cultural rules where direct communication and confrontation are avoided because this may lead to loss of face within the family group.'

As with individualism–collectivism, low and high context communication exists in all cultures, but one tends to predominate. Understanding that a client is from a high or low context culture, and the form of communication that predominates in these cultures, will make the black client's behaviour less confusing and more interpretable to the practitioner.

Immediacy and expressiveness

The 'immediacy dimension is anchored on one extreme by actions that simultaneously communicate closeness, approach, accessibility, and at the other extreme by behaviours expressing avoidance and distance' (Hecht *et al.* 1989: 167). Immediacy is the degree of perceived physical or psychological closeness between people (Richmond and McCroskey 1988). Immediacy behaviours communicate warmth, closeness and availability for communication. Examples of these behaviours are smiling, touching, eye contact, close personal distance and vocal animation (discussed in greater detail in Chapter 5). Cultures that reflect immediacy behaviours or expressiveness are often called 'high contact cultures' (Hall 1966). People in high contact cultures (e.g. Asia and Africa) stand closer and touch more (Hall 1966). People in low contact cultures (Britain and the United States) tend to stand apart and touch less. According to Patterson (1983), these patterns permeate all aspects of everyday life and affect relationships. An understanding of the above patterns of behaviour will enable social and health care workers to communicate more effectively with black clients.

Emotional and behavioural expressiveness

Emotional expressiveness refers to the communication of feelings and thoughts. It 'can refer to both one's own and one's partner's expression, with lack of expressiveness on either one's part seen as dissatisfying' (Hecht *et al.* 1989: 392).

Hecht *et al.* (1989) report that African Americans perceive emotional expressiveness as important to their communication satisfaction with whites (European Americans). Other independent variables – related to communication satisfaction – identified by black people include: acceptance, authenticity, negative stereotyping, understanding, goal attainment and powerlessness (see Hecht *et al.* 1989 for a detailed review). The authors report that 'one respondent was dissatisfied [with the communication process] because she did not express her own emotions' (p. 392). She felt that she had to maintain control.

Kochman (1981) discusses the significance of expressive, stylish and performance-oriented behaviours in African American culture. Kochman (p. 193) notes that 'Black presentations [(communication styles)] are emotionally intense, dynamic, and demonstrative; [whereas] white presentations are more emotionally restrained.' White people use 'the relatively detached and unemotional discussion mode to engage an issue, black people use the more emotionally intense and involving mode of argument' (p. 193). He described expressive and performance-oriented behaviours among African Americans as spontaneous, intuitive, improvisational, emotional, rhythmic, assertive, confrontive, direct and animated. He described white culture as a low stimulus culture: dispassionate, nonchallenging and impersonal. Africans and African Caribbeans tend to be emotionally expressive, while whites have a more emotionally self-restrained style and often attempt to understate, avoid, ignore, or diffuse intense or unpleasant situations. Blacks and whites have conflicting attitudes on the appropriateness of more or less potent forms of expressive behaviour. One of the dominant stereotypes of African Caribbeans in British society is that of the hostile, angry, prone-to-violence black male. It is not unusual for white practitioners to describe their black clients as being 'hostile and angry' (for example, see Littlewood and Lipsedge 1989; Fernando 1991). According to Sue and Sue (1990: 64),

> Black people may misinterpret white communication styles, it is more likely that whites will misinterpret black styles. The direction of the misunderstanding is generally linked to the activating of unconscious 'triggers' about racist stereotypes and fears they harbour.

Thus, in contexts where Eurocentric norms prevail, black people will find their more intense expressive behaviour and the more animated communication style criticized and pathologized.

Cultures vary in what is considered 'appropriate channelling' of emotions. There are many cultural groups in which restraint of strong feelings is highly valued. For example, traditional Asian cultures emphasize that maturity and wisdom are associated with one's ability to control emotions and feelings. Counsellors working with Asian clients need to consider cultural factors that dictate against public disclosures and feelings because these may have serious consequences for the counselling process. In Eurocentric approaches to counselling, emotional expressiveness (i.e. to be in touch with one's feelings and to be able to verbalize one's emotional reactions) is frequently a goal and is highly desired.

Self-disclosure

Self-disclosure refers to the client's willingness to tell the practitioner what she/he feels, believes or thinks. Interethnic comparisons of self-disclosure patterns show that European Americans are more disclosive than African Americans (Diamond and Hellcamp 1969) and Asians (Segal 1991). Indeed, Segal (1991: 239) describes Indians as being 'reserved and reluctant to discuss their problems outside the family'. Most forms of counselling tend to value one's ability to self-disclose and to talk about the most intimate aspects of one's life. Indeed, self-disclosure has often been discussed as a primary characteristic of the healthy personality. The converse of this is that people who do not self-disclose readily in counselling are seen as possessing negative traits such as being guarded, mistrustful and/or paranoid. Intimate revelations of personal or social problems may not be acceptable to many Asians, since such difficulties reflect not only on the individual, but also on the whole family. According to Segal, for most Indians 'family integrity is sacred, and any threat to it is viewed as a failure on the part of the parents' (p. 239). An individual's emotional problems bring shame and guilt to the Asian family, preventing any family member from reporting such problems to others outside the family. Segal indicates that 'even when counseling is sought voluntarily, [Indians] often feel they have been "reduced" to a level beneath their dignity' (p. 239). Thus, the family may exert strong pressures on the Asian client not to reveal personal matters to 'strangers' or 'outsiders'. Similar conflicts have been reported for Hispanic (Laval *et al.* 1983) and for American-Indian clients (Everett *et al.* 1983).

Leong (1992: 219) addresses the disadvantage Asians sometimes encounter in group work:

> In many Asian cultures, there is a strong cultural value that involves humility and modesty in social interactions. This value is often expressed in the form of deferential behavior and not drawing excessive attention to oneself and one's personal concerns . . . The group climate of open and free self-expression may then be experienced by these Asian Americans as an uncomfortable and culturally alien demand.

Social and health care workers unfamiliar with these cultural ramifications may perceive their clients in a very negative light. They may erroneously conclude that the client is repressed, inhibited, shy or passive. On the other hand, Asian clients may perceive the 'direct and confrontative techniques [of white practitioners] in communication as "lacking in respect for the client", and a reflection of insensitivity' (Sue and Sue 1990: 51).

Black people may also be reluctant to disclose to white practitioners because of hardships they have experienced via racism (Vontress 1981). We must not underestimate the impact of racism and discrimination on the 'way in which Black people relate to each other and to the outside world' (Boyd-Franklin 1989: 10). Few, if any, black individuals can live in Britain and the US and not be affected by racism and discrimination. According to Davis and Proctor (1989: 24), 'virtually all minorities in the United States [and Britain] have prior negative experiences with whites that contribute to their tendency toward concealment of true feelings'. The authors note that 'While white practitioners tend to minimize the importance of racial or cultural factors, minorities wonder why whites cannot acknowledge the impact of color in a racist society' (p. 13). For black people, 'race is a significant part of history and personal identity' (p. 16). Thus, the reality of racism in British society needs to be acknowledged in any counselling or social work relationship involving a black client (Phung 1995).

Sue and Sue (1990: 63) note that 'too often minorities are placed in situations where they are asked to deny their true feelings in order to perpetuate White deception'. Social and health care workers' statements that black people are oversensitive or paranoid may represent a form of denial. For example, when a black person makes comments about a white practitioner such as 'I feel some bias against black people', white practitioners are quick to dismiss such statements, by accusing the client of being oversensitive. White practitioners tend to negate or invalidate 'what might be an accurate appraisal of nonverbal communication' (Sue and Sue 1990: 63) (see Chapter 5).

Some black clients, because of their previous experiences and current expectations, may sense that whites cannot be trusted, that they will ultimately harm or cheat them. Asante (1979: 384) argues that:

Some blacks [believe] that increased understanding of them by whites will only lead to greater manipulation by those [whites] in power . . . any serious attempts at black–white communication must be played against the traditional patterns of communication between the two groups in which motives have been suspect and in which blacks have had to strategically develop subversive and in-group communication symbols and signals which could only be understood by other blacks.

This use of communication by black people was an answer to their perceived insincerity of whites. It was used partly to exclude white people, as well as being a reaction to the norms established by whites. The result is 'the transference of inauthentic information, based not so much upon what is available, but rather upon what is expedient in a climate of suspicion' (Asante 1979: 384).

A common theme of mistrust of white counsellors has been reported among African Americans, Asian Americans, Hispanic Americans and Native Americans (Vontress 1981; Sue and Sue 1990; Everett *et al.* 1983). A black client's reluctance to open up to a white practitioner may reflect a greater unwillingness to disclose him or herself to a representative of the white world (Vontress 1971). Black and other minority clients have been conditioned to be cautious and mistrusting of white practitioners. Harrison (1975: 132) pinpoints this problem in his comments on the black client: 'The hesitance of blacks to fully disclose themselves, often viewed as "playing it cool", suggests a cautiousness and initial lack of trust in the person to whom one is to disclose.' It therefore follows that 'establishing rapport with the [client] is more difficult, requiring sensitive and skillful counselor [(social work)] intervention in order to facilitate authentic communication' (p. 132). Sometimes black people do not fully trust black social workers, feeling that these workers have sold out to the white establishment.

Ridley (1984) in the US describes two major factors influencing self-disclosure in the black client. The discussion is aimed at black clients. However, the dynamics apply to clients of other minority groups. The first is cultural paranoia (defined by Ridley (1984) as a healthy psychological reaction to racism) and the second is functional paranoia (defined by Ridley as an unhealthy condition that is itself an illness). Cultural paranoia is similar to Grier and Cobbs's (1968) concept of healthy paranoia and is considered to be an adaptive response to an oppressive environment. Hesitancy about self-disclosure therefore occurs because there is concern about being misunderstood, hurt or taken advantage of if personal information is shared. The black client limits self-disclosure because of past experiences with racism or because of the present attitude of the white practitioner. The client may display suspiciousness and anticipate prejudice on the part of the counsellor. This may be displayed by being aloof and passive. A danger exists that the individual in this category will be evaluated as suffering from personal pathology. Functional paranoia is an unhealthy psychological condition. Black clients who have a pervasive suspicion fit this category. They would not disclose to any counsellor regardless of 'race'. Ridley (1984) pointed out the need for clinicians to differentiate between functional and cultural paranoia in black peoples' patterns of self-disclosure within the therapeutic relationship. Using these two dimensions, Ridley provided a four-mode typology that categorizes clients according to their type of paranoia and patterns of self-disclosure (see Ridley 1989). In Mode 1, the intercultural nonparanoiac discloser is a client who is low on both functional and cultural paranoia. This client typically self-discloses to practitioners of any 'race'. This acknowledges the fact that some interethnic relationships are effective. Nevertheless, this type of client is a rarity (Ridley 1984). In Mode 2, the functional paranoiac is a client who has a true clinical paranoid disorder. This client does not disclose to any counsellors, including members of the same 'race'. In Mode 3, the healthy cultural paranoiac is a client who attempts to protect himself or herself from racism and discrimination. This client is typically nondisclosing to white counsellors but open to counsellors of his or her own community. Many minority clients seem to fall into this category. In Mode 4, the confluent paranoiac is a client who has both a strong reaction to racism and a traditional paranoid condition. This is the most difficult black client to treat because of the complex interaction of cultural and functional paranoia. Like the functional paranoiac, this client does not disclose to counsellors of any 'race' (Ridley 1984).

The majority of black clients exhibit an appropriate reaction to racism. Many Mode 3 clients are classified as Mode 2, functional paranoiacs. Misunderstanding the black client's reluctance to self-disclose contributes significantly to the overrepresentation of minorities in pathological categories. There is evidence that the diagnosis of schizophrenia, especially of the paranoid type, is being misapplied to black people (Kleiner *et al.* 1960; Litttlewood and Lipsedge 1989).

In general, black people tend to disclose more when they are interviewed by someone from their own ethnic group (Davis and Proctor 1989). However, some Asians may reject practitioners who belong to the same ethnic group, due to concerns about breach of confidentiality.

Thomas (1995: 190) suggests that

> the children of African and Asian heritage [in Britain] communicate with white [therapists] by putting forward a 'proxy self'. This communication by proxy served the function of protecting the black child in a society where adults or people with power over them might be harmful to their psychological and emotional development. If we were living in a racism-free society, there would be no 'race' obstacle for black

children to overcome on the route towards therapy [and communication] with White professionals.

A black child or adult will tend to reveal the 'real self' only 'when some safety [in the relationship] is established' (Thomas 1995: 188). White social work and health care workers need to be aware of the effects of racism on black people's self-disclosure patterns.

Summary

This section has discussed some of the taxonomies that can be used to describe cultural variations. These taxonomies include Hall's high and low context cultural patterns and Hofstede's four dimensions – power–distance, uncertainty avoidance, individualism–collectivism, and masculinity–femininity – along which the dominant patterns of a culture can be ordered. Taken together, these taxonomies provide multiple frames of reference that can be used to understand intercultural communication. Other culture-bound values discussed were emotional/behavioural expressiveness and self-disclosure patterns.

Intracultural differences and interethnic communication

Acculturation

The construct of acculturation has been used by psychologists in their efforts to describe within-group cultural differences. Acculturation may be defined 'in terms of the degree of integration of new cultural patterns into the original cultural patterns' (Paniagua 1994: 8). It therefore refers to the interaction between a dominant and a nondominant culture in which one is affected much more profoundly than the other. Psychologists have considered acculturation along a number of dimensions. One area of research has sought to understand the psychological impact of migration and acculturation (see Berry 1980 for a detailed review). Another line of research has focused on 'levels of acculturation' as a way of delineating within-group cultural differences. This paradigm suggests that a person arriving in the United States or Britain, from Asia or Africa, gradually moves along the continuum from the nondominant pole toward the dominant pole, although numerous factors including age, gender and social class (Szapocznik *et al.* 1978) are thought to affect the rate at which this occurs. Paniagua (1994) notes that different acculturation scales have been developed to measure acculturation levels among different cultural groups, and presents examples of acculturation scales across four multicultural groups.

Ruiz (1981) has suggested a modification to the general 'levels of acculturation' – that is, that acculturation may be situational. Thus, a person might behave in a manner more closely associated with the dominant culture at work, but act in a way more congruent with the nondominant culture while at home. Keefe and Padilla (1987: 16) proposed that 'the acceptance of new cultural traits and the loss of traditional cultural traits varies from trait to trait'. For instance, the authors found that although it is true that some traits (e.g. first language ability) do diminish progressively from generation to generation, other traits (e.g. the extended family) actually seem to go stronger from the first to the fourth generation of Mexican American families. There is little research on differences between first and second generation Asians and African Caribbeans living in Britain. According to Thomas (1995: 176), 'generational changes in culture exist although there is also continuity of culture across generations'. This has also been noted by Afshar (1994) in her study of three generations of Pakistani women.

The construct of levels of acculturation provides an important way to begin to think about intracultural differences. It is important for white social and health care workers to determine the potential impact of different levels of acculturation upon interethnic communication.

Conclusion

What are the implications of above work for social and health care services? Sue and Sue (1990: 60) note that 'for effective counselling [and communication] to occur, both the worker [(professional)] and the client must be able to send and receive both verbal and nonverbal messages accurately and appropriately'.

In this chapter a number of cultural differences between black and Euro-American cultures and the relationship between these differences and interethnic communication were discussed. It also explored intracultural differences within the black community.

Each of Hofstede's four dimensions provides insights into the influence of culture on the communication process. As frames of reference, Hofstede's dimensions provide mechanisms to understand interethnic communication events. For instance, the consequences of the degree of power–distance that a culture prefers are evident in the relationship between the client and social worker. Clients raised in high power–distance cultures are expected to comply with the wishes and requests of their social workers and doctors, and conformity is regarded very favourably. Even the language systems (for example the Korean language) in high power–distance cultures emphasize distinctions based on a social hierarchy. Witte and Morrison (1995: 227) note that 'in many cultures [for example Asian], authority figures cannot be disagreed with, challenged, or contradicted'. Thus, 'differences in communication styles between healers and patients, especially in terms of politeness behaviour, may lead to miscommunication and misunderstandings' (p. 227).

A white practitioner with a monocultural perspective will view any behaviours, values and lifestyles that differed from the Euro-American norm as deficient (cultural racism). He or she will, for example, view certain nonverbal behaviours (lack of eye contact) as deviant behaviour. As discussed in Chapter 5, eye contact during verbal communication is expected in Western culture because it implies attention and respect toward others. Among Asians, however, eye contact is considered a sign of lack of respect and attention, particularly to authority and older people. Cultures differ in their values on individualism versus collectivism; low and high context communication; immediacy and expressiveness; uncertainty avoidance; emotional and behavioural expressiveness; and self-disclosure. People from different cultures have different patterns of communication. Asians, coming from a high context culture, often rely on nonverbal communication, while Euro-Americans rely more on words. Asians' oral messages frequently are more implicit and depend more on context (people and situations), while Euro-Americans' verbal messages are explicit and less concerned with context. Members of Asian cultures are more likely to be offended by direct and explicit messages and prefer indirect and implicit messages (Witte and Morrison 1995). Since Asians value harmony, they may tend to avoid any direct conflict with individuals, groups and organizations. Therefore attempts to use any conflict or confrontation approaches in the helping process may be counterproductive.

There may be clear rules regarding how older members of the family should be addressed by the younger members. This attitude will influence the doctor–patient or social worker–client relationship because if the patient or client is not used to challenging authority figures they will conform to everything suggested by the doctor or social worker. Problems with medical regimens may occur unintentionally or intentionally due to these politeness norms.

It is important for practitioners to understand these cultural factors and incorporate them in their interaction with black clients. As noted by Cayleff (1986: 346), cultural misunderstandings 'may precipitate difficulties in communication . . . and dramatically alter a [client's] willingness or ability to maintain a therapeutic program'.

White social work and health care workers need to be aware that a client's racial/cultural identity status has a direct impact on the type of world-view a client adopts, and that this world-view, in turn, determines how the client perceives and interacts with others. Gushue's (1993) model of nondominant culture identity provides a useful insight into within-group cultural differences in black communities.

Eleftheriadou (1996) discusses some of the issues involved in communicating with patients from different cultural backgrounds. These are: an awareness of one's own values so that one does not impose them on the patient; knowledge about the patient's cultural background and in particular those cultural differences that might affect treatment; respect for the patient's culture; being open-minded about cultural practices which are unfamiliar to the medical practitioner; and 'accommodating cultural ideas in the [patient's] treatment without compromising the quality of care provided for the patient' (Eleftheriadou 1996: 89). However, white practitioners must not let their assumptions about other cultures become so fixed that they expect all black clients from a particular culture to think or behave in the same way. As already noted, the literature reviewed here does tend to generate models which offer generalizations about broad areas of cultural difference, and the heuristic value of such insights must always be tempered by a cautious application to specific cases.

Practitioners and clients may have different world-views, or attitudes, about a number of topics. These include spiritual beliefs and practices; familial experiences and values; beliefs about health, illness and treatment; beliefs and stereotypes about the client's culture. For example, it may be difficult for a medical practitioner to understand why a black patient (from a collective culture) wants relatives to be present at all consultations, for in Western individualistic cultures there is generally more emphasis on individuality and privacy. According to Witte and Morrison (1995: 224), 'a collectivist orientation means that the family makes treatment and health-related decisions, not the patient'.

The white practitioner should not impose his or her cultural values on the client but, rather, work to 'create common ground in relation to the treatment'. In dealing with areas such as death in the family, the practitioner needs to consult the patient's relatives in order to gain a better understanding of culturally appropriate practices.

A study of the health needs of ethnic minorities in the Brighton, Hove and Lewes area found that the participants felt that religious and cultural needs were not addressed by health workers (Yazdani and Anjum 1994). Many women experienced embarrassment being treated by male professional health workers. McAvoy and Sayeed (1990) also noted that Asian women, especially Muslims, prefer to be treated by a female doctor. The authors emphasize that 'cultural awareness and understanding, tact and sensitivity on the part of doctors and other health professionals are required in order to avoid conflict or misunderstandings' (p. 60).

Yazdani and Anjum (1994) found that the area of mental health was particularly problematic. Many participants felt that there was a great unmet need for 'appropriate psycho-social support'. For example, an African Caribbean woman was not able to find a black woman counsellor in the local area, and did not want to see a white counsellor. The woman stated that 'Half the problem is Them – that's why I don't want to see a white counsellor.' One African Caribbean man felt that the NHS was a racist institution, with doctors who were white middle class men who may have negative stereotypes and attitudes towards black people. He stated: 'I have a very real fear of being diagnosed as schizophrenic if I presented with any form of emotional distress.' He felt there was a need for black male counsellors.

Eleftheriadou (1996) lists some dos and don'ts for white doctors in cross-cultural doctor and patient communication. The dos include: the use of open questions; exploring the racial and cultural background of clients – only if necessary; being honest about issues that are unclear to the doctor; and showing respect for cultural differences. The don'ts include: doctors pretending to understand cultural patterns that they are unclear about; being judgemental about cultural patterns; making assumptions about how the patient's cultural patterns might relate to the onset of illness or to the outcome of treatment; assuming that cultural issues are unimportant. Some of the factors listed above can equally apply for social workers in cross-cultural social worker and client interaction.

According to Sue *et al.* (1992: 110),

> To become a culturally skilled helper [(practitioner)], one must (1) be aware of one's own cultural heritage and of biases, values, and pre-conceived notions that can intrude in helping relationships, (2) acquire knowledge of culturally diverse groups that will pave the way for grasping the worldviews of culturally different clients, and (3) develop a range of intervention strategies and skills that are appropriate, relevant, and sensitive to diverse groups.

Thomas (1995: 175) suggests that 'The lack of understanding of other people's cultures can at times be at the root of much conflict or lack of engagement [in interethnic communication].' A culturally competent system of care will acknowledge and incorporate at all levels the importance of culture, the assessment of cross-cultural relations, vigilance toward the dynamics that result from cultural differences, the expansion of cultural knowledge, and the adaptation of services to meet culturally unique needs.

Annotated bibliography

Davis, L.E. and Proctor, E.K. (1989) *Race, Gender, and Class: Guidelines for Practice with Individuals, Families, and Groups.* Englewood Cliffs, NJ: Prentice-Hall.
An excellent text on some of the major dimensions and subtleties underlying the issues of 'race', gender and social class and how these might impact upon practice.
Robinson, L. (1995) *Psychology for Social Workers: Black Perspectives.* London: Routledge.
A unique book whose primary achievement is to draw together research material and literature on black perspectives in human behaviour from North America and Britain.

4

The role of language in interethnic communication

Introduction

The book has so far discussed several communication attributes that affect the outcome of interethnic contacts: the communicator's racial identity attitudes, beliefs, attitudes, values and culture.

This chapter discusses the actual means whereby all the above attributes are expressed. There are two basic means of communication: verbal and nonverbal. This chapter will discuss the verbal means of communication – that is, language – and the manner in which its uses and forms affect interethnic communication. It examines the role of Black English in interethnic communication. It discusses the implications of interacting with Asian clients who may have English as a second language, or who may not speak English at all. The chapter also discusses the effects of racist language in interethnic settings. A social and health care worker who employs racist language may be unaware that his or her expressions are racist or that they are being perceived as racist by nonwhite receivers. Finally, we conclude by discussing the implications for social work and health care practitioners.

Language and ethnic identity

The issue of language and identity has been dealt with in a number of ways. Giles and Johnson (1981) contend that language is vital to any group's identity and is particularly salient for ethnic groups. Drawing on social identity theory (Tajfel 1982; Turner 1987), Giles et al. (1977) developed ethnolinguistic identity theory to explain how members of language communities maintain their linguistic distinctiveness, and how and when language strategies are used. Other authors (for example Jenkins 1982; Smitherman-Donaldson 1988) have related specific language and dialect to identities. Jenkins (1982) notes that within the African American community there are linguistic markers of identity, and members of the group are often catalogued by their language characteristics.

Social identity theory assumes that individuals seek positive social identities in intergroup encounters. Social identity is 'that part of an individual's self-concept which derives from his [or her] knowledge of his [or her] membership in a social group (or groups) together with the value and emotional significance attached to that membership' (Tajfel 1978: 63). That part of the self-concept not accounted for by social identity is personal identity. Language is a vital aspect of the social identity of any group, particularly ethnolinguistic groups (see Giles and Johnson 1981 for a detailed review).

The basic tenets of ethnolinguistic identity theory revolve around techniques and processes for maintaining distinctiveness that include a variety of speech and nonverbal markers (e.g. vocabulary, slang, posture, gesture, discourse styles, accent) that create 'psycholinguistic distinctiveness' (Giles and Coupland 1991) (see Giles and Coupland 1991 for a detailed review). People use linguistic distinctiveness strategies when they identify strongly with their own group and are insecure about other groups (Giles and Johnson 1981).

The following example cited by Giles and Coupland (1991) illustrates within-group differences in language attitudes and behaviours among Indians living in Leicester, whose community language is Gujerati. One respondent stated:

> If I didn't speak Gujerati, I would feel drowned . . . I would suffocate if I didn't speak Gujerati. If an Indian tries to speak to me in English I always ask 'can't you speak Gujerati?'. If he can't I feel distant from him.
>
> (Giles and Coupland 1991: 104)

However, another respondent stated: 'I was at a polytechnic in London and a year passed before I spoke any Gujerati. Even when I met a Gujerati from Leicester, we got to know each other in English and wouldn't dream of speaking anything else' (Giles and Coupland 1991: 104). Ethnolinguistic identity theory takes into account between-group and within-group differences in language and ethnic attitudes. The theory enables us to analyse who uses which language strategy, when and for what purposes. For instance, in the examples cited above, the first respondent may identify herself as a 'Gujerati', while the second would probably self-identify as 'British'. van Dijk (1993: 60) argues that:

> a dominant group's language can define situations, can impose certain meanings on situations . . . Members of sub-dominant groups unwittingly and often unknowingly are thus ensnared in language which is pejorative [which] can lead to great loss of self-esteem. [Thus the] thrust towards a redefinition of terms by oppressed groups is a thrust towards a regaining of esteem, and an increase in confidence.

And according to Ryan *et al.* (1982: 1):

In every society the differential power of particular social groups is reflected in language variation and in attitudes toward those variations. Typically, the dominant group promotes its patterns of language use as dialect or accents by minority group members reduce their opportunities for success in the society as a whole.

Romaine (1995) argues that questions of language are also questions of power. Certain ways of speaking are perceived as superior largely because they are used by the powerful. In Britain, those people who speak English are evaluated according to their various accents and dialects. Dialects are versions of a language with distinctive vocabulary, grammar and pronunciation that are spoken by particular groups of people or within particular regions. Dialects can play an important role in interethnic communication because they often trigger a judgement and evaluation of a speaker. Dialects are measured against a 'standard' spoken version of the language. The term 'standard' does not describe inherent or naturally occurring characteristics. Edwards (1982: 22) suggests that 'there is nothing intrinsic, either linguistically or aesthetically, which gives Standard English special status'. However, other dialects of English are frequently accorded less status and are often considered inappropriate or unacceptable in education, business and government. For example, speakers of Black English are sometimes unfairly assumed to be less reliable, less intelligent and of lower status than those who speak Standard English (Doss and Gross 1994). Language disadvantage is not only experienced by black people. According to d'Ardenne and Mahtani (1990: 65), 'social class and education are just as likely to produce alternative forms of English which promote prejudice among listeners'. We make judgements about the quality or intelligence of a person on the basis of the way he or she speaks rather than what he or she says. Thus, as noted earlier, individuals who speak differently (i.e. in a language viewed to be nonstandard or inferior) may be perceived as possessing inferior or undesirable traits. Conversely, people who speak like the positively viewed in-group (white, middle class) will be perceived as possessing positive attributes. Our attitudes toward other languages and dialects influence how we respond to others, whether we learn other languages, when we use other languages or dialects, and whether we accommodate to people with whom we are communicating. d'Ardenne and Mahtani (p. 64) note that 'English-speaking counsellors [and social and health care practitioners] expect their clients to share their manner of speech. When they do not, [they] may devalue their clients, either by believing that they are intellectually slow or that they are uneducated.'

Research studies repeatedly demonstrate that speakers' accents are used as a cue to form impressions of them (see Giles and Johnson 1981). Studies find that accented speech and dialects provoke in listeners stereotyped reactions, so that the speakers are usually perceived as having less status, prestige and overall competence. These negative perceptions and stereotyped responses sometimes occur even when the listeners themselves use a non-standard dialect when they speak. Negative judgements that are made of others simply on the basis of how people speak will be a barrier to effective interethnic communication.

There also appears to be strong evidence that the response to the language of a group of people is closely correlated with the perception of that group. Breinburg (1986: 146) found that 'teachers' perception of black children of Caribbean background appeared to be negative and stereotyped, and this finding significantly correlated with the response to the mother tongue and speech patterns of black people of Caribbean origin'.

The language or dialect we speak influences how others judge us and whether they are willing to help us (Gaertner and Bickman 1971). For example, people speaking a standard dialect are more likely to receive help on the phone than people speaking an ethnic dialect. Speakers using a standard dialect also are rated higher on competence, intelligence, industriousness and confidence than speakers using a nonstandard dialect (see Bradac 1990 for a review). The effects of alternative forms of language use on interethnic communication competence are discussed in the following section.

Black English

For several decades, the language of many black people (African Americans and African Caribbeans) has been of interest to linguists, sociologists and psychologists. Often referred to as Black English (BE) or Ebonics, numerous studies have been conducted to delineate its distinguishing features.

Some authors treat Black English as a dialect of today's so-called 'Standard' English (that is, Euro-American, White English) under the assumption that Africans came to the US with no knowledge of English and developed the dialect while learning the mainstream language (Weber 1991). Others argue that it is a Creole language formed out of Standard English and native African languages (Stewart 1970; Jenkins 1982; Labov 1982; Smitherman-Donaldson 1988), evolving from largely West African pidgin forms (Stewart 1970; Traugott 1976). Some of those in this latter group have argued that the dialect position demeans the language system and the African slaves by assuming that their native language disappeared rather than merging with that spoken by slave owners (Weber 1991). From this perspective the study of Black English has been highly politicized because of the tendency to describe the language as a deviant or deficient form of Standard English (Smitherman 1977; Smitherman-Donaldson 1988). Viewing Black English as a dialect stems from a Eurocentric vision that only describes what is 'missing' and what is grammatically 'incorrect'. For this reason I will use Black English rather than Black Dialect to denote the language form.

Dillard (1972) sees Black English as being a mixture of African languages (West African languages of Efik, Yoruba, Ibo, Mande, Twi, etc.) and Standard English, developing through a systematic, orderly process of pidginization-creolization-decreolization (Dillard 1972). Pidginization, in this instance, refers to the language of the slaves which no one spoke originally but which resulted from the mixing of speakers of a large number of languages where no one language dominated and where various forms of such mixtures were spoken within a speech community (Dillard 1972). And decreolization refers to the influence of the English used by whites on the Creole of the slaves (Dillard 1972: 83). Black English is sometimes informally referred to as 'patois'.

The African influences in both early and current forms of Black English are seen most in sentence structure and in semantics. Sentence structures have been influenced profoundly by the rules of the African languages. Although the vocabularies of the enslaved members of multiple tribes were different, most of these languages shared the same structural patterns. For example, subject nouns are followed by a repeated pronoun ('my father, he ...'), questions omit 'do' ('what it come to?') and verbs do not vary form to indicate tense, but context clarifiers are used instead ('I know it good when he ask me') (Smitherman 1977).

Black English cannot be called incorrect English. It is now recognized as a legitimate language form with a unique and logical syntax, semantic system and grammar (Stewart 1970; Smitherman 1977; Jenkins 1982; Smitherman-Donaldson 1988) that varies in its forms depending upon which African language influenced it and in which region it was developed (Smitherman 1977). Smitherman (1977) cites some examples. These include: indicating habitual action through verb structure, notably using the form 'be' as a verb; and indicating remote past through verb structure, notably using 'been' with stress. For example, 'We had been [(pronounced with stress)] finished our schoolwork'; the White English equivalent might be: 'We had finished our schoolwork a long time ago' (for a detailed description of Black English see Dillard 1972; Smitherman 1977; Baugh 1983). The idea that Black English is 'inferior' is nothing more than symbolic racism. Black speech symbolizes Black people, and the treatment of such speech as 'inferior' is testimony to the more widespread belief that Black people are inferior (Fairchild 1997). This racism is also institutionalized in educational settings that treat the language of Black people as 'substandard' or in need of remediation. Although we may agree that life and work in 'mainstream' Britain and the United States requires 'mainstream' communication practices, we should firmly reject the idea that the language of black people is inherently inferior.

In sum, research on Black English has concluded that it is a legitimate variant of English that operates according to its own rules of syntax, grammar and the derivation of meaning. As such, Black English should be accorded an equal status relationship with Standard English. Yet, 'studies indicate that teachers, [social workers and health practitioners] and the public, continue to harbour negative attitudes and beliefs about the nature of Black English and its role in education' (Fairchild and Edwards-Evans 1990: 78).

Though Black English first served an adaptive function, it has now achieved cultural significance, often serving as a symbolic rejection of Standard English. Since the speaking of Standard English by blacks can be interpreted to mean that they agree with or identify with the norms of whites, blacks often deliberately reject Standard English out of a type of psychological consciousness and also out of peer group pressure (Dillard 1972). For instance, slaves 'turned the language as it was presented to them to their own purposes, and in fact to the precise purpose which their owners tried to prevent' (Grier and Cobbs 1968: 60). Psychologically they realized that if they mastered and used the language in the same way as whites, this would have shown that blacks agreed with the system which had defined them as inferior; it would have shown that they consented to the caste definition of the system. Through their style of language, blacks could disguise their real feelings, and because of shared experiences it achieved a cultural significance. It transcended the immediate to reach symbolic proportions. This language acquired an identity of its own and became abstracted from those who created it. It prompted group solidarity and unity among blacks. When we view the language of blacks in this context, it may be thought of as protest, as the power to redefine, as a clandestine way of excluding non-blacks, and as a way of uniting black people.

While much of the use of Black English may result from such a consciousness, an important unconscious use of it is also recognized:

> One important unconscious use of 'patois' rests on the Negro's perception, and, in fact, his white confrere's perception, as well, that the true status of the races in the United States at this time is that Negros are regarded as slaves who are no longer officially enslaved.
>
> (Grier and Cobbs 1968: 105)

Thus, traditionally, it was believed that Black English vernacular was both a reference point that black people held in positive regard and a language to be held in high ethnic esteem (Garner and Rubin 1986). The lingusitic elements of Black English are believed to represent important markers of group identity and group solidarity (Smitherman 1977).

Black English is characteristic of some African American talk (Seymour and Seymour 1979; Jenkins 1982; Smitherman-Donaldson 1988). Of course not all black people speak in Black English vernacular. Some individuals use Standard English or a mixture of Black English and Standard English. There are also variants in Black English usage. Some Black English forms were not as salient nor as commonly used as others (Edwards 1992). African Americans having strong ties to their neighbourhoods and the social networks there are more likely to use vernacular linguistic variants (Edwards 1992).

Speech that marks the individual as a member of the group can be important for in-group acceptance. Here the use of African American language markers promotes identity and may be reinforced by group members. This is true for black people in countries other than the United States. For example, in London, black teenagers' use of Creole is embedded in standard London dialect to mark and represent group language in certain contexts (Hewitt 1986). In this way Creole use is equated with black group identity: teenagers may feel the need to display some facility with the socially marked forms (this is linked to the earlier discussion on ethnolinguistic identity theory). Hewitt (1986) suggests that for this reason self-reports of language may overreport use of this language form.

In the United States, the Black English of the African American underclass is not only diverging from Standard English but from the English of the African American middle class as well (Smitherman 1991). The children of the black underclass 'are rejecting the bourgeois sociolinguistic character of the schools and dropping out or being forced out of school' (Smitherman 1991: 262). Smitherman (p. 262) argues that 'a language policy for the African American community must stress the legitimacy of Black English, and call for its use as a co-equal language of instruction'. He also stresses that language policy 'must reinforce the need for standard English' (p. 263). Acknowledging the validity of Black English in no way suggests teaching Black English in place of Standard English. It can and should serve to facilitate the teaching of Standard English. African linguists have argued for mother tongue instruction as a 'passport to literacy', both for Africans (e.g. Bamgbose 1976) and African Americans (e.g. Bokamba 1981). A language policy for the African American community must stress the legitimacy of Black English, and call for its use as a co-equal language of instruction, particularly in African American underclass schools. In December 1996, the Oakland Unified School District in the United States noted in their policy on Standard English language development that language skills were directly related to academic success. They therefore declared Black English as a unique language form and as a means to help young black people bridge the gap to Standard English (Fairchild 1997).

As suggested earlier, the dominant white culture has selected Standard English as preferred usage and relegated other forms, Black English among them, to nonstandard, lower prestige status (Jenkins 1982). This rejection of Black English as a legitimate linguistic style has harmed the development of child speakers (Seymour and Seymour 1979). Some children who speak Black English have been inaccurately diagnosed as communicatively handicapped, mentally retarded or learning-disabled (Seymour and Seymour 1979). These children were diagnosed using tests written in Standard English and standardized with its native speakers. The poor performance of these children may result from the nature of the tests rather than any inherent deficiencies. These problems continue into adulthood. Black youngsters were also seen as having restricted opportunities for cognitive development because they had 'restricted' language forms (Thomas and Sillen 1972). However, Thomas and Sillen (1972) found that the language and abstract thinking of these children were fully developed in their own form of English.

Speech style is one of the dimensions on which black people (African Caribbeans and African Americans) experience conflict about their ethnic identity and self-concept. They often react to the stigma attached to their dialect and speech style with ambivalence, having received messages from their in-group supporting its use and from mainstream culture rejecting Black English as incorrect and deviant speech. Thus, many African Americans are ambivalent toward their own speech (Jenkins 1982), calling it 'slang' and treating it as substandard (Hecht and Ribeau 1991). This makes it difficult for them to form and maintain a positive identity (Jenkins 1982) (Chapter 1 refers to the relationship between racial identity attitudes and use of Black English). This ambivalence may manifest itself in many forms, prominent among which is code or style switching (Seymour and Seymour 1979; Jenkins 1982).

The notion of code switching is based upon a concept of two or more fixed and discrete linguistic systems, between which speakers alternate either randomly (Labov 1972) or in ways that show meaningful patterning (Gumprez 1982). People may switch languages to show warmth and group identification (Gumprez and Hernandez-Chavez 1972). People may also switch codes to increase the distance between themselves and others (Scotton 1993).

In this chapter, code or style switching refers to the selective use of Black English and Standard English depending on the situation. In code or style switching black people learn to identify what is acceptable in different situations and modify their speech to the appropriate style (Baugh 1983). Code switching takes place for various reasons. According to Hewitt (1986: 111), 'the act of [code] switching conveys at least as much information about the state of the interaction as the nature of the codes employed'. In London, topic and function trigger switches from black Creole forms to Standard English dialect (Hewitt 1986). As discussed above, 'any context in which a form of rivalry exists, or is produced by the interaction, increases the chance of creole being employed by the interactant' (p. 111).

Chaika (1982) notes that people sometimes switch codes for emphasis or to see if a stranger belongs to the in-group. She argues that:

> the switch from one language to another, in itself, has meaning. No matter what else a switch means, it reinforces bonds between speakers. Such switching can obviously only occur between those who speak the same language. It may be done in the presence of non-speakers as a way of excluding them, just as jargon may.
>
> (Chaika 1982: 238)

African Americans are likely to include the use of slang, lots of laughter, in-group gestures, Black English, and assumed intimacy in conversations with other African Americans; in black–white conversations there is restraint and an awareness of grammar (Cheek 1976).

The importance of code switching is apparent in a study of successful and unsuccessful black (African American) job interviewees (Akinnaso and

Ajirotutu 1982). African American interviewees who were able to adopt more culture-general discourse strategies were perceived more positively. The interviewees who appropriately opened and closed their narratives and demonstrated the ability to stylistically signal talk as interview talk were perceived more positively. These candidiates assumed a problem-solving mode and used a narrative form to illustrate their strengths. The less successful candidates showed a more traditional stylistic form: the telling of stories that seemed to be an end in themselves rather than a way to illustrate qualifications for the job. Also, unsuccessful candidates used more back channel cueing ('um hum', 'um um', 'yeah' and 'OK') and vowel lengthening (see Chapter 5 for discussion of nonverbal communication and interethnic communication). Some authors have suggested that the African American who speaks both Standard English and some form of Black English is the prototype for success (Seymour and Seymour 1979; Jenkins 1982).

Doss and Gross (1994) studied the effects of Black English and code switching on intraracial perceptions among African American college students. Doss and Gross found that Standard English was preferred to Black English and code switching among middle class African Americans. The authors argue that subjects' preferences for Standard English may reflect a rejection of Black English stereotypes rather than Black English vernacular (also see Garner and Rubin 1986). The stereotype associated with Black English is 'inconsistent with stereotypic perceptions of the upwardly mobile middle-class individual' (Doss and Gross 1994). Minority group members (in Cross's pre-encounter stage of racial identity development) have frequently tended to derogate the in-group and display positive attitudes toward the dominant out-group (see for example, Giles and Powesland 1975; Milner 1975, 1981). Doss and Gross's (1994) findings appear inconsistent with the findings of some previous studies (for example Smitherman 1977) but in agreement with others (for example Garner and Rubin 1986; Doss and Gross 1992). Although Garner and Rubin (1986) found that their African American subjects held Black English in high regard, they held in low regard anyone who did not know how to switch from Black English to Standard English. Linguistic competency requires the use of both language systems. Persons who do not know when to use 'slang', 'image' and 'street vernacular' for effect rather than as the major form of communication and who do not use Standard English appropriately for the context are held in low regard and viewed as uneducated (Garner and Rubin 1986).

More recently, when the Oakland Unified School District in California recognized Black English as a language form, most of the criticisms against this move was levelled by the black middle class (Fairchild 1997). Davidson (1997: 5) points out that this reaction 'is a measure of Black self-hatred. Too many Blacks despise black behavior, culture or any suggestion that they are not White . . . [Thus] any group of Black people attempting to practice self-determination can expect to be attacked by some mainstream Blacks. This is inherent to White supremacy.' As noted in Chapter 1, an individual at the pre-encounter stage of racial identity development (Cross 1971) may choose not to use Black English and may feel embarrassed by those who do.

The white mainstream are ambivalent about Black English. Tests of white perceptions of 'sounding black' indicate that negative evaluations do not pervade all judgements. Many whites have negative attitudes toward speakers of any form of Black English (Seymour and Seymour 1979). In one study, Johnson and Buttny (1982) found that white listeners' response to black speakers who 'sounded black' and to speakers who sounded white depended on the content of the speech. When the content was narrative or experiential there were no differences attributable to speech style. However, when the topic was abstract and intellectual, 'sounding black' produced lower ratings from whites. Findings indicate that whites do not have uniformly negative global predispositions toward black speech, but selectively bias their evaluations to be consistent with cultural stereotypes. Thus, speakers of Black English may be disadvantaged in situations requiring expertise.

The African Caribbean experience

Creole and Patois, sometimes referred to as Black English, are commonly understood to refer to specific Caribbean languages or dialects used by people of African descent in the Caribbean and elsewhere. In most parts of Britain this is of Jamaican derivation. The Caribbean-based Creole, or Patois as it is often called, is an important feature among African Caribbean youth.

In order to understand the importance of Creole, it is important to appreciate the nature of the relationship between the black (African Caribbean) community and the dominant white society. Racial and ethnic hostility expressed in racist language employed by the white dominant society can result in hostile feelings on the part of the oppressed group. The use of Creole among African Caribbean people can be seen as a reaction to the values and standards of the dominant culture. As noted in an earlier section, it is a means of expression that serves both to express hostile reactions and to preserve the integrity of the group. It enables African Caribbeans to communicate with each other while maintaining secrecy from the white dominant society. Wong (1986: 105) notes that Patois and Creole are languages that developed because they were 'necessary for intra-community communication that excluded others. The language became at once a source of pride as well as a barrier behind which the community survived.'

According to Grier and Cobbs (1968: 61), 'the "jive" language and the "hip" language . . . is used as a secret language to communicate hostility of blacks for whites, and great delight is taken by blacks when whites are confounded by the language'. In the United States, Grier and Cobbs noted that 'The indirectness of southern language patterns suited the needs of the oppressed black minority perfectly. In the circumlocution so necessary to the beleaguered blacks, it became a refined art' (p. 124).

Creole, as a source of strength and pride, functions as a means of maintaining the identity and group solidarity of the African Caribbean community. The language or dialect people select thus reinforces their social identities. It enables black people to fight the inherent racism in British society (Wong 1986).

African Caribbean teenagers use Creole to establish in-group identity and to act aggressively (Hewitt 1986). For example, among some groups arguments produce increased use of Jamaican pronounciations. Teenagers seem to equate strength and assertiveness with Creole and use it strategically with authority figures such as police, teachers and social workers. Where there is a power differential, Creole use takes on political and cultural significance because it denotes assertiveness and group identity. Hewitt (1986: 109) noted that:

> Certain contacts with the police, . . . or in conflicts with teachers (Gilroy and Lawrence 1986) or with youth workers (Brandt 1984) may foster the use of creole largely because of its association with strong and dauntless assertiveness. Where the 'race'/power dimension is also present, this connotation may be further supplemented by a concept of black group identity, so that the power of individual assertiveness may be translated into an assertiveness concerning group (i.e. 'race') relations.

The adoption of Creole by many African Caribbean adolescents is also a reaction against Standard English, which is seen by many as militating against African Caribbean people (see the section on racist language). Racist attitudes to any language spoken by African Caribbean people, as well as the racist overtones and nuances of the English language itself, have contributed to the adoption of Creole by many second generation young African Caribbean people (Wong 1986). For many African Caribbean adolescents, 'Patois is a powerful social and political mantle which . . . becomes an aggressive and proud assertion of "racial" and class identities' (Wong 1986: 119). Thus, the acquisition of competence in Creole is an expression of racial identity and solidarity as well as a demonstration of determination to acquire status and power (Wong 1986). The secrecy and hostility inherent in the existence of different language codes present obvious but nevertheless strong barriers to effective interethnic communication.

In a comparative study of two generations of African Caribbeans and Asians, Modood *et al.* (1994) explored the attitudes of first generation African Caribbeans toward the use and transmission of Creole and Patois languages. Half of the first generation of African Caribbeans in the sample felt that it was not important for them or their children to maintain an oral Creole or Patois tradition. The group felt that the use of such language was limited as a mode of communication to other Caribbean peoples only, and would not therefore offer employment opportunities to their children.

However, the other half of the African Caribbean group sampled felt that it was important for their language to be transmitted to their children as part of a cultural identity. Hewitt (1986: 105) found that many black parents equate Creole use with economic failure and discouraged children from using Creole. These parents did not want it taught at schools.

The second generation of African Caribbeans in Modood *et al.*'s (1994) study felt that it was important to maintain their oral tradition as part of their cultural identity. Thus, one respondent said: 'It gives me a sense of identity, it gives me something I can relate to.' Another respondent stated that 'It is an expression of blackness' (p. 38). Where Creole use is equated with African Caribbean group identity, youngsters often feel the need to display some facility with socially marked Creole forms (Hewitt 1986). Hewitt suggests that for this reason self-reports of language may over-report use of this language form. One 16-year-old reported to Hewitt (p. 107): 'I feel black and I'm proud of it, to speak like that.'

Most of the second generation respondents in Modood *et al.*'s (1994) study felt that it was essential for African Caribbeans to be able to communicate in Creole and Patois. Those African Caribbeans who were unwilling or unable to use Creole or Patois were viewed negatively by some of the respondents. They were considered to be out of touch with 'where they were coming from'. These respondents also felt that Caribbean languages should be offered in schools.

Teachers tend to notice use of Patois among pupils in early or mid-adolescence and then view it as an effort to build a new counterculture when in fact, as Bones (1986) argues, it is a renewal, a culture that is a counter to white encroachment and is made to last well beyond adolescence. Sutcliffe (1986: 8) notes that:

> With [a] raising awareness of racism, particularly during mid-adolescence, there comes a raising of black consciousness: an awareness that black people can express their identity through their own language, music, lifestyles and can find solutions to their problems within the community. One of the clearest markers of this process is the growing use of Creole.

By ignoring or being hostile to languages other than Standard English, schools have contributed to, not alleviated, academic failure (Sutcliffe 1986). Politzer and Hoover (1976) showed that teachers demonstrated lower academic expectations for speakers of Black English than for speakers of Standard English. Studies have shown that teacher attitudes affect the students' attitudes and behaviours (see Jenkins 1982). Teachers who expect failure typically demand less from students, provide less information and feedback to students, and generally engage in conscious and unconscious behaviours that produce failure. Teachers must accept each child's language or dialect as legitimate (Freeman 1982). In so doing, teachers must use teaching techniques that meaningfully communicate with children in ways that provide for academic enrichment.

Dalphinis (1985: 195) argues that 'A recognition of Creoles as languages, rather than dialects would decrease the alienation of pupils of Caribbean origin from the school.' By refusing to legitimize the use of Creole as a language in its own right, schools negate the African Caribbean child's linguistic competence. The effect of this is that the teaching of English in most schools has become a process of dismantling the child's linguistic competence rather than adding a second language to his/her first language.

Teachers could exert much more influence on their African Caribbean pupils by treating Black English as a foreign language. English could be learned as a second language; there is nothing to indicate that proficiency in Black English would minimize one's proficiency in English, or vice versa. When people feel secure about the legitimacy of their native language, including Black English (see Williams 1982), there is a greater willingness to learn a second language.

Dalphinis argues that English as a Second Language (ESL) teaching methods should be used with pupils who have difficulty in Standard English. However, ESL teaching methods are not considered applicable to African Caribbean pupils because Creole has been 'defined by others [(white dominant society)] as a dialect, while their errors in standard English are considered at best inconsistent errors in standard English, and at worst, as evidence of their cognitive deficiency' (Dalphinis 1985: 197).

The devaluation of Black English in British and American society is consistent with the devaluation of African Caribbean people in general, and must be addressed. White practitioners who view Black English as a legitimate code spoken by many African Caribbean people, notwithstanding the importance of learning English, are likely to attain greater satisfaction from communication with speakers of Black English than are those who see the language as negative.

Bilingual issues and interethnic communication

According to Yates (1972: 50):

> Using a second language successfully requires more than a grasp of a complex linguistic system. Speakers must also have a shared communicative style which is based on social and cultural values which prevail in society . . . Without this awareness they are more likely to undervalue the individuals who speak English and, even more critical, to reject them because of failure to measure up to majority social and cultural values or norms of behaviour.

People make a positive or negative evaluation about the language that others use. Generally speaking there is a pecking order among languages that is usually buttressed and supported by the prevailing political order. In Britain, 'there is a temptation to disparage others' language forms as deficient. [But] as with the concept of culture [(see Chapter 2)], others' language forms are different, not deficient' (Lago and Thompson 1996: 56). Since many Western societies place such a high premium on the use of English, it is a short step to conclude that minorities are inferior, lack awareness, or lack conceptual thinking powers. Ahmed and Watt (1986: 99) quote a Sikh woman who speaks three Indian languages but cannot speak English: 'You know, in this country if you don't know English they make you feel you are nothing, and that attitude makes you feel so small and insignificant.' On the other hand, those who speak English are evaluated according to their various accents and dialects.

The use of Standard English to communicate with one another may unfairly discriminate against those from a bilingual background. Not only is this seen in the educational system, but also in the social work and health care interview. The bilingual background of many Asians may lead to much misunderstanding. When clients have to communicate in a language that is not their native language, important aspects of experience may be left out. Marcos and Alpert (1976) report that if bilingual individuals do not use their native tongue in counselling, many aspects of their emotional experience may not be available for treatment. For example, because English may not be their primary language, they may have difficulties using the wide complexity of language to describe their particular thoughts, feelings and unique situation. Clients who are limited in English tend to feel they are speaking as a child and choose simple words to explain complex thoughts and feelings. If they were able to use their native tongue, they would easily explain themselves without the huge loss of emotional complexity and experience (Marcos and Alpert 1976).

In counselling, heavy reliance is placed on verbal interaction to build rapport. The presupposition is that participants in a counselling dialogue are capable of understanding each other. Vontress (1971) points out how counsellors often fail to understand a black client's language and its nuances for rapport building. This applies to the social worker interview. A black client's brief, different or 'poor' verbal responses may lead many social workers to impute inaccurate characteristics or motives to him/her. The client may be seen as uncooperative, sullen, negative, nonverbal or repressed on the basis of language expression alone. White (1984) believes that understanding black communication styles and patterns is indispensable for counsellors and other practitioners working in the black community. Failure to understand imagery, analogies and nuances of cultural sayings may render the counsellor ineffective in establishing relationships and building credibility.

Marcos and Urcuyo (1979) advised monolingual clinicians to use care in the evaluation of the bilingual client's sparse use of words – behaviour which is often misinterpreted as evidence of lack of motivation, emotional withdrawal, or depression. An alternative hypothesis for the patient's observed behaviour is the effect of bilingualism, and monolingual practitioners should be sensitive to this possibility. Interviews conducted in a client's second language add additional responsibilities to the role of the

social and health care worker, who must sort out linguistic and paralinguistic data provided by the client and determine which are meaningful for
analysis and which are merely the results of using a second language.
Clients can also fail to perceive many of the linguistic devices which therapists use in the course of therapy, such as vocal cues, intonation, pauses
and emotional tone (Marcos and Urcuyo 1979).

Some American data suggest that bilingual multicultural clients may be
rated as being more psychopathological when they are interviewed in English than when they are interviewed in their native language. Marcos *et al.*
(1973) asked mental health professionals to rate videotapes of Hispanic
clients communicating in Spanish and Hispanic clients communicating in
English. The raters detected more psychopathology during the English
interview. These authors suggest that when bilingual culturally diverse
clients are instructed to speak English rather than their native language,
they may appear tense, uncooperative and more emotionally withdrawn.

Martinez (1986) points out that many Hispanic clients who speak minimal or no English first think in Spanish, then translate into English to themselves, and finally respond to the therapist in English. Many changes in the
client's verbal and nonverbal behaviour during this process may be interpreted as psychopathological. For example, Hispanic clients with little
command of Standard English would answer a question or remark from a
therapist with a simple and restricted verbal output that may be interpreted
as a case of 'impoverishment of thought'. Similar observations have been
made about the potential effect of nonstandard English versus the effect of
Standard English on the evaluation of psychopathology. Russell (1988)
cites a study in which white and black (African American) therapists
observed an actor (playing the role of a client) describing his mental problems in Black English and Standard English. The study found that black
therapists reported less psychopathology when the actor spoke in Black
English and more psychopathology when the actor spoke in Standard English; the inverse findings were reported by white therapists.

Black people in Britain find that their problems are misconstrued because
of differences in language, culture, beliefs, diagnostic models and racism.
Language barriers become more significant in mental health as the process
of diagnosis is dependent upon communicating feelings and experiences. It
is difficult to achieve this communication effectively through the use of an
interpreter. The inappropriateness of diagnostic tools, added to the problems of communicating in different languages, has led to several cases of
misdiagnosis (Ahmed and Webb-Johnson 1995). A number of studies (see
Ho 1976) found that bilinguals (Chinese English; Korean English) presented different personalities depending on whether they were responding
in English (their second language) or in their native language.

As discussed in Chapter 3, Asians are likely to come from a collectivistic,
family-oriented culture. However, the English language 'is more limited in
defining family relationships when compared with languages from family-
centred cultures' (d'Ardenne and Mahtani 1990: 67). For example, in

Hindi, there are four different words for 'aunt' and four different words for 'uncle' (Rack 1982). Thus, 'in counselling [or interviewing] a client from this family-centred culture, the counsellor [or social worker] working only in English is limited in her understanding of the subtlety of family relationships' (d'Ardenne and Mahtani 1990: 67)

In Britain, those who speak English often lack sympathy for and patience with those who do not. There is evidence that doctors communicate differently with black patients. As discussed above, black patients who do not speak English fluently may be perceived as less intelligent than the majority (white) culture. Doctors 'tend to provide more directive information to a patient who is not fluent in English than would be given to a patient who is fluent and can therefore articulate their fears and questions easily' (Eleftheriadou 1996: 52).

In a study on the health and social care needs of black communities in the Brighton, Hove and Lewes area, Yazdani and Anjum (1994) reported that communication was a major problem for people who could not speak English, with implications for diagnosis/needs assessment and health promotion work. Communication problems created feelings of frustration and alienation in service users. For instance, one Bengali woman in the study stated:

> My main problem is communication. Because of the language problem often I feel dumb and can't express my positive or negative feelings . . . I stayed in hospital for 2 weeks. Two of the nurses neglected me. Of course I didn't know whether it was because of my colour or because of the communication problem . . . I am still not sure about the exact medical term of the operation.
>
> (Yazdani and Anjum 1994: 19)

Social and health care workers need to respond patiently to clients who have a limited knowledge of English. They need to be aware of the jargon in their speech and provide a clear definition of technical terms. They must withhold judgements and negative evaluations; instead, they must show respect for the difficulties associated with learning a new language. White social workers and health care interviewers tend to assume that black people are familiar with the dominant ways of conducting interviews. If a black client gives what is felt to be an irrelevant answer to a question, this is likely to be put down to the client's uncooperativeness, and so forth, and not to the possibility of miscommunication. Thus, black clients may be denied valuable services 'through misconceptions based upon cultural insensitivity and dominance' (Fairclough 1989: 64). Doctors and social workers may attribute the difficulty they experience in dealing with black patients and clients to the clients' 'incompetence or unco-operativity or some other stereotyped trait, rather than to different dialect or discourse norms, perhaps low proficiency in a second language or stress in an unfamiliar environment' (Giles and Coupland 1991: 123). Similar problems may arise for working class clients.

According to Sue *et al.* (1992: 79), 'promoting bilingualism rather than monolingualism should be a major goal to the provision of mental health [and social] services: it is an expression of personal freedom and pluralism'.

Mares *et al.* (1985), working in the field of health care, have suggested some practical ways in which practitioners can communicate more effectively with people who speak little or no English or who speak as a second language. These are: (1) to reduce stress – for example, practitioners should allow more time for interviewing the client than they would for an English-speaking client, and practitioners should also give plenty of nonverbal reassurance; (2) to simplify English – for example, practitioners should speak clearly but must not raise their voice and must not use slang or idioms; (3) to check back properly – for example, practitioners need to develop a regular pattern of checking that what they have said has been understood.

The use of interpreters

The term 'interpretation' emphasizes the exchange of connotative meaning between languages so that both affect and meaning are conveyed; whereas 'translation' refers to the exchange of the denotative meaning of a word, phrase or sentence in one language for the same meaning in another language. The 'translator should be someone with cultural knowledge and appropriate professional background' (Lago and Thompson 1996: 61). Most of the literature and studies on intercultural/interethnic communication refer to 'interpreting' services.

One stereotyped image which exists about Asian people is that 'they do not speak English'. However, a large proportion of the Asian community speak English as a second language and many people speak two or three languages as well as English. Asian women who do not work outside the home, and older Asians who migrated to Britain in their later years, are more likely not to speak English. These groups have also been identified as most vulnerable to health and emotional problems (Beliappa 1991).

A substantial minority of Asians will be entering old age with a poor grasp of English and using health services of which they know little (Donaldson and Odell 1984), where they will find, in the main, inadequate help from trained interpreters. While it is a statutory obligation of health authorities to provide services meeting the needs of all their population, the fact is that most have been unable to meet this ideal.

Yazdani and Anjum's (1994) study cited above illustrates the problems associated with communication difficulties. The participants in the study felt that they could not make themselves understood properly – which had implications, for example, in making a diagnosis. In another study of social and health authority services – 38 social services departments (SSDs) and 39 district health authorities (DHAs) – for elderly people from black and minority ethnic communities, Askham *et al.* (1995) found that half of both the SSDs and DHAs used no specifically funded interpreting services (merely relying on families, phrase books or cards, or volunteers from their staff or community groups). All SSD respondents were aware of the inadequacy of interpreting services, and two-thirds said they were reviewing or intending to review them. However, less than half the DHAs reported such intentions, and even these were mainly to do with improving leaflets rather than providing interpreters. The authors also interviewed 83 Caribbeans and 89 Asians. Two-thirds of the Asian sample said that communication was an issue for them. For example, 'more interpreters' was one of the two main answers given by Asians, the other being 'more Asian staff', to a question about how, if at all, people thought services could be improved. Ninety-eight per cent of service users said it was important to them that those looking after them spoke their first language. Yet only 5 per cent of Asians said they had ever made use of interpreters when consulting doctors etc.; only 40 per cent said they had ever been asked in hospital whether they needed help with interpreting, and only 34 per cent in outpatient clinics. In an earlier survey of health authorities (1978), all the respondents mentioned language as a major obstacle to health care (Bhatti, in Wandsworth CRC 1978).

The following examples (from Askham *et al.*'s 1995 study) illustrate the anxiety and distress caused by communication difficulties. A 52-year-old Asian woman said: 'I was frightened of the tall, male nurse who just pushed me onto the bed. Also I couldn't say anything because he didn't speak my language' (p. 88). A 56-year-old Asian woman said: 'I go to hospital for regular check-ups but I don't understand anything. If I don't understand they should be patient, not angry. They should have an interpreter . . . it will give us comfort and confidence in hospital.' Finally, a 67-year-old Asian woman said: 'I need an interpreter to go everywhere as I cannot speak English. I have difficulty obtaining DSS benefits, housing, health services, and even going to the GP because of the language' (pp. 86–7).

People who are suffering from illness or distress are more likely to express themselves only in their mother tongue. The subject of interpreting is therefore of great significance in health and social services. Interpreting is frequently carried out by husbands or wives, other relatives, friends and children.

Many Asian people frequently take their children to hospital to interpret. This brings its own problems. For example, in the gynaecological department, taking your children to interpret would seem utterly shameful for most parents. It cannot be assumed that people would wish to ask friends or acquaintances to interpret for them in highly personal and confidential situations. The disadvantages of using family members as interpreters should be recognized (Rack 1982; Shackman 1985; Dominelli 1988; Yazdani and Anjum 1994). For example, social services tend to use children to translate for their elders (Dominelli 1988). In sensitive situations this can result in distress and humiliation and/or vital information not being elicited. Dominelli (1988) cites an example in which a child is used for interpreting. A Sikh woman who spoke Punjabi but virtually no English was referred by a health visitor to social services – because the woman was suffering from post-natal depression. However, 'as there were no Punjabi-speaking social workers, a white social worker visited the woman and used the woman's 9 year old daughter as a translator' (Dominelli 1988: 102). In Yazdani and Anjum's (1994) study, one Sudanese woman stated: 'I always use my son or daughter as interpreter in the GP surgery' (p. 19). Rack (1982: 199) argues that 'under no circumstances should children be asked to interpret medical details for their parents'. He goes on to say that:

An adult relative or friend is less objectionable, but if he [or she] has no familiarity with medical and psychiatric matters he [or she] will find his [or her] task very difficult, and may intrude consciously or unconsciously his [or her] own interpretation of the problem, or report not what the patient says, but what he [or she] thinks he [or she] means.
(Rack 1982: 200)

Dominelli (1988) has noted that the inappropriate use of interpreters and translators has continued for several decades in order to cut costs because they are cheaper to employ than qualified black social workers. And she has argued for the development of a comprehensive translation service being necessary in establishing anti-racist social work.

Lago and Thompson (1996) list some of the advantages and limitations in using professional interpreters. The advantages of using interpreters are as follows:

[It] infers respect for the client's preferred language; signals to the client the [practitioner's] wish to understand fully the client and their predicament; [and] acknowledges that the client will be able to be maximally fluent and descriptive of their situation in their own language.
(Lago and Thompson 1996: 61)

However, some of the problems that may arise in using interpreters include: the possibility of bias as communication is dependent on a third party; meanings can be changed in the process of translation – the messages that leave both the practitioner and client have the potential to be modified and indeed changed through the interpreter. Vasquez (1982) refers to this as 'role exchange' whereby the interpreter assumes more the role of practitioner. Interpreters are sometimes unfamiliar with the terminology used. An interpreter's presence may embarrass the patient when the problem is perceived as a taboo subject. Breach of confidentiality is a serious issue – some Asians reject interpreters who belong to the same community at interviews. And finally, an interpreter might wrongly reinterpret the patient's ideas, or abbreviate responses. Other disadvantages include: the practitioner's inability to assess intonation, pauses and emotionality in the client through the use of a translator (Marcos 1979). Thus even with a correct translation, the lack of subtle nonverbal cues makes assessment difficult (Gomez *et al.* 1982).

Interpreting in the area of mental health is a particularly complex and demanding task which requires a high level of sensitivity as well as linguistic expertise. Words are culturally loaded and have different meanings and concepts in different languages. The interpreter has to decode within the cultural context what is being expressed behind the words in order to communicate the full message to the professional. An Asian counsellor observes: 'Asians feel that because of the language barrier they can't express themselves fully and they get misdiagnosed as mentally ill. It might just be that they are stressed or depressed.'

Shackman (1985) has provided a useful checklist of practical ways of assisting the process of communication through an interpreter. She recommends that interviewers: check that both the interpreter and client do speak the same language or dialect; allow time for a pre-interview discussion with the interpreter to establish the content of the interview and the way in which they will work together (issues to be discussed include goals of the evaluation, areas of focus, sensitive topics, confidentiality and objectivity); use straightforward language; throughout the interview check that the client has understood what has been said; and have a post-interview discussion with the interpreter about the interview. In the counselling process, practitioners 'will need to consider much more systematically how to manage such three-way situations [(the counsellor, client and interpreter)] in order that they can fully involve translators and prepare clients for the impact of this new working situation' (Lago and Thompson 1996: 63). Cox (1976) has included among his qualities of a good interpreter the ability to understand the culture of both the professional and the client, a thorough knowledge of the languages used, a familiarity with the terminology used and an unhurried approach.

I wish to conclude this section with a quote from Ahmed (1989: 2):

Linguistic skill is an essential prerequisite of social work and other caring [and health] professions, without which they can neither communicate nor provide an effective service. Not speaking the language of the client, then, is the problem OF professionals, not of clients. It becomes the problem FOR clients, when their right to services is denied due to lack of language provision, when they get trapped in the forces of language, 'race' and power, that perpetuates racism, both personal and institutional.

Racist language

Dominelli (1988: 6) argues that 'the very language we use is riddled with racism. When social workers speak of Britain, they usually mean white, "English" Britain.' A very good example of the racist attitudes inherent in much language usage is revealed in the connotations associated with the words 'black' and 'white' in the English language. The notions of 'black' as evil and 'white' as good and pure are deeply embedded within the symbolism of the art and literature of European culture. Williams (1964: 721) states that 'an abundance of informal evidence can be offered to support the observation that, in our culture, the word (and color) black carries a negative or "bad" connotative meaning, while the word white carries a positive or "good" meaning'. Kloss (1979) noted that the word 'black' has numerous negative connotations for the average person – including evil, sin, excrement, hostility and violence. Howitt and Owusu-Bempah (1994) found 55 negative connotations of the word 'black' as compared to only 21 for the word 'white' in the dictionary. Conversely, the authors found 9 and 19 positive connotations of black and white respectively. White practitioners need to be aware of the 'implicit racism in the word [black]' (Dominelli 1988: 6).

The white practitioner's choice of language sends messages continuously to the client about his or her values. The language used will betray the practitioner if he or she does not genuinely respect his or her client's culture. For example, is negative language being used, such as in blatant derogatives ('nigger', 'Paki'), colour symbolism (white as good, black as bad), political evaluations ('underdeveloped', cultural 'deprivation'), and in ethnocentric descriptions ('huts' in Africa). Or conversely, are positive terms being used when they would not be used for whites in the same context (blacks being called 'quite intelligent'). Are the religions of other cultures treated with respect? Is black people's culture trivialized or ridiculed? Finally, is a distinction made between 'us' and 'them', in such a way that black people are not part of 'us' or Britain.

White practitioners need to be familiar with how their clients refer to themselves and their own communities. For example, terms such as 'immigrant', 'alien' and 'coloured' may all seem to the white worker as innocuous, but may have strong emotional connotations for black people. In historical terms, these words have been used in a derogatory and discriminatory way (d'Ardenne and Mahtani 1990). Terms that white people employ to 'put down' black people, to define a subjugated position for blacks, are also racist, even though they are frequently employed on an unconscious level. The use of such terms as 'you people' when referring to black people causes great anger in interethnic interaction. According to Lago (in Lago and Thompson 1996: 10) the use of phrases such as 'You're one of them' – are 'inferred slants/strong reference to something other, you're not sure of what/but it has negative vibes'. Any language that, through a conscious or an unconscious attempt by the user, places a particular racial or ethnic group in an inferior position is racist at base and is almost certain to produce angry responses highly disruptive to interethnic communication. White practitioners need to engage in frequent and frank interethnic interactions with black people who will tell the white practitioner which expressions cause hostile responses.

The racism in language such as that expressed in words like 'nigger', 'Paki' is so obvious that they are seldom heard in interethnic encounters in social service and health settings. More common today is the subtle racism in language. A refusal on the part of white people to say 'black' or African Caribbean' instead of 'coloured', and a constant reference to black groups as 'you people' are all interpreted by black people in interethnic settings as indications of racist attitudes on the part of the white language user. The language of racism, be it overt or subtle, is a deterrent to effective interethnic communication. Words such as 'nigger', 'Paki', have such emotional-connotative meaning that they disrupt or often terminate the possibility for interethnic communication.

van Dijk (1987) undertook a study of how highly prejudiced attitudes are transmitted through discourse. By interviewing white Dutch racists, van Dijk showed that much of their discourse involved both expressing the negative attitude and simultaneously avoiding the possibility of being charged with racism. This involved a number of strategies, among which were:

1 Credibility-enhancing moves, in which the person would make statements designed to show that they 'knew' what they were talking about;
2 Positive self-presentation: this refers to 'negative comparison between us and them: we are the victims (engender empathy) of unfair competition; denial of racist reasons for dislike, stressing "good reasons" for dislike' (van Dijk 1987: 295). Thus, the person would disclaim being racist but provide reasons for disliking the minority group in question based on what they claimed to be 'good' reasons, like unfair competition;
3 Negative other-presentation, in which the disliked group was described as engaging in negative or illegal behaviour. Ethnic minority groups are 'accused of stealing, mugging, cheating on welfare, lack of hygiene, laziness, [etc.]' (van Dijk 1987: 300).

The use of these strategies, van Dijk argued, meant the speaker's racist attitudes were communicated in a way which made it more difficult for the recipient to accuse the speaker of racism directly: they were defining the context of social interaction in such a way as to make these unpleasant attitudes appear socially acceptable. van Dijk concludes (p. 394) that

> The general norms or values [of a racist society] may be inconsistent with racism, but actual discourse, such as everyday talk and the media, as well as commonsense interpretations and evaluations are not based on systematically developed knowledge and beliefs about the processes of prejudice and discrimination. People have not learned to contradict racist thought and talk . . . The prevailing practices, also in communication, are protective of the status quo, and hence of the dominance of the White majority.

Indeed one of the perplexing difficulties of everyday racist thought and utterance is that it may be contradictory, ad hoc and lack apparent theoretical coherence: which of course makes it all the more difficult to confront and negate through rational argument (see, for example, Essed 1991; Wetherell and Potter 1992).

Conclusion

Social workers and health care workers need to have an understanding of the relationship between racial identities (see Chapter 1) and use of Black English. A black person with high pre-encounter attitudes may choose not to use Black English and may feel embarrassed by those who do. Instead, he or she may use Standard English exclusively. On the other hand, an individual at the immersion–emersion level of racial identity development embraces black culture and history and may choose to use Black English in order to gain self-esteem and racial pride.

White practitioners need to respect the right and need of black people to establish and maintain their own languages. It is important to develop the self-concept and self-worth of black children and young people by allowing them to preserve and perpetuate their own languages. The problem introduced into the interethnic communication situation by the existence of codes – for example, Black English, needs to be acknowledged by white practitioners. According to d'Ardenne and Mahtani (1990: 64), 'Black clients who speak another form of English are even less likely to be understood by their counsellors [and other service providers] than those who speak another language and require interpreters.'

White practitioners in interethnic interaction should have an understanding of different language habits – different denotations, connotations, grammar, accents and concepts of the function of language. A sensitivity to such differences and a willingness to make the adjustments necessary for common understanding is a big step toward resolving the difficulties resulting from linguistic diversity. White practitioners should resist judging and evaluating a black person's language, since ethnocentric judgements will interfere with effective communication.

Interpreters are often an undervalued and 'abused' section of service providers. Interpreting must be considered a central rather than a peripheral part of social and health services. There is also a need to raise the status of this activity within the National Health Service. As a long-term objective, social and health services need to recruit more bilingual professionals.

Finally, white practitioners who want to communicate with black people in a productive fashion must become as sensitive to their offensive racist expressions as black people have become. The major challenge facing white social and health care workers is to become more sensitized to the racism inherent in white language usage and to make a conscious effort to discard the overt and covert language of racism. The use of overt or subtle racism in language in interethnic interviews will result in anger and hostility toward the practitioner and disrupt or often terminate the possibility for interethnic communication. Social and health care workers need to modify their personal linguistic habits in order to ensure effective interethnic communication.

Annotated bibliography

Giles, H. and Coupland, N. (1991) *Language: Contexts and Consequences*. Buckingham: Open University Press.
This book provides a theoretical approach for the study of culturally relevant interpersonal and intergroup processes across a wide range of language situations.
Hewitt, R. (1986) *White Talk Black Talk: Inter-racial Friendship and Communication Among Adolescents*. Cambridge: Cambridge University Press.
This book studies the relations between black and white adolescents in south London. It examines the sociolinguistic impact of the Jamaican Creole used by young black people on the language and culture of young whites.
van Dijk, T. (1987) *Communicating Racism: Ethnic Prejudice in Thought and Talk*. Newbury Park, CA: Sage.
This book offers a fascinating analysis of elite racist discourse. It is based upon the author's own empirical studies and shows that elites play a primary role in the reproduction of ethnic dominance and racism in the popular culture of Western societies.

5

Nonverbal communication in interethnic settings

Introduction

> Cities throughout the world today increasingly include minorities
> defined by 'race', ethnicity, language, class, religion, and sexual orien-
> tation. Encounters with 'difference' now pervade modern everyday life
> in urban settings.
>
> (Rosaldo 1989: 28)

This chapter discusses the importance of nonverbal communication in
interethnic settings. Much communication between members of different
ethnic groups is nonverbal. According to some authors, only 30–40 per cent
of what is communicated conversationally is verbal (Condon and Yousef
1975; Ramsey and Birk 1983). Nonverbal behaviour is undeniably important in communication, within a culture or across cultures. Nonverbal language is highly culture-bound (Argyle 1975; Schneller 1985) and the
contribution of nonverbal communication itself, relative to that of verbal
language, is also highly culture-dependent.

This chapter will explore the significance of nonverbal behaviours and
communication among black and white people. The meanings we interpret
from nonverbal behaviours are culturally conditioned. The differences in
nonverbal behaviour among cultures can cause breakdowns in intercultural communication (Dodd 1987). We need to be aware that:

> Cultural differences in nonverbal behaviour can ... be a source of mis-
> communication (LaFrance and Mayo 1976). Also, if someone does not
> behave in an expected manner then ... the perceiver might be tempted
> to make an internal attribution. [Hence] in a society where there is
> limited emotional expression a member of a more expressive culture
> might be inferred to be 'over-emotional'.
>
> (Hinton 1993: 177)

In this chapter I will discuss the impact of racism and discrimination on black people's presentation of self to others and impression management. The importance of nonverbal communication in interethnic settings is significant because the lack of trust between ethnic communities has caused interethnic communicators to reject the values of verbal communication and to search for nonverbal cues as indicators of real meaning and response in interethnic communication situations. Finally, implications for social workers and health care workers are discussed.

Nonverbal behaviours

Most researchers in the field of nonverbal communication categorize nonverbal communication into the following areas: kinesics or body movements (i.e. gestures, movements of the body, e.g. hands, arms, head, feet and legs); facial expressions (e.g. smiles); eye behaviour (e.g. blinking, direction and length of gaze, and pupil dilation); posture, touching behaviour (e.g. stroking, hitting, holding); paralanguage (e.g. vocal qualities, including moans, loudness of voice, pauses, silences, hesitations); physical characteristics (e.g. physique, body shape, general attractiveness, body or breath odours, hair, weight, height and skin colour); proxemics (e.g. people's use and perception of personal and social space); artefacts (e.g. perfume, clothes, spectacles, etc.); and environmental factors (e.g. architecture, furniture, lighting, crowding, music and noise, smells, weather, or related factors that could affect the communication process). Research into nonverbal behaviour is of two types, related either to studying the meaning attributed to nonverbal behaviour or to assessing its frequency.

This section will discuss some of the characteristics of nonverbal communication which are of special importance in interethnic communication. Nonverbal cues are often the best indicators of an individual's true attitudes or intentions, irrespective of what has been said. Unlike spoken language, which is used as often to conceal thought as it is to express thought, and which people largely control for their own purposes, much nonverbal behaviour seems impossible to control. Individuals are not aware of most of their own nonverbal behaviour, which is enacted mindlessly, spontaneously and unconsciously (Burgoon 1985; Samovar and Porter 1985; Andersen 1986). Social and health care workers must accept that at least some of the time their nonverbal behaviour and their spoken words may not seem to match.

What is the basis of our evaluation of a client's appearance, walk, posture and eye contact? By what means do white social and health care workers judge black clients? If social and health care workers use the criteria of their 'race' or culture, their assessment of the client may be inappropriate since a certain type of nonverbal expression may mean one thing to the social worker but have a completely different meaning for the black client. Social and health care workers interviewing black clients may make judgements of them unaware that the behaviour has a cultural/racial basis that they are misinterpreting. Thus, interactions between members of different cultures may be problematic if the meaning of their behaviour is misinterpreted (Argyle 1988). A good example to consider is cultural differences in eye-contact behaviour. If a client failed constantly to look you in the eyes, you may interpret this behaviour as being disrespectful. However, such behaviour may communicate a great amount of respect for what he/she perceives as the status difference between him/herself and the social worker. Other differences between cultures include factors such as people's use of personal space (for example, how close it is appropriate to stand in conversation with another person) and touch (for example, when and how often you touch another person).

There has been a rapid increase in research and publications in the subject of nonverbal communication. However, the majority of studies have been carried out in the USA. Little research has been directed toward black people's nonverbal communication patterns in Britain.

High and low context

As noted in Chapter 3, Hall (1976) proposed the concept of high and low context cultures. In low context cultures (for example the US and Britain), verbal messages are elaborate and highly specific and tend also to be highly detailed and redundant. Verbal abilities are highly valued. Low context cultures have been associated with being more opportunistic, more individual rather than group oriented (Smith 1981). In high context cultures, most of the information is either in the physical context or internalized in the person. Very little is in the coded, explicit, transmitted part of the message. High context cultures are more sensitive to nonverbal messages; hence they are more likely to provide a context and setting and let the point evolve. Black cultures have been described as high context. Many blacks require fewer words than their white counterparts to communicate the same content (Stanbeck and Pearce 1981; Jenkins 1982; Weber 1985). Sue and Sue (1990: 58) note that 'Asian Americans, Blacks, Hispanics, and other minority groups in the US emphasize high context cues'.

This notion of context poses problems when social work and health care clients are from cultures that differ in context level. When white social and health care workers (from low context cultures) interact with clients of high context cultures (African and Asian), the social and health care workers are liable to have difficulty in communicating because the high context messages do not contain sufficient information for practitioners to gain a true or complete meaning. Social and health care workers may interpret a high context culture message according to their low context disposition and reach entirely the wrong meaning. Black clients are more adept at reading nonverbal behaviour. People in high context cultures have an expectation that others are also able to understand the unarticulated communication; hence, they do not speak as much as people from low context cultures.

Thus, what is not said may be more important in determining meaning than what *is* said.

White practitioners' attributions about the nonverbal communication of black people can sometimes be wrong. However, understanding that a client is from a collectivistic or individualistic culture or a high or low context culture will make his or her behaviour less confusing and more interpretable.

The following section explores how ethnicity/culture may influence the following areas of nonverbal behaviour: kinesics (facial expressions), touching behaviour, perception of time, proxemics, paralanguage, silence, posture and gesture. It is important to be aware that not all nonverbal behaviours described below are exhibited by all black people; and behaviours or patterns may be modified by class, age or gender.

Kinesics

This is the study of body language. It refers to 'gestures, facial expressions, eye contact, body positions, body movement, and forms of greeting and their relation to communication' (Dodd 1987: 173). Some kinesic behaviours are culture-specific and therefore need to be studied within a cultural framework (Dodd 1977; Knapp 1980).

We can detect emotions from facial expressions. The research carried out by Ekman *et al.* (1972) on facial expressions in various cultural groups is useful. Ekman and Friesen (1967) argue that facial behaviours are both universal and culture-specific. According to Ekman, 'What is universal in facial expression of emotions is the particular set of facial muscular movements triggered when a given emotion is elicited' (in Harper *et al.* 1978: 100). The authors note that facial expressions can also be culture-specific. Thus, because of cultural norms and individual expectations, eliciting events for the same emotions can vary from person to person. Wolfgang (1984) found that whites in Canada decoded facial expressions representing the fundamental emotions more accurately of whites (Anglo-Saxons) than of blacks (West Indians).

A major nonverbal facial feature relates to maintaining eye contact in a dyad ('gaze behaviour'): looking at or looking away from the person being addressed. I will examine visual behaviour, which is one of the most studied aspects of nonverbal behaviour.

In black (African American) nonverbal behaviour visual behaviour (eye contact, gaze, staring, etc.) plays a major role. In particular, it plays an important role in interpersonal communication, interpersonal attraction and arousal. The research carried out by LaFrance and Mayo (1976) demonstrates that African Americans tend to have lower eye contact and gaze than whites. African Americans look at others while listening with less frequency than whites (Harper *et al.* 1978; Smith 1983; Hanna 1984). During a conversation whites look at their partners for 55 per cent of the time, compared to 42 per cent for blacks, which amounts to 33 seconds per minute for whites and 25 seconds per minute in the case of non-whites. When European Americans speak they tend to look at their partner less than they do while listening (Kendon 1967; LaFrance and Mayo 1976; Atkinson *et al.* 1979). Consequently, white people look less and blacks look more while speaking. But while listening whites look more and blacks look less. When these patterns are combined we can anticipate that when a European American is speaking the individuals interacting will not be looking at each other frequently. This may be interpreted as boredom, lack of interest and low involvement by a social worker or other white professional interviewing black clients. When a black person is speaking, there is more mutual eye contact than either would expect (LaFrance and Mayo 1976) and this may be interpreted as intensity, hostility or power. Ickes (1984: 331) suggests that: 'A common outcome of this clash of cultural expectations is that black and white participants both experience their visual interaction as somewhat awkward and uncomfortable.'

LaFrance and Mayo (1976) suggest that white authority figures (e.g. administrators, teachers, educators, etc.) often misread African American eye behaviour (for example, inferring that black people are uninterested, less honest, withhold information, and have poor concentration). According to LaFrance and Mayo it is important to use a cultural framework when interpreting eye contact and gaze. White people tend to associate eye contact and eye gaze with affiliation, positive attitudes between communicators, trustworthiness, forthrightness and sincerity (Hanna 1984). In white culture, members expect direct eye contact as a sign of listening and showing respect for authority. Black people, on the other hand, may associate eye contact and gaze with negative overtones and a lack of respect.

Hanna's (1984) data showed some African Americans were reluctant to look directly in the eye of persons who occupied an authority position. Many black children are taught not to look another person (particularly older persons) in the eye when the older person is talking to them. To do so is to communicate disrespect. Avoiding eye contact is a non-verbal way of communicating a recognition of the authority–subordinate relationship of the participants in a social situation. In contrast, white children are socialized to do just the opposite; looking away from a speaker is seen as disrespectful. Patterns of eye contact learned in childhood seem to be relatively unaffected by later experiences (Jandt 1995). Thus, 'in many countries there are elaborate patterns of eye avoidance which are often linked to considerations of deferential respect, many of which [white practitioners] would have very little insight into' (Lago 1989: 146).

Johnson (1971: 18) observed that 'Black people can express with their eyes an insolent, hostile disapproval of the person who is in the authority role. The movement of the eyes is called "rolling the eyes" in the Black culture.' 'Rolling the eyes' is a nonverbal way of expressing impudence and disapproval of the person who is in the authority role and of communicating every negative label that can be applied to the dominant person (Johnson 1971).

Hemsley and Doob (1978) investigated the relation between credibility and gaze behaviour in an experimental setting. White subjects were exposed to film fragments depicting a witness in court. In one fragment the witness looked directly at the judge while testifying; in the other the witness gazed at the floor. The content of the testimonies was identical. Results showed that the testimony was perceived to be more credible if the witness maintained eye contact with the judge. These reviews generally reveal a consistent pattern of meanings attributed to gaze behaviour. Individuals within the dominant culture in the US and Britain who frequently look their discussion partner in the eye are not only considered to be more credible, but are also judged to be more congenial, attentive, competent, more skilful socially and more assertive. Credibility increases with the use of eye contact – at least in the US and Britain (Robinson 1995).

Garratt et al. (1981) made an inventory of the style of police questioning preferred by black and white subjects. The results suggest that white subjects prefer a police officer to look at them during questioning, while blacks would rather not. Blacks experience frequent eye contact as impolite. Ickes (1984) moreover notes that blacks consider continued eye contact as provoking, arrogant and disdainful. Thus, black people may appear to be indifferent or uninvolved in their interactions with whites (Asante and Noor-Aldeen 1984; Ickes 1984). North American whites, on the other hand, are more likely to experience such interactions as somewhat difficult and burdensome and therefore tend to talk, look at the other and smile more (Ickes 1984). Ickes (1984) concludes that, compared to blacks, North American whites either anticipate or perceive greater difficulty and awkwardness in these initial interethnic interactions and feel a particular responsibility and concern for making the interaction work. These patterns may reflect over-accommodation on the part of European Americans (Giles and Coupland 1991).

In Asian cultures, direct eye-to-eye contact is avoided during a conversation, particularly if the other person is of the opposite sex; this behaviour should not be taken as avoidance of the issue being discussed. For example, among Muslim women 'sitting with somewhat bowed head and downcast eyes is a sign of great modesty' (McAvoy and Sayeed 1990: 61). In Britain a person who fails to establish eye contact is often seen as being evasive or unassertive (Mercer 1984). American Asians 'tend to regard eye contact as disrespectful; restraint in the use of eye contact is regarded as a sign of deference. There is a greater use of peripheral vision' (Kadushin 1990: 288).

One study showed that Arabs, Latin Americans and southern Europeans focused their gaze on the eyes or face of their conversational partner, whereas Asians, Indians and Pakistanis tend to show peripheral gaze or no gaze at all (Harper et al. 1978). Too much eye contact is also considered threatening to the Japanese (Argyle et al. 1981).

Studies have shown that there are gender differences in visual behaviour. Overall, LaFrance and Mayo (1976) found that looking while listening occurred least for black males and most for white females. The eye and

visual literature shows that, overall, females use eye contact more frequently than males (Smith 1983).

Females may establish more eye contact when compared to males, 'as a
way to show sensitivity and emotional expression' (Majors 1988: 281).
These sex differences also seem to be generally consistent across age.

To summarize, eye-contact patterns may account for some of the dispar-
ities in level of involvement in conversations between white workers and
black clients. As noted earlier, European Americans may interpret the
behaviour of a person from another culture as inattentive or rude due to the
differences between cultures in gaze behaviour (Argyle 1988). Differences
in white and black visual behaviour have clear applications in the social
work and health care interview. Instead of assuming that the client's
averted eyes indicate lack of understanding, a social or health care worker
more familiar with patterns of black nonverbal behaviour might well
attribute it to a culturally learned behaviour pattern.

Touching

Touch, or the study of haptics, provides a rich area of intercultural communication insight. Many white people feel uncomfortable when a person
from a culture whose members touch a lot greets the white person 'by
touching the shoulders and arms for what seems like a long time' (Dodd
1987: 11). Conversely, many members of a 'haptically active' host culture
feel equally uncomfortable when the white person maintains a lack of touch
and distance, since this behaviour is perceived as unfriendly and cold. Some
cultures (Arab, Jewish, Mediterranean) are highly touch oriented while
others are nontouching cultures (German, English) (Mehrabian 1971).
Africans and African Americans, as contrasted with whites, touch others in
a wider variety of different situations. Heinig (1975) reported that African
American students touched teachers more than their white counterparts.
Willis *et al.* (1976) showed that touching behaviour among African Americans was much greater than the touching behaviour among white children
(Hanna 1984). Hall and Hall (1990: 11) have noted that 'in northern
Europe one does not touch others. Even the brushing of the overcoat sleeve
used to elicit an apology.'

Different cultures encode and interpret touch behaviour in different
ways. Low contact cultures include the United States and Britain, and high
contact cultures include Asia and Africa (see Chapter 3 for discussion of
high and low contact cultures). Research (e.g. Watson 1970) comparing
touching behaviours in Latin America (high contact) and the United States
(low contact) reveals that people in the Latin American cultures engage in
much more tactile behaviours than people in the United States. According
to Patterson (1983: 145),

> These [high and low contact cultures'] habitual patterns of relating to
> the world permeate all aspects of everyday life, but their effects on
> social behaviour define the manner in which people relate to one

another. In the case of contact cultures, this general tendency is manifested in closer approaches so that tactile and olfactory information may be gained easily.

People in collectivistic cultures (such as Asian, African and African Caribbean) tend to engage in more tactile interaction than people in individualistic cultures. African Americans touch other blacks more than they touch European Americans, and this is even more evident after successes in sports (Smith *et al.* 1980; Halberstadt 1985). Smith *et al.* (1980), for example, found a higher rate of touching among African Americans than whites in expression of congratulations on a bowling team. This pattern is particularly true of lower socio-economic class African Americans. For example, in a study of touching behaviour, Hall (1974) found working class blacks, as opposed to middle class whites and working class Hispanics, showed a greater tendency towards bodily contact in interpersonal interactions. It has also been observed that interethnic dyads touch less than intraethnic dyads among both European Americans and African Americans (Willis *et al.* 1976).

There are ethnic and gender differences in touching behaviour (Smith 1983). These variables will have an effect on the initiation and the receptivity levels of touch behaviour, as well as on the variations of nonverbal touch forms. In a study of touching behaviours among African Americans and white female pairs, Willis and Hoffman (1975) observed that there was 'more frequent touching in same sex and same "race" dyads than in dyads of other "race"/sex combinations' (Smith 1983: 58). Willis *et al.* (1976) found that touching was more likely to occur in black–black dyads, with females touching more frequently than any other group. Black females use touching behaviours in order to communicate intimacy (Willis *et al.* 1976), while males use touching more for status and power (Eakins and Eakins 1978; Smith 1983). Leathers (1986: 137) states that 'in both intimate and professional relationships men are expected to touch women much more frequently than they are touched by women, and they do so'. Same-sex touching is female-dominated since men tend to restrict tactile contact with other men. Unlike males, females are conditioned by society to show feelings and emotions (Eakins and Eakins 1978; Smith 1983). Also, most research shows that females are touched more by others than males are touched by others. As noted above, touching for males may connote dominance or possession toward others. As Henley and Thorne wrote, 'the wholesale touching of women carries the message that women are community property' (Eakins and Eakins 1978: 394). Henley (1986) suggests that male–female dyads are 'mixed' in the sense that there is an unequal distribution of status and power between men and women in our society. Therefore, just as any superior is freer to touch any subordinate than vice versa, so are men freer to touch women than vice versa. Class differences in touching have been found, with people in higher income groups touching less than those in lower income groups (Henley 1977).

Time

Chronemics is the study of how we perceive, structure, use and react to time. It includes perceptions of when someone is 'on time' and the significance of being 'late'. Our perception of time is culturally determined and differs greatly among different groups.

The study of meanings, usage and communication of time is probably the most discussed and well-researched nonverbal code in the intercultural literature (Hall 1959, 1976, 1984; Burgoon and Saine 1978; Malandro and Barker 1983; Gudykunst and Kim 1984). According to Poyatos (1992: 366), 'many misunderstandings and ill feelings develop because of our different conceptualization of time lapse, the meaning of "punctuality", "tomorrow", "later", . . . or the need to plan ahead of time'.

Hall (1994: 266) differentiates between monochronic and polychronic time. Polychronic time 'stresses involvement of people and completion of transactions rather than adherence to present schedules. Appointments are not taken as seriously and, as a consequence, are frequently broken.' Monochronic time 'is not inherent in man's biological rhythms or his creative drives' (p. 266). Monochronics usually think in a linear fashion. For instance, monochronics schedule appointments linearly, arrival, meeting, conclusion, action, and they move through this same pattern all day long. When a monchronic is placed in a polychronic situation, stress and poor communication usually result.

Most Euro-Americans have a monochronic attitude toward time (Hall 1984) and often prefer to do one thing at a time. They consider time as a valuable commodity that can be measured, saved, spent, wasted, bought and lost. How to get things done effectively is their primary concern, and the surrounding circumstances are not as important. They set measurable objectives and evaluate the outcome in terms of effectiveness and efficiency. They separate the objectives into different periods with immediate, short-term and long-term goals, so they can terminate a project should it not achieve its preset objectives. In contrast, it is argued that Asians usually do not schedule their time as strictly. Asians are often involved simultaneously in several activities. They are satisfied with having a general guideline or plan and believe that everything has its own time.

In the 'US [and Britain] promptness is highly prized . . . People make attributions regarding the person depending on how prompt or late that person is' (Brislin and Yoshida 1994: 47). A large share of white peoples' relationships are governed by the clock. If black people arrive late for an appointment, they are labelled as being 'irresponsible', 'lazy', 'never on time'. Deviation from the set of rules people have learned in their culture regarding time 'tends to provoke strong emotional reactions' (Brislin and Yoshida 1994: 47). This can result in interethnic misunderstandings.

In Asian, African and African American culture, orientations to time are driven less by a need to 'get things done' and conform to external demands than by a sense of participation in events that create their own rhythm. As

Daniel and Smitherman suggest (1976: 32) about time in African American culture, 'Being on time has to do with participating in the fulfillment of an activity that is vital to the sustenance of a basic rhythm, rather than with appearing on the scene at, say "twelve o'clock sharp".' The key is not to be 'on time' but 'in time'. Thus, African Americans 'often use what is referred to as BPT (black people's time) or hang loose time; maintaining that priority belongs to what is happening at that instant' (Samovar 1994: 18). However, black people are capable of code switching with time just as with language. For example, the black professional may well be monochronic in the work setting but polychronic in other settings, such as social and leisure activities.

Norms in the less time-oriented cultures seem to address the issue of people first, schedules second. Cultural rules in these cases are centred around internal relationships rather than external schedules. Interethnic communication problems between 'time-oriented cultures and less time-oriented cultures involve task-oriented people, externally shaping their relationships with time and schedules, and relationship-oriented people, motivated by saving face and social lubrication' (Dodd 1987: 48). Consequently, the white practitioner communicating with the black client 'may experience unexplainable rebuffs – such cool relationships are expected when [white practitioner's] cultural time rules do not match those of the cultural system in which [white practitioners] are communicating' (p. 48).

Proxemics

Hall (1955, 1964) was the first researcher to study personal space, systematically referring to the study of spatial usage as proxemics. Proxemics is a term that describes the study of the individual's use and perception of social and personal space. Personal space can be viewed 'as that area around each individual which is treated as a part of himself or herself' (Baron and Byrne 1991).

Various studies have indicated that cultures differ greatly in their use of personal space, the distances they maintain, and their regard for territory, as well as the meanings they assign to proxemic behaviour (Hall 1976; Samovar et al. 1981; Gudykunst and Kim 1984).

According to Hall (1983) Euro-Americans prefer the following ranges of distances: very close (3 to 6 inches) for top secret; close (6 to 12 inches) for very confidential; near (12 to 20 inches) for confidential; neutral (20 to 36 inches) for personal subject matters; neutral (4½ to 5 feet) for information of nonpersonal matter; public distance (5½ to 8 feet) for public information/business conversation. Little (in Hall 1974) found that members of Mediterranean cultures (e.g. Greeks, southern Italians) prefer closer interpersonal distances than northern Europeans.

In a number of studies, Halberstadt (1985) found that black Americans establish closer distances than European Americans. These closer distances begin in childhood when black American children establish closer distances in play and other activities (Aiello and Jones 1971; Duncan 1978). Hall (1974: 180) observed that:

> The flow and shift of distance between people as they interact with each other is part and parcel of the communication process. The normal conversational distance between strangers illustrates how important are the dynamics of space interaction. If a person gets too close, the reaction is instantaneous and automatic – the other person backs up. And if he [or she] gets too close again, back we go again.

The distance we expect others to stand from us when we are talking varies between contact and noncontact cultures (Hall 1966) (see Chapter 3 for discussion of contact and noncontact cultures). People in contact cultures (e.g. Asians and African Caribbeans) expect others to stand only inches away, while people from noncontact cultures expect others to stand at least 'an arm's length' away.

The degree to which a culture is individualistic or collectivist has an impact on the nonverbal behaviour of that culture in a variety of ways. People from individualistic cultures are comparatively remote and distant proximically. Collectivistic cultures are interdependent and, as a result, they work, play, live and sleep in close proximity to one another. Gudykunst and Ting-Toomey (1988: 125) suggest that 'members of individualistic cultures tend to take an active, aggressive stance when their space is violated, while members of collectivistic cultures tend to assume a passive, withdrawal stance when their personal space is violated'. Just as with ethnicity, so also with gender and age, it is difficult to make rigid culture-general statements about 'typical' behaviours. Male–male, female–female, and male–female dyads most often respond differently within a single culture. Rosegrant and McCroskey (1975) analysed US black and white contacts and found that: males established greater interpersonal distance from males than they did from females, than females did from males, or than females did from females; female blacks established closer distances than female whites or either black or white males. African American females lean toward each other more than white females or African American male dyads (Smith 1983). African American women use leaning as a way to convey intimacy and rapport (Smith 1983). It is often said that the male's need and desire for control of greater territory and space (LaFrance 1981) is a subliminal expression of dominance and status. It is therefore not unusual for males to believe they are entitled to more personal space. Eakins and Eakins (1978) noted that males (compared to females) usually have larger houses, cars, land-holdings, offices, desks. Eakins and Eakins also reported that males used more personal space in their body spread. Women's territory is perceived as smaller by both females and males. Women seem to have become accustomed to, and tolerant of, invasions of their personal space.

Aiello and Jones (1971) indicate that the need for space increases with age. Children interacted the most proximally, adolescents at an intermediary distance, and adults at the greatest distance. Curt and Nine (1983) noted that in Puerto Rico (a contact culture), people of the same sex and age touch a great deal and stand quite close together; whereas people of the opposite sex and age do not touch at all and tend to stand further apart than Americans do.

White social workers and health care practitioners should note that the nonverbal behaviours of touch and distance can signal involvement, connection and intimacy for Asians and African Caribbeans clients through a symbolic language which may differ extensively from their own culturally familiar nonverbal behaviour.

Paralanguage

Paralanguage deals with how something is said and not what is said. It deals with the range of nonverbal cues surrounding common speech behaviour (Knapp 1978). Paralanguage includes all that accompanies language: pitch, range, rhythm, tempo and articulation; vocalizations – vocal characterizers: laughing, crying, sighing, etc.; vocal qualifiers – intensity, pitch heights, extent. Other vocal cues include pauses, silences, dialect or accent, speech rate, duration of utterance and interaction rates. Paralanguage is very likely to be revealed in conversation conventions such as how we greet, address and take turns in speaking.

The volume and intensity of speech in conversation are also influenced by cultural values (Sue and Sue 1990). Practitioners need 'to be aware of possible misinterpretations as a function of speech volume. [Thus,] speaking loudly may not indicate anger and hostility; and speaking in a soft voice may not be a sign of weakness, shyness, or depression' (p. 57).

Sue and Sue (1990: 57) note that 'directness of a conversation or the degree of frankness [(paralanguage)] varies among various cultural groups'. For instance, many Asians 'converse in an indirect or circular pattern, contrasting markedly with the direct, linear orientation of English [people]. Such an approach can be misinterpreted as indicating shyness, verbosity, or evasiveness' (McAvoy and Sayeed 1990: 61).

However, the most relevant element in paralanguage in terms of interethnic communication is the impact that accent or dialect patterns have upon communication receivers. Accents and dialects carry with them stereotypes of the speakers employing them, and these stereotypes affect interethnic interaction. The interethnic implications of vocal stereotypes are enormous. Many black people are not only physically stereotyped, but they are vocally stereotyped as well (see Chapter 4).

Silence

As noted above, paralanguage includes the use of silence. There are complex rules regarding when to speak or yield to another person (Jensen 1973). A practitioner working with culturally different clients needs to be aware of these rules in order to communicate effectively.

The intercultural implications of silent behaviours are diverse because the value and use of silence as communication vary markedly from one culture to another. The Western tradition is relatively negative in its attitude toward silence and ambiguity, especially in social and public relations. In a Western context, silences can convey all the various kinds and degrees of messages that may be described as cold, oppressive, defiant, disapproving or condemning, calming, approving, humble, excusing and consenting (Samovar *et al.* 1981).

Triandis (in Giles *et al.* 1992) argues that the differences in beliefs about talk between Chinese and European Americans are due to individualism–collectivism:

Individualists have a choice among many groups . . . to which they do belong, and usually belong to these groups because they volunteer. Collectivists . . . are born into a few groups and are more or less stuck with them. So, the collectivists do not have to go out of their way and exert themselves to be accepted, while individualists have to work hard to be accepted. Hence, the individualists often speak more, try to control the situation verbally, and do not value silence.

(Giles *et al.* 1992: 11)

The above analysis could also apply to differences in beliefs about silent behaviours between Asians and the white population in Britain. Traditionally, Eastern societies such as India have valued silence more than Western societies. Oliver (1971: 264) observed that 'silence in Asia has commonly been entirely acceptable, whereas in the West silence has generally been considered socially disagreeable'. In India silence is used to promote harmony, cooperation and other collectivistic values. Silence is a sign of interpersonal sensitivity, mutual respect, personal dignity, affirmation and wisdom (Jain and Matukumalli 1993).

Social and health care workers should, therefore, pay more attention to the cultural views of silence and the interpretations given to silence in communication interactions. Intercultural misunderstanding can occur if practitioners do not know when, where and how to remain silent.

Posture

Mehrabian (1971) describes a person's posture as essential to understanding interethnic communication – he termed this posture the 'power metaphor'. It is expressed in terms of body expansion or contraction:

For dominance or status, the communication code seems to be based on a power or fearlessness metaphor. Power coexists with large size (for example, strutting versus shuffling, expansive versus small, and controlled postures and movements). Absence of fear (the opposite of vigilance) is implied by relaxation versus tension and by the ability to turn one's back to another.

(Mehrabian 1971: 55)

The implications of postural communication for interethnic communication are significant. The lack of trust between black and white people and the constant state of vigilance observed by participants – black and white – are expressed in the extreme body tensions present in many interethnic situations (Mehrabian 1971). There is rarely the same degree of total body relaxation in interethnic groups as there is in ethnically homogeneous groups (Mehrabian 1971). Social and health care workers need to be aware of the implications of postural communication for interethnic communication.

Gesture

Gesture is an important form of communication in interethnic settings. Gestures are movements of the body, usually the hands, that are generally reflective of thought or feeling. Like language, gestures are culture-specific and differ in each culture. But when we use them, especially in interethnic contexts, we do not readily think about the fact that they may have a different meaning to someone else. Some scholars have attempted to catalogue in great detail the use of gestures in different cultures (for example, Kendon 1987).

The 'secret' black (African American) handshake unites members of one racial group in a common cause (see Majors 1991). This symbolic gesture systematically excludes those outside the racial and ethnic group in much the same way as does a different language code (see Chapter 4).

McAvoy and Sayeed (1990: 61) suggest that 'eye-winking can cause grave offence to many Asians, especially if directed at a woman by a man' . . . [and] the "thumbs up" sign symbolizes defiance, not success or good luck'. Another gesture, 'pointing the index finger during conversation, often used for emphasis or discipline in Western culture, is regarded as bad manners by many Asians' (p. 61). When social and health care workers use gestures in intercultural contexts, they need to be aware that their gestures may have a different meaning for the client. Being unaware of these differences can cause problems. According to Barna (1990: 30), 'the lack of understanding of nonverbal signs and symbols, such as gestures . . . is a definite communication barrier'.

The impact of racism and discrimination on black people's presentation of self to others and impression management

One of the most commonly held assumptions is that nonverbal behaviour operates primarily at the unconscious or unawareness level (Argyle 1975) and therefore to be trusted more than words, because it is more spontaneous and difficult to censor or falsify (Mehrabian 1972). Nonverbal language may contradict the verbal message, usually unconsciously, creating a state of 'double-edged' or inconsistent communication (Mehrabian 1971).

Empirical data show that in many such cases it is exactly the nonverbal component which determines the final impact of the message (Knapp 1978).

We tend to regard nonverbal communication as the 'true' indicator of a communicator's meaning, because nonverbal behaviour (frequently unconscious or reflexive) is more difficult to control than verbal behaviour. Therefore, our true emotions will often 'leak' through in hints of nervousness, anger, boredom and other feelings. If white practitioners 'are unaware of their own biases, the nonverbals are most likely to reveal their true feelings' (Sue and Sue 1990: 62). Hall (1976) has also stressed that on one level, the verbal communication can convey one meaning, while on another level, the nonverbal, command level, a very different meaning can be conveyed. Such inconsistencies can result in 'miscommunication' – something is communicated, even though it is not what was intended, and often it is not what was thought to have been communicated (Hall 1976).

Research suggests that black people and women (white and black) are 'better readers of nonverbal cues than White males' (Sue and Sue 1990: 62). As noted above, this may be mainly due to black people's high context orientation, but it could be a matter of psychological survival (Sue and Sue 1990). In order to survive in a white-dominated society, black people have 'to rely on nonverbal cues more often than verbal ones' (p. 62). Thus, if white social and health care workers have not dealt adequately with their own racism, the black client will be quick to detect any racist biases.

Black people often see nonverbal messages as more credible than verbal messages. When a contradiction occurs between the verbal and nonverbal messages, black people tend to believe the nonverbal messages more. A common saying among African Americans is:

'If you really want to know what White folks are thinking and feeling, don't listen to what they say, but how they say it'. Such a statement refers to the biases, stereotypes, and racist attitudes that whites are believed to possess, but that they consciously or unconsciously conceal.
(Sue and Sue 1990: 60)

In discussing nonverbal communication among black people, Boyd-Franklin (1989: 97) used the terms 'vibes' as follows:

Black people, because of the often extremely subtle ways in which racism manifests itself socially, are particularly attuned to very fine distinctions among such variables in all interactions . . . Because of this, many Black people have been socialized to pay attention to all of the nuances of behavior and not just to the verbal message. The term most often applied to this multilevel perception on Black culture is 'vibes'.

Certain nonverbal behaviours in black individuals have taken on unique characteristics as a consequence of the 'history of conflict' with white people (for example slavery, racism, discrimination). Black people use different roles because of their distrust of white people and in an attempt to survive. Majors (1991: 273) considers that 'survival, pride, solidarity, camaraderie, entertainment, and bitterness have become the impetus for and raison d'etre of many culture-specific nonverbal behaviours in present day African American culture'. Majors (p. 270) argues that in order

> To cope with the 'invisibility' and frustration resulting from racism and discrimination, many African American people have channeled their creative talents and energies into the construction and use of particular expressive and conspicuous styles of nonverbal behaviours (e.g. in their demeanour, gestures, clothing, hairstyles, walk, stances, and handshakes, among other areas). For many African American people these unique, expressive, colorful, stylish and performance-oriented behaviours are ways to act 'cool', to be visible and show pride. Elsewhere these behaviours have been referred to as 'Cool pose'.

Messinger *et al.* (in Majors 1991) provide us with a good example of how black people use different roles. They quote Sammy Davis Jr. as saying, 'As soon as I go out the front door of my house in the morning, I'm on . . . but when I'm with the group, I can relax. We trust each other.' Thus, 'there are times when, although "off stage", he [(Davis)] feels "on stage"'. The authors conclude with a citation from another author, Bernard Wolfe, who asserts that we can most probably expect 'members of any oppressed group [to have] similar experiences' (Majors 1991: 74). It is highly probable that black people in Britain have similar experiences. From this perspective, black people will regard presentations of self to others and impression management as the key to control and survival.

Conclusion

Gudykunst and Kim (1992: 186) indicate that 'To communicate effectively with strangers [(black clients)], [social and health care workers] must learn to accurately interpret their nonverbal behaviour and their violations of [black clients'] expectations.'

Social workers and health care practitioners need to recognize the profound influence of nonverbal behaviours in the communication process and then realize how their own cultural background influences the way they interpret nonverbal behaviour. While these processes are usually unconscious and automatic, that does not mean that practitioners cannot improve on them to be more flexible and inclusive of different cultural systems of behaviour. Poyatos (1992: 375) suggests that counselling 'requires very specific nonverbal skills and much sensitiveness to the counselee's nonverbal communication, as it can involve all types of persons and from any culture, which in the final analysis applies to any of the other helping professions [e.g. social workers]'.

Black clients can get conflicting messages from nonverbal behaviour. The words coming out of a white practitioner's mouth may tell the client one thing, but the practitioner's nonverbal behaviours (for example, tone of voice, gaze) may tell the black client something else. The problem in interethnic communication is that nonverbal languages are silent. Our interpretational processes are unconscious and automatic. We may not attend to them very much, but messages are being transmitted. More often than not, the nonverbal language of black people is different from what white practitioners are accustomed to.

White practitioners need to study how black people react to and express distrust towards white people in order to understand and analyse the nonverbal behaviours and communication styles of black people. Suppose that a white social and health care worker was making an assessment of a black client, he or she might misinterpret the client's nonverbal characteristics (for example the client's posture, eye contact, etc.). If the white social and health care worker uses the criteria of his or her culture, the assessment may be inappropriate since a certain type of nonverbal expression may mean one thing in the white worker's culture but have a completely different meaning in the culture of the applicant. For example, in the helping context, where the social and health care worker is perceived as an authority figure, Asian clients may behave submissively. Avoidance of eye contact between persons of higher social status is an Asian cultural norm and should not be misunderstood by white practitioners to indicate dishonesty or lack of confidence.

As suggested earlier, members of low context cultures (for example, Britain) tend to communicate in a direct fashion, whereas members of high context cultures (for example, Asian and African Caribbean cultures) tend to communicate in an indirect fashion. Thus, black clients may suffer frustrations in communication because of the assumption that 'It need not be mentioned; everyone in the relationship knows it.' On the other hand, white practitioners place more reliance on the explicit code or message content and place less reliance on the nonverbal part of the message. Both sides are therefore often unaware of their different roles and expectations.

As noted earlier, the manner in which different cultures view time exerts a great influence on their lives. For instance, if white practitioners examine situations in their lives that seem frustrating or nonproductive, they 'may find that all or part of the problem involves monochronic/polychronic conflicts' (Dodd 1987: 87). Thus, an understanding of the differences of monochronic and polychronic time orientations may help to resolve some of the inherent problems in these situations.

Differences in the rules we all have concerning the use of space in interpersonal contexts can pose major problems in interethnic communication situations. Like other nonverbal behaviours, our use of space and our interpretation of the use of space around us often happens automatically and unconsciously. White practitioners have internalized these unspoken cultural rules and act on them automatically. Practitioners need to take these nonverbal behavioural differences into account when understanding and interacting with people of different cultures. When talking to black people, white practitioners must realize that what would be a violation of a worker's personal space in his or her culture is not so intended by the black person. Practitioners may experience feelings that are difficult to handle; they may believe that the black person is overbearing. However, the black person's movements are only manifestations of his or her cultural learning about how to use space.

Differences in the overall amount of touching that cultural groups prefer can lead to difficulties in interethnic communication. In general, white practioners may be perceived as cold and aloof by black clients, who in turn may be regarded as aggressive, pushy and overly familiar by the white service providers.

Argyle *et al.* (1981) proposed a 'games' model for understanding interaction in social situations. Just as you need to know the rules of a game (for example tennis), you need to know the rules, goals, roles and expectations of the client in the interethnic communication situation. For instance, they need to know which nonverbal behaviours reflect positive intimacy, affiliation, confidence; which ones are reinforcing; and which reflect nonverbal involvement of black clients. Literature that addresses nonverbal behaviours among Asian and African Caribbean cultures is limited at best. If we are to appreciate and understand Asian and African Caribbean communication styles, much more research on nonverbal behaviour is needed.

The variables of age, sex and social class are essential to consider in discussions on nonverbal communication. Although white social work and health care workers must be aware of cultural differences in nonverbal behaviour they must be careful not to stereotype nonverbally the people from different cultures into cultural slots. It is important to note that not every black person will exhibit the nonverbal behaviours described above.

Dodd (1987: 195) puts forward some skill suggestions for improving nonverbal communication:

1. Observe and discover specific kinesic behaviours for any one culture . . . 3. Notice spatial positions. 4. In practicing eye contact, observe what is appropriate within different contexts. 5. If you think you acted incorrectly, ask people, if it seems appropriate, what you did wrong.

Studies suggest that white therapists can improve their effectiveness with clients if they pay attention to clients' non-verbal behaviour (Argyle *et al.* 1981). Studies have also shown that formal training in nonverbal behaviour interpretation can help intercultural communication processes and outcomes. For example, Garratt *et al.* (1981) trained police officers to engage in gaze and visual attentive behaviour patterns that were similar to those found with African Americans in previous studies. The police officers then used these patterns when interviewing male African American undergraduate subjects. The subjects rated the trained officers more favourably than the untrained officers.

Social workers and counsellors need to help black clients explore the relevance of racial or cultural issues to their own concerns, especially when the

concern relates to the client's experiences in a potentially racist or discriminatory environment (e.g. Casas 1984; Helms 1990a; Sue and Sue 1990;
Atkinson *et al.* 1993). Thompson *et al.* (1994: 155) found that for black
women

> Counselor content orientation [(exploration of clients' problems as
> they relate to cultural and racial issues)] related significantly to depth
> of disclosure and willingness to self-refer, with participants reveal-
> ing more intimately and reporting a greater willingness to return to
> counselors when exposed to the cultural as opposed to the univer-
> sal content orientation [(exploration of clients' problems as they
> relate to issues shared universally – i.e. by humanity – irrespective of
> culture)].

Black people have encountered too many situations in which double messages are given to them, where the verbal and non verbal messages of the
white practitioners are different. An awareness of the communicative
power of one's unconscious physical expression will enable white practitioners to deal with the difficulties that arise in interethnic settings as a
result of unspoken expressions of emotions and attitudes.

Overcoming the black client's mistrust is the greatest contribution that
social workers and health care professionals can make to the 'working
alliance'. White practitioners must be alert to themes of concealment, suspicion and disguise. According to Gelso and Fretz (1992), trust is the
client's most important contribution to the 'working alliance' between the
client and the counsellor. But trusting a white counsellor is often difficult
for black clients. Black people have an understandable distrust of mental
health professionals because of psychiatry's view and treatment of black
people (see Littlewood and Lipsedge 1989; Fernando 1995). If effective
interethnic communication is to take place, the establishment of trust is
imperative. Toward this end, white practitioners must demonstrate their
goodwill; that is, they must convey that they are well-meaning individuals
who have chosen to work with people whom they value. In particular they
must be as free as possible of racism. Trust is also enhanced by the worker's
demonstration of the skills necessary to address the black client's problems
(Davis and Proctor 1989).

It is not, however, sufficient for a white social or health care worker just
to have a knowledge of black people's nonverbal behaviour. In order to
communicate effectively with black people, white social and health care
workers must address their racist attitudes, beliefs and feelings. Thus,
'attempts to teach effective cross-cultural counselling [(communication)]
will be doomed to failure unless [practitioners] address their own white
racism' (Sue and Sue 1990: 73). For many white practitioners, 'racism is a
very painful topic, and they are likely to react negatively to it' (p. 74). However, a worker who has not adequately dealt with his or her own biases and
racist attitudes may unwittingly communicate them to his or her black
client (Ridley 1995). Indeed, 'the primary task of white social [and health

care workers] wishing to implement anti-racist practice is to change their own racist attitudes and practices' (Dominelli 1988: 40).

Annotated bibliography

Argyle, M. (1988) *Bodily Communication*. London: Methuen.
  An introductory text on nonverbal communication.
Dodd, C.H. (1987) *Dynamics of Intercultural Communication*. Dubuque, IA: William C. Brown.
  A useful text on intercultural communication.

6

Interpersonal perception and interethnic communication

Introduction

This chapter focuses on the relationship between perception and intereth-nic communication. It argues that perception – the means of selectively receiving and organizing our experience – is at the core of any interethnic encounter. It examines the actual means whereby the communicator's stereotypes, perceptions, prejudices and attributions contribute to the suc-cess or failure of communication between black and white groups. This chapter explores the relationship between racial identity stages and dispos-itions toward prejudice.

Many problems erupting in interethnic communication settings can be attributed to our tendency to perceive selectively and perpetuate stereo-types. This chapter explores in detail the manner in which the stereotype functions as a barrier to effective interethnic communication.

Social and health care workers need to be aware that they will bring to any interethnic communication situation the capacity and predisposition to 'perceive' based on a combination of what really exists 'out there' and the set of expectations existing in 'the world inside our heads'. Our percep-tions affect not only our own behaviour but may also affect the personality and behaviour of the perceived person.

Definitions

Perception

Fellows (1968: 218) has defined perception as 'the process by means of which an organism receives and analyses information'. Chaplin (1975: 336) has defined perception as 'a group of sensations to which meaning is added from past experience'. Porter and Samovar (1994: 14) have defined perception as 'the internal process by which we select, evaluate, and organize stimuli from the external environment'. These definitions describe two events in which we participate when interacting with our environment. First, we 'receive' information. This reception refers to sensation or the process by which information comes to us through our senses. However, we do more than just receive or sense stimuli; we also analyse what we sense. Such an analysis process has two components: attention and organization (Fellows 1968: 5). The process of attention refers to the process whereby we systematically choose those stimuli to which we will attend, as we cannot possibly sense all there is to be received in the environment. In order to make sense of the various elements we have selected, we must engage in a process of organization. Thus, we convert the experience of our sense receptors into a 'useful and consistent' (Fellows 1968: 5) picture. Perception is an active, not a passive process. It is one in which the perceiver adds his/her own meaning to the data provided by his/her senses.

Stereotype

The term 'stereotype' has been extensively used by laypeople and academics from a wide variety of disciplines. Many of the viewpoints generally expressed in present-day literature regarding stereotypes originated as far back as 1922 with Walter Lippman, one of the first to define and employ the construct of the stereotype. Present-day literature has maintained Lippman's 'point that the "real environment" is too complex for us to understand it fully directly and therefore we perceive the world more simply: stereotypes are part of this process of simplifying the world in order to be able to deal with it' (Hinton 1993: 66). The process of stereotyping involves three stages:

> The first is identifying a set of people as a specific category . . . [this might be] . . . skin colour, sex, age . . . The second stage involves assigning a range of characteristics to that category of people . . . The final stage is the attribution of these characteristics to every member of the category . . . this overgeneralization . . . brings out the prejudiced nature of stereotyping as all group members are placed in the 'strait jacket' of the stereotype.
>
> (Hinton 1993: 66)

The dynamics of stereotyping ascribe to a single individual the characteristics associated with a group of people, or extend to a group the characteristics attributed to a single individual. The stereotype generally represents a negative judgement of both the group and the individual; it emphasizes negative differences. For black people, negative stereotyping has revolved around skin colour, assumed low intelligence or pathological behaviour. Stereotyping occurs in the context of racism as a means of explaining black people as inferior.

Stereotyping is particularly spurious when (1) characteristics are assigned to people because they are assumed to be inferior, (2) stereotypes lead to a 'self-fulfilling prophecy' or (3) people who stereotype are dogmatic and unwilling to open themselves up to new information that might contradict their beliefs. Once rigidly formed, stereotypes are highly resistant to change (Axelson 1993).

Prejudice

Allport (1954: 7) defined prejudice as 'a judgement based on previous decisions and experiences. While prejudice can be positive or negative, there is a tendency for most of us to think of it as negative. Allport (1979: 9) defined negative ethnic prejudice as 'an antipathy based on a faulty and unflexible generalization. It may be felt or expressed. It may be directed toward a group as a whole, or toward an individual because he [or she] is a member of that group.' The following three components are contained in this definition: prejudice is negative in nature and can be individually or group focused; prejudice is based on faulty or unsubstantiated data; and prejudice is rooted in an inflexible generalization (Ponterotto 1991).

It is useful to think of the strength of our prejudice as varying along a continuum from low to high, rather than in terms of a dichotomy, 'either I am prejudiced or not'. People who are highly prejudiced tend to ignore information not consistent with their faulty and inflexible generalization. Highly prejudiced people tend to alter their beliefs to justify their attitude when confronted with contradictory information. Allport (1979) refers to this process as rationalization.

Prejudice differs from its behavioural counterpart, discrimination. Prejudice 'includes internal beliefs and attitudes that are not necessarily expressed or acted upon' (Ponterotto and Pedersen 1993: 11). Direct discrimination involves behaving in such a way that members of an outgroup are treated disadvantageously. An individual who discriminates 'takes active steps to exclude or deny members of another group entrance or participation in a desired activity' (p. 34). Discrimination may exist in the absence of prejudice due to social pressures to conform (Pettigrew 1981) or as a consequence of routine institutional practices.

Racial identity models and prejudice

This section will examine the probable relationships between different racial identity stages (discussed in Chapter 1) and dispositions toward prejudice. I will first examine the relationship of white racial identity development to prejudice toward black clients. Some authors argue that the topic of white racial identity development is of such importance that it should be the focus of education in general, and of counsellor training in particular (for example Ponterotto 1991). I would also add that it should be the focus of social work and health care training. As described in Chapter 1, Helms's (1990a) model of white racial identity consists of six stages organized into two major phases. Phase 1, incorporating the first three stages, is called the 'abandonment of racism', and Phase 2, incorporating the last three stages, is termed 'defining a nonracist white identity'. A growing body of research has focused on the relationship of white racial identity attitudes to racism. Carter (1990) found a significant relationship between white racial identity attitudes and racism among white college students. Contact attitudes (for example, evaluating black people according to white criteria) and reintegration attitudes (for example, a belief in white racial superiority) were related to higher levels of racism (Carter 1990). As noted in Chapter 1, a person at the contact level of development denies the importance of 'race' and racial issues. Helms (1990a: 57) notes that for people high in contact attitudes, 'Negative race-related conditions [(unemployment, poverty)] are assumed to result from black people's inferior social, moral, and intellectual qualities.'

Carter (1990) found that white women with high contact attitudes were unlikely to endorse racism but were likely to ignore 'race', which itself can be racist when 'race' is salient to the other individual. In not recognizing that blacks and whites are different, white women with a predominance of contact attitudes may be eliminating an important aspect of their (and others') racial identities (Katz and Ivey 1977). In the United States and Britain 'ignoring "race" is a significant omission in that "race" is a particularly salient characteristic in Black and White interactions' (Carter 1990: 49).

To sum up, Carter's (1990) study suggests that both white men and women may be expressing racist attitudes, but they may do so in different ways. White men at all levels of racial awareness seem to hold racist beliefs and attitudes. White women exhibit racist beliefs and attitudes primarily when their level of racial awareness is low in that they may deny the importance of 'race'. Racism may be a product of racial/cultural ignorance (Katz and Ivey 1977). Whether the ignorance is naive (as in contact attitudes), hostile (as in reintegration attitudes), or influenced by all levels of racial identity attitudes, it may be time for white practitioners to examine their own racial/cultural awareness or identity. Carter's (1990) study suggests that white practitioners need to explore and discover their racial identity. However, Carter (p. 49) states that

> the findings of the study should be interpreted with caution . . . similar studies should be undertaken in other settings . . . It is possible that [whites] who live in different geographic regions [of the US] may develop racial identity and/or express their racial beliefs differently.

Pope-Davis and Ottavi (1992) replicated Carter's (1990) study on a sample of white university faculty members. The authors found that high contact attitudes for white men were related to endorsement of racist beliefs. Reintegration attitudes were also predictive of racism among white university faculty members. Block *et al.* (1995: 84) noted that reintegration attitudes resembled 'old-fashioned racism . . . the tendency to endorse pre-Civil War negative "racial" stereotypes about blacks and to be opposed to all aspects of integration'. And in another study, Pope-Davis and Ottavi (1994) found that disintegration and reintegration attitudes were associated with racism among college students. Contact attitudes were more characteristic of women than men (Pope-Davis and Ottavi 1994).

Claney and Parker (1989) examined the relationship of white racial identity to comfort with black people. The authors found a curvilinear relationship between white identity attitudes and college students' reported comfort with African Americans. Students in the first and last stages reported being more comfortable with black people, while white students in the middle stages were more uncomfortable around blacks. Block *et al.* (1995) found that individuals characterized by high disintegration attitudes were likely to endorse racist attitudes and were not comfortable with black people in work and social situations. These results are consistent with Helms's (1984) white racial identity model that postulates early stage naivety around racial issues and final stage appreciation and acceptance of racial diversity (Helms 1984). The above studies demonstrate that white individuals in contact, disintegration and reintegration stages are more likely to be negatively prejudiced toward black people.

Although it is crucial to consider the links between white racial identity development and dispositions toward prejudice, it is also important to consider the feelings that black and other minority clients hold toward themselves and toward the white majority. The racial/ethnic identity models described in Chapter 1 depict a stage where black/minority individuals identify with the white majority culture. Thus, in Cross's (1991) model – the extreme racial attitude to be found within the pre-encounter stage is anti-blackness, 'Their vision of blackness is dominated by negative, racist stereotypes, and on the other side of the coin, they may hold positive racial stereotypes of white people and white culture' (Cross 1991: 55). Individuals in Stage 1 are therefore more likely to be negatively prejudiced toward one's own racial/ethnic group and to have a positive prejudice toward the white dominant culture. In Cross's encounter stage (second stage), individuals may be beginning to develop positive prejudice toward their own racial group and a concurrent negative prejudice toward the white majority. Individuals in the third, (immersion–emersion) stage are likely to have a high level of positive prejudice toward their own racial/ethnic group coupled with a high level of negative prejudice toward the white majority group. Immersion is 'a strong, powerful, dominating sensation, which is constantly being energized by rage (at white people and culture)' (Cross 1991: 93). The major characteristic of the fourth stage is the development of a secure racial/ethnic identity coupled with an appreciation of other cultures. Thus, an appreciation and respect of other racial/ethnic groups may not be very likely if one does not develop a positive racial/ethnic identity (Ponterotto 1991).

Prejudice and communication

van Dijk (1984) found that individuals who hold highly prejudiced attitudes tend to qualify verbally the views they express of other groups so that they appear reasonable. For example, if individuals are going to make a negative comment about blacks they preface their comment with a claim of not being prejudiced. The following interview from van Dijk's (1984) study illustrates this: the interviewer asked 'Did you ever have any unpleasant experiences [with foreigners]?' and the interviewee responded by stating: 'I have nothing against foreigners. But their attitude, their aggression is scaring. We are no longer free here. You have to be careful' (p. 65). van Dijk (p. 70) found that prejudiced talk clusters in four categories: '(1) they are different (culture, mentality); (2) they do not adapt themselves; (3) they are involved in negative acts (nuisance, crime); and (4) they threaten our (social, economic) interests'. This study was carried out in the Netherlands but this type of prejudiced talk may be overheard among white social and health care workers in Britain (see for example, Dominelli 1988; Stubbs 1988).

The way we talk about people who are different is, in large part, a function of how we want to be seen by our in-group. van Dijk (1984: 154) notes that

> people 'adapt' their discourse to the rules and constraints of interaction and communication in social settings. Especially when delicate topics, such as 'foreigners', are concerned, social members will strategically try to realize both the aims of positive self-presentation and those of effective persuasion. Both aims, however, derive from the position of social members within their group. Positive self-presentation is not just a defense mechanism of individuals as persons, but also as respected, accepted, and integrated social members of ingroups.

While van Dijk (1987) finds direct expression of prejudice in topics of conversations when those conversations are held within the boundaries of an ethnic group (e.g. minorities as criminal, lazy, etc.), less direct expressions are found in argument forms (e.g. arguments about immigration, affirmative action, learning English). It is interesting to note that these indirect forms may be used in a variety of cultures. In addition to van Dijk's (1987) comparative study, Wodak (1991) discusses indirect forms of anti-Semitism in Austria, and Stern (1991) notes such forms in Germany.

Indeed in the last few decades as the extremist right and neo-fascist political groupings in Europe have made directly racist utterances socially unacceptable in polite society, more subtle modes of racist discourse have become widespread in national politics and everyday conversation. Reeves (1983) describes this as 'discursive de"racial"ization'; by which he means the process whereby people speak purposely to each other about racial matters while avoiding the overt deployment of racial language. What this concept reminds us is that such strategies are not just a feature of individual psychology but that they are necessarily social and ideological processes. The shared understanding of what is not being said, but which is to be inferred, must be socially constructed. The euphemistic terms and the superficially nonracial agendas which form the fabric of discursive deracialization must of course be shared by all those engaged in the dialogue. They must be learned, and given value through shared usage. They are in fact social constructs whose denotative meaning has added value to the extent that they effectively disguise their latent meaning. Thus the management of racist discourse is both a personal discursive strategy and a sophisticated expression of the dynamic fluidity of racist ideology.

Perception and communication

This section examines the way we make sense of our world – our perceptions and attributions – and its application to interethnic communication. We will first consider the selective and interpretive nature of perception and its influence on interethnic communication. Next, we will look at attribution theory and its application to interethnic communication.

Forgas (1985: 21) maintains that person perception 'is the first crucial stage in any interaction between people. We must first perceive and interpret other people before we can meaningfully relate to them.' It is important to note that there may be inter-group differences in perception between blacks and whites. A basic belief is that people behave as they do because of the ways in which they perceive the world and that these behaviours are learned as part of their cultural experience. We tend to notice, reflect on and respond to those elements in our environment that are important to us. As Comer (1972: 115) points out, 'there are situations in American [and British] life in which the "Black mind" sees it one way and the "White mind" sees it another or does not see it at all'.

If we had to pay attention to all of the stimuli in our environment, we would experience information overload. In the interest of not overloading ourselves with too much information, we limit our attention to those aspects of the other person or the situation that are essential to what we are doing. We might, for example, limit our attention to the colour of a person's skin. Watts (1966: 29) states that 'to notice is to select, to regard some bits of perception, or some features of the world, as more noteworthy, more significant than others'. Our perceptions of other people are also highly selective. Our presuppositions and expectations influence the cues that we select from the environment and what we see. Each of our perceptions are unique: they are based on our culture, our ethnicity, our sex, our background experiences and our needs. Our perceptions overlap with those of others to the extent that we share common experiences (e.g. culture). The problems for our communication with others arise because we mistakenly assume that we perceive others in a unbiased fashion. But our perceptions are highly selective and biased. Our past experiences are one source of bias. Our previous experiences with a particular person also can bias our perception of her or his current behaviour. Our emotional states also bias our perceptions. Sue and Sue (1990: 47) note that 'it is highly improbable that any of us can enter a situation or encounter people without forming impressions consistent with our own experiences and values'.

Perception also involves categorizations. Categorization allows 'us to structure and give coherence to our general knowledge about people and the social world, providing typical patterns of behavior and the range of likely variation between types of people and their characteristic actions and attributes' (Cantor *et al.* 1982: 34). When we categorize something, we group people or objects by features they have in common and ignore features they do not have in common. Our categorizations are based on only selected features of the person. In categorizing, we have to ignore some features in order to classify a person or object. Once we have created the category, we assume that things within the category are similar and that things in different categories are different. What creates problems in communication is the rigidity with which we maintain the boundaries between categories. People with rigid categories try to classify each thing and person into a single category. If we hold our categories rigidly, we do not recognize individual variations within our categories or consider recategorizing someone based on new information. Thus, if white people's categories are rigid, they see all black people as alike. To communicate effectively with a black person, white practitioners must be able to recognize how he or she is like other black people and how he or she is different from other black people. For example, if white practitioners' categories are rigid, they might categorize a black client as aggressive and refuse to consider reclassifying the client, even when confronted with consistent evidence that he or she is not aggressive. If our mental structures are flexible and elastic, we can 'break away from the mental cages in which we so often lock ourselves' (Zerubavel 1991: 122). In order to communicate effectively with black clients, social workers and health care workers need to have flexible categories.

First impressions and the persistence of perceptions

As soon as we observe anything about a person, we begin to form an impression of that person. Out of the many stimuli, we select only the more noticeable ones upon which we build our first impressions. Once we have formed this first impression, later observations will be influenced by our first impression. The first impression of a client determines the social and health care worker's behaviour toward the client. The client, in turn, behaves in a manner consistent with the worker's behaviour, and this consequently reinforces the worker's initial impression. For example, if a white social worker perceives a black client as hostile and responds to his or her own perception with defensiveness or hostility, the black client will tend to respond to the white social worker's response with hostility. Thus, the first impression of the white social worker is then confirmed, perhaps a self-fulfilling prophecy. The black client may have been hostile or friendly from the outset. However, the white practitioner's predisposition to select any feature that could be interpreted as hostility almost predestines the black client to grow into the hostile expectation of the white practitioner. Thus, our perceptions affect not only our own behaviour but may also affect the personality and behaviour of the perceived person. Our expectations can dictate how others behave toward us and hence reinforce our perceptions.

As Sue and Sue (1990: 35) note, 'what you think you see or expect to see is probably what you will see'. Thus, if a white social and health care worker expects hostility and resentment, then he or she will probably interpret communication behaviour in that light. Practitioners tend to see behaviour that confirms their expectations, even when it is absent. Hamilton *et al.* (1992: 149) suggest that

> perceivers can influence a person with whom they interact by constraining the person's behaviour. However, perceivers typically do not recognize this influence or take it into consideration when interpreting the target's behaviour. Although a target person's behaviour may be affected by perceiver-induced constraints, it is often interpreted by the perceiver as a manifestation of the target's personality.

First impressions are very difficult to change, even in the face of contradictory evidence. Nicolson and Bayne (1990: 5) suggest that 'the most direct way of countering the disproportionate power of first impressions is first to become aware of them and then to treat them as hypotheses: to check the evidence on which they are based, and to look for further evidence'.

Attribution theory

Attribution theory is a fairly recent development which attempts to explain how people perceive one another (Hartley 1993). This theory is particularly interested in how people decide the cause of other people's actions (Brislin and Yoshida 1994). It can also be used to examine how we explain our own actions. Studying attributions allows us to examine the biases that operate as people explain others' behaviours, which, in turn, affect their own behaviour. When white practitioners make attributions on 'automatic pilot' (Gudykunst 1994), they make errors, especially in interethnic communication situations.

Cross-cultural research on attributions is especially important in furthering our understanding of intercultural and interethnic interactions. However, most of the knowledge in this area is derived from research conducted almost exclusively in the United States. Research on attributions in the United States has centred on several issues. One issue concerns the types of attributions that people make, especially in relation to the locus of their attributions of causality. For example, a widespread concept in attribution research involves the distinction between internal and external attributions. Internal attributions are those that specify the cause of behaviour within a person; external attributions are those that locate the cause of behaviour outside a person. Research on attribution bias – the tendency to make certain types of attributions despite lack of evidence – has led to several popular concepts in social psychology, including fundamental attribution error, defensive attributions, and self-serving bias. Fundamental attribution error refers to a bias toward explaining the behaviour of others using internal attributions but explaining our own behaviours using external attributions (Jones and Nisbett 1971; Watson 1982). For example, we may attribute another person's failure at school to low intelligence or ability (internal) and our own failure to bad luck or bad teachers (external). Self-serving bias is the tendency to attribute our successes to personal factors and our failures to situational factors (Bradley 1978). Finally, defensive attributions refer to the tendency to blame victims for their misfortune, so that one feels less likely to be victimized in a similar way (Thornton 1984).

These attributional styles and theories have an impact both on our own behaviour and on our understanding of the behaviour of others. The attributional styles and biases described above are derived from research conducted almost exclusively in the United States with white participants. However, research conducted in other cultures shows that people of other cultures do not interpret their world the way Euro-Americans do; that is, they do not share the same attributional biases. For instance, several studies have found that the self-serving bias that tends to characterize Americans is not found in other cultures. Of these, Moghaddam *et al.* (1990) showed that Indian women who had immigrated to Canada were more likely to attribute both successes and failures to internal causes. Kashima and Triandis (1986) showed that Japanese people use a much more group oriented, collective approach to attributional styles with regard to attention and memory achievement tasks. Unlike their American counterparts, Japanese people attributed failure to themselves more and attributed success to themselves less. Kashima and Triandis (1986) interpreted this finding as suggestive of American and Japanese cultural differences in the degree of responsibility-taking. As these studies exemplify, attributional styles may be quite different across cultures. Duda and Allison (1989) suggested that the definitions of success and failure are ethnocentrically biased. How white Americans view success and failure (in terms of personal achievement on the basis of competition with others) is different from how people of other cultures define them (see Chapter 2, for differences between individualistic and collectivistic cultures). Duda and Allison (1989) also suggested that the meanings of the specific elements in theories and research on attribution may differ among cultures (for example, effort, work, luck). Different meanings assigned to these elements have implications for the meanings of the attributions associated with them.

A number of studies have found biases in white attributional styles. Tom and Cooper (1986) examined the attributions of 25 white primary school teachers for the performance of students varying in social class, 'race' and gender. The results indicated that the teachers were more likely to take account of the successes of middle class, white students and discount their failures, relative to students of other social classes or 'race'. Other researchers (for example Graham 1984; Graham and Long 1986) have also found that attributions are influenced by social factors such as social class as well as 'race' and culture.

Pearce (1994) investigated biases in white trainee counsellors' attitudes to clients from different cultures. The trainees were faced with a vignette of a case history of a client. The only indication of the client's ethnicity was the single stimulus item (i.e. Asian, white or West Indian). This cue influenced the trainee's perceptions and resulted in biased responses. The studies supported the contention that white trainees would show a favourable pattern of attribution for the white client, while biased attributions would be made for some out-group clients. Although the case history of the four clients was identical except for the cue indicating the culture to which the client belonged, the trainees' attributions 'warm', 'friendly' and 'helpful' were applied by trainees only to the white client. The case history of the clients provided limited information, but this did not prevent the sample from making implicit value judgements about how the client ought to behave. Pearce's study suggests that counsellors and other practitioners need to become aware of their own biases, values and assumptions. Pearce (1994: 427) concludes that 'further studies should indicate to the respondents [(counsellor trainees)] the implications of their positive and negative attributes towards clients of different clients'.

These findings of different attributional styles across cultures are especially important in furthering our understanding of interethnic interactions. The consequences for incorrect attributions are potentially severe. Interpreting the causes of behaviour accurately, especially with regard to intentions and good will, is important to the success of any type of interaction. White practitioners should take into account the influence of cultural factors on behaviour in their attributions of others as well as their own behaviour. Then white practitioners will have taken an important step toward improving interethnic communication and understanding. As 'people are enculturated into a society, they learn to make fairly accurate attributions about others' behaviours. Problems, however, arise in intercultural [and interethnic] encounters where the same attributions should not necessarily accompany the same behaviours' (Brislin and Yoshida 1994: 44).

Social attribution refers to how members of one social group explain the behaviour of their own members and members of other social groups. Pettigrew (1979: 464) defines the ultimate attribution error as 'a systematic patterning of intergroup misattributions shaped in part by prejudice'. Thus, our tendency to attribute behaviour to dispositional characteristics is strengthened when a member of an out-group is perceived to engage in negative behaviour. In contrast, when members of an out-group engage in what is perceived to be positive behaviour, our tendency is to treat the person as an exception to the rule and we may disregard dispositional explanations for the behaviour. We attribute the behaviour to situational factors.

Stereotypes and interethnic communication

This section examines the result of prejudice and selective perception – the stereotype – and the manner in which it functions as a barrier to effective communication between black and white people. Stereotypes affect interethnic communication for they determine how white practitioners react to and interact with black clients.

Hamilton *et al.* (1992: 142) point out that:

> stereotypes operate as a source of expectancies about what a group as a whole is like (e.g. Hispanics, [Asians, African Caribbeans]) as well as about what attributes individual group members are likely to possess. Their influence can be pervasive, affecting the perceiver's attention to, encoding of, inferences about, and judgements based on that information. And the resulting interpretations, inferences, and judgements typically are made so as to be consistent with pre-existing beliefs that guided them.

Psychological studies confirm anecdotal notions of stereotypes and specify the ways in which those stereotypes operate. England (1972, cited in Dodd 1987) studied the white stereotypic attitudes toward Mexican Americans. Two groups of white matched samples were shown a series of eight slides. The first group were shown a Mexican American male in various scenes – 'in a yard behind a frame house, carrying trash cans, raking leaves around a tree, and putting the leaves into a wagon. He was dressed in a work shirt, work pants, and a work hat' (Dodd 1987: 75). The second group were shown identical scenes, but the man in the slides was a white man. The two groups were asked a number of questions about the two men in the slides. The results revealed significant differences in the way the Mexican American and white man were perceived. Thus, the Mexican American was perceived as 'having a larger family and less education than the [white man]' (p. 75). This study suggests that 'the perception of ethnic background alone precipitates significant differences in assessing a person's characteristics, a finding that has been documented numerous times' (p. 75).

The tendency to rely on stereotypes to ease the difficulty of interacting with the unfamiliar is very strong for all people, regardless of racial or ethnic identity. It is easier for us to draw on preconceptions when in doubt than it is to make the effort to seek out and know individuals.

Consider your own stereotypes of people in the following groups: Asians, African Caribbeans, Chinese. Many are created by direct experience with only one or two people from a particular group. Others are probably based on secondhand information and opinions, output from the mass media, and general habits of thinking; they may even have been formed without any direct experience with individuals from the group. Yet many people are prepared to assume that all people from a group share the stereotypical traits. When stereotypes are used, the individual is hidden. Rather than using stereotypes as 'best guess' generalizations of a group of people from which we will then interact with individuals and adjust accordingly, we often use stereotypes as a rigid type of knowledge about all people of that group, regardless of individual differences or evidence to the contrary. The danger of stereotypes is that they are impervious to logic or experience. All incoming information is distorted to fit our preconceived notions. For example, 'people who are strongly anti-Semitic will accuse Jews of being stingy and miserly and then, in the same breath, accuse them of flaunting their wealth by conspicuous spending' (Sue and Sue 1990: 47).

Interethnic communication competence requires an ability to move beyond stereotypes and to respond to the individual. Although stereotypes are helpful in ordering the complexity of human experience (Lippman 1922; Hinton 1993), they interfere with meaningful interaction, because they predispose to interaction between preconceptions rather than between the participants themselves. Hinton (1993) points out that when a system of stereotypes is well fixed, attention is called to those facts that support it and diverted from those that contradict it. As noted at the beginning of this section, such a process is termed 'selective perception'. Consciously, and more often unconsciously, people are impressed by those facts that fit 'the pictures in their head'. Being preconditioned to perceive selectively, consciously or unconsciously, people perceive the data supporting their stereotype and selectively ignore those aspects of the perceived individual that contradict their expectation (Allport 1979). The consequence of stereotyping is that the vast degree of differences that exist among the members of any one group may be overlooked and therefore not taken into account in the interpretation of messages.

Stereotypes have to be learned; they do not suddenly appear through instinct. As noted earlier, stereotypes are formed through personal experience, through the passed-on experience of 'relevant' others: family, teachers, friends and through the influence of the mass media. The tendency to adopt the stereotypes of others is particularly strong when one has not had sufficient personal experience with the stereotyped person or group to contradict the cognition passed on by the influential model figure. Thus, stereotypes may be created and perpetuated in individuals merely by communication of verbal labels from generation to generation with no actual interaction with the people who are the target of the stereotype (Brislin 1993).

We need, however, to remember our ability to challenge stereotypes. We can control the effects of automatic processing. This occurs especially in conditions where we want to present a 'nonprejudiced' identity (Devine 1989). Devine (p. 15) argues that conscious control of our reactions when our stereotypes are activated is necessary to control our prejudice: 'Nonprejudiced responses are a function of intentional controlled processes and require a conscious decision to behave in a nonprejudiced fashion. In addition, new responses must be learned and well practiced before they can serve as competitive responses to the automatically activated stereotype-congruent response.' This position is consistent with Langer's (1989) notion that mindfulness is necessary to reduce prejudice.

We can draw at least four generalizations about the stereotyping process (Hewstone and Giles 1986). First, stereotyping is the result of our tendency to overestimate the degree of association between group membership and psychological attributes. Second, stereotypes influence the way we process information. Research indicates that we remember more favourable information about our in-groups and more unfavourable information about out-groups. This, in turn, affects the way we interpret incoming messages from members of in-groups and out-groups. Third, stereotypes create expectations regarding how members of other groups will behave. Stereotypes are activated automatically when we have contact with strangers (Devine 1989). Unconsciously, we assume that our expectations are correct and behave as though they are. We therefore try to confirm our expectations when we communicate with members of other groups. Fourth, our stereotypes constrain others' patterns of communication and engender stereotype-confirming communication. Thus, stereotypes create self-fulfilling prophecies. We tend to see behaviour that confirms our expectations even when it is absent. We ignore disconfirming evidence when communicating on 'automatic pilot'. If we assume someone else is not competent and communicate with him or her based on this assumption, she or he will appear incompetent (even if actually competent).

Word *et al.* (1974) demonstrated the power of self-fulfilling stereotypes in interethnic interviews. In one study, white interviewers displayed more grammatical and pronunciation errors, spent less time, and showed less immediacy with blacks than with whites. Essentially, they were less friendly, less outgoing and more reserved with blacks. In another study, white confederates behaved in either the immediate or more reserved interview styles observed in the first study. White interviewees subjected to the more reserved styles were more nervous and performed less adequately than those exposed to the immediate style: 'the two investigations suggest that in interethnic encounters, "racial" stereotypes may constrain behaviour in ways that cause both blacks and whites to behave in accordance with those stereotypes' (Snyder *et al.* 1982: 67). Thus, stereotyped groups and individuals implicitly may come to deliver what is expected of them.

Inaccurate stereotypes, in turn, can lead to inaccurate predictions about the behaviour of people from the other culture (Gudykunst and Hammer 1988). According to Barna (1994: 341),

> Stereotypes are stumbling blocks for communicators because they interfere with objective viewing stimuli – the sensitive search for cues to guide the imagination toward the other person's reality. They are not easy to overcome in ourselves or to correct in others, even with the

presentation of evidence. Stereotypes persist because they are firmly established as myths or truisms by one's own national culture and because they sometimes rationalize prejudices. They are also sustained and fed by the tendency to perceive selectively only those pieces of new information that correspond to the image held.

Hecht *et al.* (1989) identified negative stereotyping as one of the primary issues African Americans perceived as salient to their communication satisfaction with European Americans (Hecht and Ribeau 1987; Hecht *et al.* 1989; Hecht and Ribeau 1991). Black people believed that stereotyping was a fact of life in the United States. Negative stereotyping 'involved conversations in which the communication partner racially categorized the respondent and ascribed characteristics of his/her ethnic group to the respondent rather than treating the person as an individual' (Hecht *et al.* 1989: 392). An African American female reported dissatisfaction when her white conversational partner 'seemed to say to me that she (a third party) was black and you know how they are' (p. 392). Several black respondents also discussed a form of negative stereotyping that could be labelled as 'indirect stereotyping'. This type of stereotyping occurred when the European American dyadic partner talked to the black person about what were believed to be 'black' topics (such as sports or music); this occurred during dissatisfying conversations. This type of stereotyping can also occur in the social work context when social workers are trying to establish a relationship with a black client. One black respondent labelled people who brought up 'black' topics as 'patronizing or unaware' (Hecht *et al.* 1989). Other forms of 'indirect stereotyping' included 'over-accommodating' or 'trying too hard'. Thus, white people's 'modification of their own behavior may appear so stereotyped or extreme that it invokes a feeling of forced behaviour or artificiality, "trying too hard"' (p. 407). Another respondent felt that many whites were 'predisposed to see the negatives in blacks'. Many of the respondents reported that they reacted with a great deal of emotion to negative stereotyping (see Hecht *et al.* 1989).

Racial stereotypes also affect white practitioners' interpretation of information about black clients. Wampold *et al.* (1982) tested this possibility in a study in which white and ethnic minority students were presented with information about hypothetical persons and asked to make judgements based on the data presented to them. White students were more susceptible than the ethnic minority trainees to the influence of stereotypes when processing information about ethnic minorities. Stereotypes prevented white students from distinguishing actual information about the client from their own prior, albeit incorrect, assumptions. Owusu-Bempah (1994) found evidence of stereotypical thinking about black families in a study of postgraduate trainees in social work. Three vignettes of children were presented to the students. The vignettes described a 13-year-old boy who had a history of behavioural difficulties both at home and school. They differed only in terms of the racial origin of the children ('black', 'white' and 'mixed parentage'). The social work students were asked to identify possible causes for the behavioural problems. Owusu-Bempah noted that '"race" was highly influential in terms of the respondents' comments'. For example, 59 per cent of the respondents noted that family circumstances contributed to the black child's problems as opposed to only 30 per cent for the white child's behavioural problems (Owusu-Bempah 1994).

A number of stereotypes operate in the encounter between black people and the state welfare agencies. These are stereotypes of African Caribbeans as aggressive, excitable and defiant, and images of Asian people as meek, passive and docile (Robinson 1995). One common stereotype assigned to Asians by whites is that Asian culture is dominated exclusively by men, with women playing a dependent, submissive role. However, Kakar (1981: 118) points out that although the wife of a family patriarch pays

> a formal, and often perfunctory deference to her husband, especially in front of strangers, she may exercise considerable domestic power, not merely among the other women of the household, but with her husband, and she often makes many of the vital decisions affecting the family's interests.

If a social or health worker expects Asian women to play a submissive role, then she/he will probably interpret the client's communication behaviour in that light. Social and health care workers must address themselves to the problem of overcoming the stifling effects of strong racial and ethnic stereotyping if multiracial and multi-ethnic communication is to occur.

The stereotypes held by mental health service providers may contribute to differential diagnosis of minority clients in mental health service systems (Wilson 1993; Fernando 1995). Wilson notes that 'knee-jerk reactions which summon up visions of violent and dangerous African Caribbeans and passive Asians, who "look after their own" do little to aid an understanding of the diverse cultural characteristics . . . and should be challenged on that basis' (Wilson 1993: 15). For white people, 'the mode of acceptable communication is considered to be low-keyed, dispassionate, [and] impersonal' (Sue and Sue 1990: 50). However, 'black styles tend to be high-keyed, animated, confrontational'. These differences in communication styles may trigger off certain stereotypes white practitioners have about black people.

Psychiatric assessment is affected by the 'race'/culture of the practitioner. Jones and Gray (1986) report that black psychiatrists' and white psychiatrists' responses reflected differences in the rate, order and frequency with which various problems were seen in black clients. The investigators suggested that white psychiatrists may be less likely to perceive depression as a presenting problem for black men because it is not consistent with racial stereotypes. It has been repeatedly stated in the Eurocentric literature that depression is rarely found among blacks in the United States and Britain. Black people may be viewed as having a primitive character structure, and as being too jovial to be depressed and too impoverished to experience objective loss (Adebimpe 1981). Black patients run a higher risk of being misdiagnosed as schizophrenics, whereas white patients showing identical behaviours are more likely to receive diagnoses of depression (Adebimpe 1981). Although 'the concept of depression is widely used, its validity in a multi"racial" society is limited by racism disguised in cultural terms' (Mercer 1992: 71).

It is often asserted that people from non-Western cultures, and particularly those from the Indian subcontinent, communicate their emotional distress in somatic or physical terms, in contrast to those from Western cultures who express their distress in psychological terms. This has led to a common stereotype among mental health professionals that South Asians are not psychologically minded and lack the capacity for insight necessary for certain 'talking therapies'. They are seen as more likely to describe physical symptoms such as aches and pains. There is, however, no conclusive evidence that Asians 'somatize' more than any other ethnic group. Beliappa (1991) found that Asians did not somatize their distress and were able to recognize the psychosomatic nature of their problems.

Literature on 'race' and psychiatric treatment continues to suggest the operation of racial bias in treatment. Black people are often stereotyped in the psychiatric literature as not being psychologically minded, as culturally deficient, and as lacking the psychological sophistication and motivation to benefit from psychotherapy (Robinson 1995). Such ideas influence the nature of the therapist–patient communication styles and relationship.

If we examine the psychological literature, we find that stereotypes of typical white (mainly middle class) clients match those characteristics (intelligent, motivated, verbal, attractive, articulate, personable, trusting, disclosive) most highly valued by therapists in ideal client populations. The question we therefore need to ask is: 'What is the degree of congruence between characteristics most highly valued in clients and those stereotypically associated with black groups?' Stereotypic attitudes of black clients conflict with the 'ideal client' characteristics. If black patients continue to be characterized as being less verbal, impulse-ridden, more concrete than abstract in thought, and having difficulty dealing with intrapsychic material, therapists might be encouraged to adopt more action-oriented, compared with insight-oriented, therapeutic strategies when working with black patients (Smith 1977). However, evidence from organizations in Britain (for example Nafsiyat Intercultural Therapy Centre and the Transcultural Psychiatry Unit at Lynfield Mount Hospital) which are providing psychotherapy to members of the Asian community shows that Asians are able to benefit from this kind of therapy. A psychotherapist's identification with white middle class values is of great significance for the outcome of psychotherapy. This identification can affect the psychotherapist's feelings and attitudes about black behaviour (Bloch 1968). Responses which seem unusual, inappropriate or even pathological to the therapist might be quite consistent with the values of the client. A client's behaviour may not only reflect his or her cultural background but also be a response to the racial feelings of the psychotherapist (Bloch 1968). Consequently, it is not only necessary for a psychotherapist to understand a client's culture before he or she can be sure that the client is behaving inappropriately, it is also necessary for the psychotherapist to be aware of whether or not he or she is unconsciously communicating negative images to the client. For example, it is common for black patients to be labelled as paranoid or at least hypersensitive to insults and other racial issues (Bloch 1968). The patient's expression of these feelings is often dismissed as defensive by the therapist, thus negating the validity of the client's perceptual world. A knowledge of Cross's (1978, 1980) model of nigrescence (see Chapter 1) will enhance the therapist's grasp of the role of defensive behaviour in therapy. Thus, a patient in the encounter phase of Cross's model may be defensive because he or she has experienced a series of events that challenge his or her previously held beliefs about himself or herself.

When black experiences are discussed, the focus tends to be on pathological lifestyles and/or a maintenance of false stereotypes. Often stereotypes about black people are carried over into the therapy situation. The negative racial attitudes held by the white therapist may destroy the entire therapy process from the time the client comes in the door until the client is released. These attitudes have serious consequences for the black client if the practitioner, unaware of the effects of racial myths on his/her thinking, continues to misinterpret, mislabel and misadvise. Various stereotypes about blacks seem to persist even when psychotherapists view the myths as untrue. As noted above, myths about aggressiveness and sexuality are particularly common. Consequently, black clients can arouse anxieties in the therapist. Although these anxieties may be too vaguely defined to be recognized by the therapist, they can nevertheless, have a profound influence on his/her behaviour during a therapy session. Such anxiety can result in distorted perceptions of the black client's behaviour, in mishandling or overemphasis of the importance of certain client feelings and/or behaviours, and in neglect of areas of exploration which might have been fruitful.

Much of the blame for the perpetuation of racial myths and stereotypes in the mental health field is attributable to the vast psychological and psychiatric literature which psychotherapists study (Robinson 1995). Black clients are often characterized by practitioners as suspicious and paranoid. Although it may be difficult for white practitioners to distinguish between fears of oppression that are founded and those that are actually pathological, practitioners should recognize that for members of historically oppressed minority groups, suspicion and paranoia may represent well-developed survival mechanisms (Ridley 1984) (see Chapter 4 for detailed discussion). However, practitioners tend to perceive rage in black clients – ignoring the fact that oppression is a daily reality for most black people – and that the rage provoked by the environment often must be repressed, displaced, sublimated or internalized. The venting of rage may often appear inappropriate if considered only in relation to the immediate precipitating event. Provocations in the life of the average black person are longstanding and cumulative. Therefore 'although the immediate provocation may be minor, when it is seen in light of myriad other precipitating events, the combination may result in the release of pent-up anger' (Jones 1979: 114).

White social work and health care workers should not consider themselves immune to racial and cultural stereotyping just because they are trained as helping/caring professionals. In the United States, Bloombaum *et al.* (1968) found that Mexican Americans, Blacks, Jews, Chinese Americans and Japanese Americans, in that order, were the most frequent objects of stereotyping of white psychotherapists. The investigators concluded that the therapists' attitudes reflect those of the culture in general.

There are also assumptions brought to interethnic communication by the participants that do not completely fit the stereotype definition. It is equally important to be aware of these as possibly blocking interethnic communication. For example, white practitioners may assume that 'colour is unimportant in interpersonal relations' or 'open recognition of colour may embarrass blacks'. These types of assumptions made by either the practitioner or the black client need to be examined and brought to a conscious level because they represent cultural differences which interfere with communication. Implicit in the assumption that 'recognition of colour may embarrass blacks' is that there is something wrong, less good about being black. The assumption communicates the feeling of racial superiority. Social workers adopting a colour-blind approach take the view that black people can be treated like white people in terms of the provision of services (Dominelli 1988). Similarly, some psychotherapists are apt to make comments such as 'I treat them all alike'; 'When I look at you I don't see a colour, I see a person – a human being.' When the issue of colour is ignored by the therapist, a very important aspect of the client's reality is being ignored. The psychotherapist who considers himself/herself to be colour blind can be just as harmful to black clients as an overt bigot. 'Colour blind' psychotherapists are ill-equipped to deal with black clients because they have chosen to pretend that a significant feature of the client's life is unimportant. Research suggests that white counsellors who acknowledge ethnic/cultural differences and the obstacles they produce, instead of projecting an image of 'colour blindness' are perceived as credible sources of help by black (African American) students (Poston *et al.* 1991).

Conclusion

White practitioners' stereotypes and assumptions about other racial groups can have significant effects on their behaviour in interethnic communication. In order to control our prejudices, Devine (1989) argues that it is necessary to control consciously our reactions when our stereotypes are activated. Thus, practitioners need to make a conscious decision to behave in a non-prejudiced way. They must also substitute their prejudiced responses with new responses (Devine 1989).

It is necessary for social and health care workers to be 'mindful' (Langer 1989) in an interethnic communication situation and not to operate automatically (i.e. to see behaviour that confirms their expectations, even when it is absent) in order to prevent miscommunication or communication breakdown. Mindfulness involves '(a) creation of new categories; (b) openness to new information; and (c) awareness of more than one perspective' (Langer 1989: 62).

White practitioners should have an awareness of how their expectations can dictate how others behave toward them and hence reinforce their perceptions. Thus, the 'image' the social worker has of the communication of another group influences interethnic interaction.

The solution to the problem of negative stereotypes, in terms of communication, is complex. Dodd (1987: 76) cites some possible guidelines which include: seeking a common code – 'frequently linguistic variations and dialectical differences cause people to close the door to further understanding and communication attempts . . . [thus] asking questions and seeking to clarify are excellent ways to begin the [communication] process'. According to Dodd (p. 76), white people need to 'make a conscious effort to suspend [negative] attitudes toward [people] from different "racial" or ethnic background' in interethnic interactions. White practitioners should attempt to build trust and suspend judgements.

Social workers and health care workers need to challenge the basis for stereotypes and the generalizations underlying them about the characteristics of the groups to which they are associated. They need to recognize individual differences within groups and the fact that no stereotype can adequately describe all people within a certain group.

Annotated bibliography

Hinton, P. (1993) *The Psychology of Interpersonal Perception*. London: Routledge. An introductory text on interpersonal perception.

Ponterotto, J.G. and Casas, J.M. (1991) *Handbook of Racial/Ethnic Minority Counseling Research*. Springfield, IL: Charles C. Thomas. This book draws together developments in the rapidly evolving field of racial/ethnic minority counselling. It examines theory, research, practice and training in ethnic minority counselling.

7

Conclusion

In this book I have argued that in order to work effectively with minority groups, social and health care workers from the majority group need to have an understanding of the communication styles and patterns of these groups.

I have attempted to articulate, from a black perspective, a framework for understanding interethnic communication. I have argued that traditional studies of interethnic communication have not had sufficient explanatory power to account for the behaviour of black people. Racism and discrimination based on skin colour is evident at all levels of United States and British society.

I have argued that racial identity development models are more relevant to understanding the interethnic communication experiences of black people in Britain than the more traditional Eurocentric theories. However, this perspective has largely been ignored by traditional Eurocentric psychology.

I have explored the relationship between racial identity development of black and white people and interethnic communication. I have tried to show that one's racial identity status has a direct impact on the type of world-view one adopts, and that this world-view, in turn, determines how one perceives and interacts with others. Currently, the training social work and health care professionals receive does not equip them to understand 'race' and racial identity and their influence on the communication process. It was clearly apparent from Robinson's (1997) study of racial identity attitudes and self-esteem among African Caribbean children in residential care in Birmingham that residential care staff found Cross's model extremely useful in therapeutic work with African Caribbean children. Little is known about how black and white people in Britain come to view and accept their identity as black and white, and how this influences interethnic communication. There is a need for research to be carried out in this area.

During the course of this book, I have argued that racial prejudice is extensive, and not even well-intentioned practitioners escape its impact on their thoughts, attitudes and values. As Ridley (1995: 39) notes, 'racism exists in numerous counseling [and social work] behaviours, bringing harm to [black] clients . . . counselors [(practitioners)], in many ways, are socialized and trained to behave as racists without even knowing it'. White practitioners need to avoid racist behaviour (overt and covert) and language in their interactions with black clients.

Power is an important variable in an interethnic communication situation. Power is linked to racism in the sense that power provides those elevated to the 'superior' position with the ability to carry out their perceptions and role definitions. Blubaugh and Pennington (1976: 39) argue that the 'ideal power relationship in interethnic communication . . . is to attribute to all "racial" groups the credibility that allows them positive influence in communication situations'.

In this book I have examined some of the cultural values of African American, African Caribbean and Asian people and their impact on interethnic communication. Cultures were characterized by their values on the dimensions of power–distance, uncertainty avoidance, individualism–collectivism, masculinity, low and high context communication, immediacy and expressiveness, emotional and behavioural expressiveness, and self-disclosure. An understanding of these dimensions will enable social and health care workers to gain a better understanding of the interethnic/intercultural communication process. I have argued that white workers with a monocultural perspective will view any behaviours, values and lifestyles that differ from the Euro-American norm as deficient.

In this book I have argued that white practitioners' values may conflict with the values of black groups. For example, many social work and counselling theories reflect Western, middle class values (e.g. individualism) that conflict with the 'familialism and group responsibility' (collectivism) valued by black people. White practitioners should strive to be aware of their own racial stereotypes and cultural values which are at odds with those of their black clients.

Social and health care workers can work more effectively with black clients if they begin from their clients' points of strength. A strengths-coping perspective tends to describe black behaviour almost exclusively as positive adaptations and does not attempt to utilize a white cultural framework as a standard for all behavioural phenomena.

Interethnic communication includes both verbal and nonverbal interaction. In this book I have identified some of the characteristics of nonverbal communication which are of special importance in interethnic communication. White practitioners need to have an understanding of the nonverbal communication styles of minority clients. Nonverbal communication styles – for example, patterns of eye contact, expression of feeling, physical distance and directiveness are likely to vary for black clients.

The white practitioner should establish a basis for client trust. As elaborated in earlier chapters, black people have experienced a history of mistreatment and have subsequently developed what is sometimes referred to as 'healthy paranoia' in their interactions with outsiders. The lack of trust among the 'race's has caused black people to reject the value of verbal communication and to search for nonverbal cues as indicators of real meaning and response in interethnic communication settings.

Black people may be reluctant to disclose to white practitioners because of their lack of trust of white people. The practitioner may, therefore, be required to exert considerable effort to establish client trust.

I have examined the role of language in interethnic communication. White social and health care workers in interethnic interaction need to have an understanding of different language habits – different denotations, connotations, grammar, accents, and concepts of the function of language. This book has discussed the important role of Black English in interethnic communication. The use of Black English among African Caribbean and African American people can be seen as a reaction to the values and standards of the dominant culture. It enables African Caribbeans to communicate with each other while maintaining a secrecy from the white dominant society.

I have explored the implications of interacting with Asian clients who may have English as a second language, or may not speak English at all. And I have stressed that white social and health care workers should avoid judging and evaluating a black person's language, since ethnocentric judgements will interfere with effective communication.

To conclude, in this text I have discussed some of the communication attributes that affect the outcome of interethnic contacts. It is my hope that the issues discussed in this text will be taught in pre-qualifying and post-qualifying courses in social work and health care. Social work education and training in Britain is under the control of white educators and practitioners (Dominelli 1988), who have failed to address satisfactorily the issues discussed in this book. The main aim of this book has been to sensitize trainers and practitioners to some of the factors that can influence interethnic communication. The literature that addresses interethnic communication from a black perspective is limited at best. If we are to appreciate and understand some of the factors involved in interethnic communication from a black perspective and its implications for social work and health care practice much more must be written, researched and published.

References

Adebimpe, V. (1981) Overview: white norms in psychiatric treatment, *American Journal of Psychiatry*, 138(3): 275–85.

Afshar, H. (1994) Muslim women in West Yorkshire: growing up with real and imaginary values amidst conflicting views of self and society, in H. Afshar and M. Maynard (eds) *The Dynamics of 'Race' and Gender: Some Feminist Interventions*. London: Taylor and Francis.

Ahmad, W.I.U. (1996) Family migrations and social change among Asian communities, in W.I.U. Ahmad and K. Atkin (eds) *'Race' and Community Care*. Buckingham: Open University Press.

Ahmed, B. (1989) Introduction to conference in interpreting in action: a report of the conference 'Language, Race and Power', Newcastle upon Tyne, May 1989. London: REU.

Ahmed, G. and Watt, S. (1986) Understanding Asian women in pregnancy and confinement, *Midwives Chronicle and Nursing Notes*, 99: 98–101.

Ahmed, S. (1996) Anti-racist social work: a black perspective, in C. Hanvey and T. Philpot (eds) *Practising Social Work*. London: Routledge.

Ahmed, T. and Webb-Johnson, A. (1995) Voluntary groups, in S. Fernando (ed.) *Mental Health in a Multi-Ethnic Society*. London: Routledge.

Aiello, J. and Jones, S. (1971) Field study of the proxemic behavior of young school children in three subcultural groups, *Journal of Personality and Social Psychology*, 19: 351–6.

Akbar, N. (1976) *Natural Psychology and Human Transformation*. Chicago: World Community of Islam.

Akbar, N. (1981) Mental disorders among African-Americans, *Black Books Bulletin*, 7(2): 18–25.

Akinnaso, F. and Ajirotutu, C.S. (1982) Performance and ethnic style in job interviews, in J.J. Gumprez (ed.) *Language and Social Identity*. New York: Cambridge University Press.

Allport, G.W. (1954) *The Nature of Prejudice*. Reading, MA: Addison-Wesley.

Allport, G.W. (1979) *The Nature of Prejudice*, 25th anniversary edn. Reading, MA: Addison-Wesley.

Andersen, P.A. (1986) Consciousness, cognition, and communication, *Western Journal of Speech and Communication*, 50: 87–101.

Andersen, P.A. (1990) Explaining intercultural differences in nonverbal communication, in L.A. Samovar and R.E. Porter (eds) *Intercultural Communication: A
Reader*. Belmont, CA: Wadsworth.

Arce, C.A. (1981) A reconsideration of Chicano culture and identity, *Daedalus*,
110: 177–92.

Argyle, M. (1975) *Bodily Communication*. London: Methuen.

Argyle, M. (1988) *Bodily Communication*, 2nd edn. London: Methuen.

Argyle, M., Furnham, A. and Graham, J. (1981) *Social Situations*. Cambridge:
Cambridge University Press.

Asante, M.K. (1983) The ideological significance of Afrocentricity in intercultural
communication, *Journal of Black Studies*, 4(1).

Asante, M.K. and Noor-Aldeen, H.S. (1984) Social interaction of black and white
college students, *Journal of Black Studies*, 14: 507–16.

Asante, M.K., Blake, C. and Newmark, E. (eds) (1979) *Handbook of Intercultural
Communication*. Beverly Hills, CA: Sage.

Askham, J., Henshaw, L. and Tarpey, M. (1995) *Social and Health Authority Services for Elderly People from Black and Minority Ethnic Communities*. London:
HMSO.

Atkinson, D.R., Morten, G. and Sue, D.W. (1979) *Counseling American Minorities: A Cross-cultural Perspective*. Dubuque, IA: William C. Brown.

Atkinson, D.R., Morten, G. and Sue, D.W. (eds) (1989) *Counseling American
Minorities: A Cross-cultural Perspective*. Dubuque, IA: William C. Brown.

Atkinson, D.R., Morten, G. and Sue, D.W. (1993) *Counseling American Minorities: A Cross-cultural Perspective*. Dubuque, IA: W.C. Brown.

Atkinson, D.R., Thompson, C.E. and Grant, S.K. (1993) A three dimensional model
for counseling racial/ethnic minorities, *The Counseling Psychologist*, 21(2):
257–77.

Austin, L.N., Carter, R.T. and Vaugh, A. (1990) The role of racial identity in black
students' attitudes toward counseling and counseling centers, *Journal of College
Student Development*, 31(3): 237–43.

Axelson, J.A. (1985) *Counseling and Development in a Multicultural Society*. Mon-
terey, CA: Brooks/Cole.

Axelson, J.A. (1993) *Counseling and Development in a Multicultural Society*, 2nd
edn. Pacific Grove, CA: Brooks/Cole.

Baldwin, J.A. (1985) African self-consciousness: an Afrocentric questionnaire,
Western Journal of Black Studies, 9(2): 61–8.

Bamgbose, A. (1976) Introduction: the changing role of the mother tongue in education, in A. Bamgbose (ed.) *Mother Tongue Education: The West African
Experience*. Paris: Unesco Press.

Barna, L. (1990) Stumbling blocks in intercultural communication, in L.A. Samovar
and R.E. Porter (eds) *Intercultural Communication: A Reader*. Belmont, CA:
Wadsworth.

Barna, L. (1994) Stumbling blocks in intercultural communication, in L.A. Samovar
and R.E. Porter (eds) *Intercultural Communication: A Reader*, 2nd edn. Belmont,
CA: Wadsworth.

Baron, R.A. and Byrne, D. (1991) *Social Psychology: Understanding Human Interaction*, 6th edn. London: Allyn and Bacon.

Baugh, J. (1983) *Black Street Speech: Its History, Structure and Survival*. Austin:
University of Texas Press.

Baughman, E.E. (1971) *Black Americans*. New York: Academic Press.

Bauman, Z. (1990) Modernity and ambivalence, in M. Featherstone (ed.) *Global Culture*. London: Sage.

Baxter, C. (1993) *The Communication Needs of Black and Ethnic Minority Pregnant Women in Salford*.

Beliappa, J. (1991) *Illness or Distress? Alternative Models of Mental Health*. London: Confederation of Indian Organisations.

Bennett, M. (1986) A developmental approach to training for intercultural sensitivity, *International Journal of Intercultural Relations*, 10: 179–96.

Bennett, M. (1991) New insights for intercultural sensitivity model, *Training and Culture Journal*, 3(5): 5–10.

Berry, J.W. (1980) Acculturation as varieties of adaptation, in A.M. Padilla (ed.) *Acculturation: Theory, Model, and Some New Findings*. Boulder, CO: Westview.

Betancourt, H. and Lopez, S.R. (1993) The study of culture, ethnicity, and race in American psychology, *American Psychologist*, 48(6): 629–37.

Block, C. (1980) Black Americans and the cross-cultural counseling experience, in A.J. Marsella and P.B. Pederson (eds) *Cross-cultural Counseling and Psychotherapy*. New York: Pergamon.

Block, C., Robertson, L. and Neuger, D. (1995) White racial identity theory: a framework for understanding reactions toward interracial situations in organizations, *Journal of Vocational Behaviour*, 46: 71–88.

Bloch, J.B. (1968) The white worker and the Negro client in psychotherapy, *Social Work*, 13(2): 36–42.

Bloombaum, M., Yamamoto, J. and James, Q. (1968) Cultural stereotyping among psychotherapists, *Journal of Consulting and Clinical Psychology*, 32: 99–103.

Blubaugh, J.A. and Pennington, D.L. (1976) *Crossing Difference: Interracial Communication*, Columbus, OH: Merrill.

Bokamba, E. (1981) Language and national development: black English in America, in G. Smitherman (ed.) *Black English and the Education of Black Children and Youth*. Detroit, MI: Wayne State University Center for Black Studies Press.

Bones, J. (1986) Reggae deejaying and Jamaican Afro-lingua, in D. Sutcliffe and A. Wong (eds) *The Language of the Black Experience*. Oxford: Basil Blackwell.

Borden, G. (1991) *Cultural Orientation: An Approach to Understanding Intercultural Communication*. Englewood Cliffs, NJ: Prentice Hall.

Bowser, B.P. and Hunt, R.G. (eds) (1981) *Impacts of Racism on White Americans*, Newbury Park, CA: Sage.

Boyd-Franklin, N. (1989) *Black Families in Therapy*. London: The Guildford Press.

Bradac, J. (1990) Language attitudes and impression formation, in H. Giles and P. Robinson (eds) *Handbook of Language and Social Psychology*. London: John Wiley.

Bradley, G.W. (1978) Self-serving biases in the attribution process: a re-examination of the fact or fiction question, *Journal of Personality and Social Psychology*, 35: 56–71.

Braye, S. and Preston-Shoot, M. (1995) *Empowering Practice in Social Care*. Buckingham: Open University Press.

Brearley, J. (1995) *Counselling and Social Work*. Buckingham: Open University Press.

Breinburg, P. (1986) Language attitudes: the case of Caribbean language, in D. Sutcliffe and A. Wong (eds) *The Language of the Black Experience*. Oxford: Blackwell.

Brislin, R. (1993) *Understanding Culture's Influence on Behavior*. Forth Worth, TX: Harcourt Brace Jovanovich.

Brislin, R. and Yoshida, T. (1994) *Intercultural Communication Training: An Introduction*. London: Sage.

Burgoon, J.K. (1985) Nonverbal signals, in M.L. Knapp and G.R. Miller (eds) *Handbook of Interpersonal Communication*. Newbury Park, CA: Sage.

Burgoon, J.K. and Saine, T. (1978) *The Unspoken Dialogue: An Introduction to Nonverbal Communication*. Boston, MA: Houghton Mifflin.

Butt, J. (1994) *Same Service or Equal Service?* London: HMSO.

Cantor, N., Mischel, W. and Schwartz, J. (1982) Social knowledge, in A. Isen and A. Hastorf (eds) *Cognitive Social Psychology*. New York: Elsevier.

Carter, R.T. (1990) The relationship between racism and racial identity among white Americans: an exploratory investigation, *Journal of Counseling and Development*, 69: 46–50.

Carter, R. and Helms, J. (1987) The relationship of black value-orientation to racial identity attitudes, *Measurement and Evaluation in Counseling and Development*, 19: 185–95.

Carter, R. and Helms, J. (1990) White racial identity attitudes and cultural values, in J. Helms (ed.) *Black and White Racial Identity: Theory, Research and Practice*. New York: Greenwood Press.

Casas, J.M. (1984) Policy, training, and research in counseling psychology: the racial/ethnic minority perspective, in S.D. Brown and R.W. Lent (eds) *Handbook of Counseling Psychology*. New York: John Wiley.

Cayleff, S.E. (1986) Ethical issues in counseling gender, race and culturally distinct groups, *Journal of Counseling and Development*, 64: 345–47.

Chaika, E. (1982) *Language: The Social Mirror*. Rowley, MA: Newbury House.

Chaplin, P. (1975) *Dictionary of Psychology*. New York: Dell.

Cheek, D. (1976) *Assertive Black Puzzled White: A Black Perspective on Assertive Behaviour*. Berkeley, CA: Impact Publishers.

Chung, D.K. (1992) Asian cultural commonalities: a comparison with mainstream American culture, in D.K. Chung, K. Murase and F. Ross-sheriff (eds) *Social Work Practice with Asian Americans*. Newbury Park, CA: Sage.

Claney, D. and Parker, W.M. (1988) Assessing white racial consciousness and perceived comfort with black individuals: a preliminary study, *Journal of Counseling and Development*, 67: 449–51.

Comer, J.P. (1972) White racism: its root form, and function, in R.L. Jones (ed.) *Black Psychology*, 1st edn. New York: Harper and Row.

Condon, J.C. and Yousef, F. (1975) *An Introduction to Intercultural Communication*. New York: Bobbs-Merrill.

Cox, J.L. (1976) Psychiatric assessment of the immigrant patient, *British Journal of Hospital Medicine*, 16: 38–40.

Cross, W.E. (1971) The Negro to black conversion experience: towards the psychology of black liberation, *Black World*, 20: 13–27.

Cross, W.E. (1978) The Thomas and Cross models of psychological nigrescence: a literature review, *The Journal of Black Psychology*, 5(1): 13–31.

Cross, W.E. (1980) Models of psychological nigrescence: a literature review, in R.L. Jones (ed.) *Black Psychology*. New York: Harper and Row.

Cross, W.E. (1985) Black identity: rediscovering the distinction between personal identity and reference group orientation, in M.B. Spencer, G.K. Brookins and W.R. Allen (eds) *Beginnings: The Social and Affective Development of Black Children*. Hillsdale, NJ: Erlbaum.

Cross, W.E. (1991) *Shades of Black: Diversity in African American Identity.* Philadelphia, PA: Temple University Press.

Cross, W.E. (1995) The psychology of nigrescence: revising the Cross model, in J.G. Ponterotto, J.M. Casas, L.A. Suzuki and C.M. Alexander (eds) *Handbook of Multicultural Counseling.* London: Sage.

Cross, W.E., Parham, T.A. and Helms, J.E. (1991) The stages of black identity development: nigrescence models, in R.L. Jones (ed.) *Black Psychology.* Los Angeles: Cobb and Henry.

Curt, C. and Nine, J. (1983) Hispanic-anglo conflicts in nonverbal communication, in I. Albino (ed.) *Perspectives Pedagogicas.* San Juan, Puerto Rico: Universidad de Puerto Rico.

Dalphinis, M. (1985) *Caribbean and African Languages: Social History, Language, Literature and Education.* London: Karia Press.

D'Andrea, M. (1992) The violence of our silence: some thoughts about racism, counseling and development, *Guidepost*, 35(4): 31.

D'Andrea, M., Daniels, J. and Heck, R. (1991) Evaluating the impact of multicultural counseling training, *Journal of Counseling and Development*, 70: 143–50.

Daniel, J. and Smitherman, G. (1976) How I got over: communication dynamics in the black community, *Quarterly Journal of Speech*, 62: 26–39.

Danna, R.H. (1993) *Multicultural assessment perspectives for professional psychology.* Boston, MA: Allyn and Bacon.

d'Ardenne, P. and Mahtani, A. (1990) *Transcultural Counselling in Action.* London: Sage.

Davidson, A. and Thompson, E. (1980) Cross-cultural studies of attitudes and beliefs, in H. Triandis and R. Brislin (eds) *Handbook of Cross-cultural Psychology*, vol. 5. Boston, MA: Allyn and Bacon.

Davidson, H. (1997) Ebonics: an overreaction, *Psychological Discourse*, 28(2): 5.

Davis, F.J. (1978) *Minority-dominant Relations: A Sociological Analysis.* Arlington Heights, IL: AHM.

Davis, L.E. and Proctor, E.K. (1989) *Race, Gender, and Class: Guidelines for Practice with Individuals, Families, and Groups.* Englewood Cliffs, NJ: Prentice-Hall.

Devine, P. (1989) Stereotypes and prejudice, *Journal of Personality and Social Psychology*, 56: 5–18.

Diamond, R. and Hellcamp, D. (1969) Race, sex, ordinal position of birth, and self-disclosure in high school, *Psychological Reports*, 35: 235–8.

Dillard, J.L. (1972) *Black English: Its History and Usage in the United States.* New York: Random House.

Dodd, C.H. (1977) *Dynamics of Intercultural Communication*, 1st edn. Dubuque, IA: William C. Brown.

Dodd, C.H. (1987) *Dynamics of Intercultural Communication*, 2nd edn. Dubuque, IA: William C. Brown.

Dominelli, L. (1988) *Anti-racist Social Work.* London: Macmillan.

Dominelli, L. (1997) *Anti-racist Social Work*, 2nd edn. London: Macmillan.

Dominelli, L. (1992) An uncaring profession? An examination of racism in social work, in P. Braham, A. Rattansi and R. Skellington (eds) *Racism and Antiracism.* London: Sage.

Donaldson, L.J. and Odell, A. (1984) Planning and providing services for the Asian population: a survey of district health authorities, *Journal of the Royal Society of Health*, 104: 199–202.

Doss, R.C. and Gross, A.M. (1992) The effects of black English on stereotyping in intraracial perceptions, *Journal of Black Psychology*, 18(2): 47–58.

Doss, R.C. and Gross, A.M. (1994) The effects of black English and code-switching on intraracial perceptions, *Journal of Black Psychology*, 20(3): 282–93.

Downs, J.F. (1971) *Cultures in Crisis*. Beverly Hills, CA: Glencoe Press.

Drury, B. (1991) Sikh girls and the maintenance of an ethnic culture, *New Community*, 17(3): 387–99.

Duda, J.L. and Allison, M.T. (1989) The attributional theory of achievement motivation: cross-cultural considerations, *International Journal of Intercultural Relations*, 13: 37–55.

Duncan, B.L. (1978) Nonverbal communication, *Psychological Bulletin*, 72: 118–37.

Eakins, B. and Eakins, G. (1978) *Sex Differences in Human Communication*. Boston, MA: Houghton-Mifflin.

Edwards, V.K. (1982) *West Indian Language, Attitudes and the School*. London: National Association for Multicultural Education.

Edwards, W.F. (1992) Sociolinguistic behaviour in a Detroit inner-city black neighborhood, *Language in Society*, 21: 93–115.

Ekman, P. and Friesen, W.V. (1967) Origin, usage, and coding: the basis for five categories of nonverbal behavior. Paper presented at the Symposium on 'Communication Theory and Linguistic Models', Buenos Aires.

Ekman, P., Friesen, W.V. and Ellsworth, P. (1972) *Emotion in the Human Face*. New York: Garland.

Eleftheriadou, Z. (1996) Communicating with patients from different cultural backgrounds, in M. Lloyd and R. Bor (eds) *Communication Skills for Medicine*. London: Churchill Livingstone.

Elliot, S., Scott, M.D., Jensen, A.D. and McDonough, M. (1982) Perceptions of reticence: a cross-cultural investigation, in M. Burgoon (ed.) *Communication Yearbook 5*. New Brunswick, NJ: Transaction Books.

Essed, P. (1991) *Understanding Everyday Racism*. London: Sage.

Everett, F., Proctor, N. and Cortmell, B. (1983) Providing psychological services to American Indian children and families, *Professional Psychology*, 14: 588–603.

Fairchild, H. (1997) On ebonics, *Psychological Discourse*, 28(2): 3.

Fairchild, H. and Edwards-Evans, S. (1990) African American dialects and schooling: a review, in A.M. Padilla, H.H. Fairchild and C.M. Valadez (eds) *Bilingual Education: Issues and Strategies*. Newbury Park, CA: Sage.

Fairclough, N. (1989) *Language and Power*. London: Longman.

Fellows, B. (1968) *The Discrimination Process and Development*. Oxford: Pergamon.

Fernando, S. (1991) *Mental Health, Race and Culture*. London: Macmillan.

Fernando, S. (ed.) (1995) *Mental Health in a Multi-ethnic Society: A Multidisciplinary Handbook*. London: Routledge.

Fishbein, M. and Ajzen, I. (1975) *Belief, Attitude, Intention, and Behavior: An Introduction to Theory and Research*. Reading, MA: Addison-Wesley.

Forgas, J. (1985) *Interpersonal Behaviour*. Oxford: Pergamon.

Freeman, E.B. (1982) The Ann Arbor decision: the importance of teachers' attitudes toward language, *Elementary School Journal*, 83(1): 41–7.

Gaertner, S.L. and Bickman, L. (1971) Effects of race on the elicitation of helping behaviour, *Journal of Personality and Social Psychology*, 20: 218–22.

Gaertner, S.L. and Dovidio, J.F. (1986) The aversive form of racism, in J.F. Dovidio and S.L. Gaertner (eds) *Prejudice, Discrimination, and Racism*. Orlando, FL: Academic Press.

Garner, T.E. and Rubin, D.L. (1986) Middle class blacks' perceptions of dialect and style shifting: the case of Southern attorneys, *Journal of Language and Social Psychology*, 5: 33–48.

Garratt, G., Baxter, J. and Rozelle, R. (1981) Training university police in black American nonverbal behaviour, *Journal of Social Psychology*, 113: 217–29.

Gelso, C.J. and Fretz, B.R. (1992) *Counseling Psychology*. Fort Worth, TX: Harcourt Brace Jovanovich.

Giles, H. and Coupland, N. (1991) *Language: Contexts and Consequences*. Buckingham: Open University Press.

Giles, H. and Johnson, P. (1981) The role of language in ethnic group relations, in J. Turner and H. Giles (eds) *Intergroup Behaviour*. Chicago: University of Chicago Press.

Giles, H. and Powesland, P. (1975) *Speech Style and Social Evaluation*. London: Academic Press.

Giles, H., Bourhis, R.Y. and Taylor, D.M. (1977) Towards a theory of language in ethnic group relations, in H. Giles (ed.) *Language, Ethnicity and Intergroup Relations*. London: Academic Press.

Giles, H., Coupland, N. and Wiemann, J. (1992) Talk is cheap . . . but my word is my bond, in R. Bolt and H. Kwok (eds) *Sociolinguistics Today*. London: Routledge.

Gilroy, P. (1993) *The Black Atlantic*. London: Verso.

Gomez, E.A., Ruiz, P. and Laval, R. (1982) Psychotherapy and bilingualism: is acculturation important? *Journal of Operational Psychiatry*, 13(1): 13–16.

Graham, S. (1984) Communicating sympathy and anger to black and white children: the cognitive (attributional) consequences of affective cues, *Journal of Personality and Social Psychology*, 47: 40–54.

Graham, S. and Long, A. (1986) Race, class, and the attributional process, *Journal of Educational Psychology*, 78: 4–13.

Grant-Thompson, S.L. and Atkinson, D.R. (1997) Cross-cultural mentor effectiveness and African American male students, *Journal of Black Psychology*, 23(2): 120–34.

Greeley, A.M. and Sheatsley, P.B. (1971) Attitudes toward racial integration, *Scientific Racism*, 225(6): 13–19.

Grier, W. and Cobbs, P. (1968) *Black Rage*. New York: Bantam Books.

Gudykunst, W.B. (1994) *Bridging Differences*. London: Sage.

Gudykunst, W.B. and Hammer, M.R. (1988) Strangers and hosts, in Y. Kim and W. Gudykunst (eds) *Cross-cultural Adaptation*. Newbury Park, CA: Sage.

Gudykunst, W.B. and Kim, Y.Y. (1984) *Communicating with Strangers: An Approach to Intercultural Communication*. New York: McGraw-Hill.

Gudykunst, W.B. and Kim, Y.Y. (1992) *Communicating with Strangers: An Approach to Intercultural Communication*, 2nd edn. New York: McGraw-Hill.

Gudykunst, W.B. and Ting-Toomey, S. (1988) *Culture and Interpersonal Communication*. Newbury Park, CA: Sage.

Gumprez, J. (1982) *Discourse Strategies*. Cambridge: Cambridge University Press.

Gumprez, J. and Hernandez-Chavez, E. (1972) Bilingualism, bidialectism and classroom interaction, in C. Cazden, V. John and D. Hymes (eds) *Functions of Language in the Classroom*. New York: Teacher's College Press.

Gushue, G.V. (1993) Cultural-identity development and family assessment: an interaction model, *The Counseling Psychologist*, 21: 487–513.

Gwyn, F. and Kilpatrick, A. (1981) Family therapy with low-income blacks: a tool or turn off? *Social Casework*, 62: 259–66.

Halberstadt, A.G. (1985) Race, socioeconomic status, and nonverbal behavior, in A.W. Siegman and S. Feldstein (eds) *Multichannel Integrations of Nonverbal Behavior*. Hillsdale, NJ: Lawrence Erlbaum.

Hall, E.T. (1955) The anthropology of manners, *Scientific American*, 192: 85–9.

Hall, E.T. (1959) *The Silent Language*. New York: Anchor Press/Doubleday.

Hall, E.T. (1964) Adumbration as a feature of intercultural communication, *American Anthropologist*, 66: 154–63.

Hall, E.T. (1966) *The Hidden Dimension*. New York: Doubleday.

Hall, E.T. (1974) *Handbook for Proxemic Research*. Washington, DC: Society for the Anthropology of Visual Communication.

Hall, E.T. (1976) *Beyond Culture*. New York: Anchor Press/Doubleday.

Hall, E.T. (1984) The hidden dimensions of time and space in today's world, in F. Poyatos (ed.) *Cross-cultural Perspectives in Nonverbal Communication*. Toronto: C.J. Hogrefe.

Hall, E.T. (1994) Monochronic and polychronic time, in L.A. Samovar and R.E. Porter (eds) *Intercultural Communication: A Reader*. Belmont, CA: Wadsworth.

Hall, E. and Hall, M. (1990) *Understanding Cultural Differences*. Yarmouth, ME: Intercultural Press.

Hall, W.S., Freedle, R. and Cross, W.E., Jr. (1972) *Stages in the Development of a Black Identity*, ACT research report 50. Iowa City: Research and Development Division, American Testing Program.

Hamilton, D., Sherman, S. and Ruvolo, C. (1992) Stereotyped based expectancies, in W.B. Gudykunst and Y.Y. Kim (eds) *Readings on Communicating with Strangers*. New York: McGraw-Hill.

Hanna, J.L. (1984) Black/white nonverbal differences, dance and dissonance: implications for desegregation, in A. Wolfgang (ed.) *Nonverbal Behavior: Perspectives, Applications, Intercultural Insights*. Lewiston, NY: C.J. Hogrefe.

Hannerz, U. (1996) *Transnational Connections*. London: Routledge.

Hardiman, R. (1982) 'White identity development: a process oriented model for describing the racial consciousness of white Americans', unpublished PhD dissertation. University of Massachusetts, Amherst.

Harrison, D.K. (1975) Race as a counselor–client variable in counseling and psychotherapy: a review of the research, *Counseling Psychologist*, 5: 124–33.

Harper, R.G., Wiens, A.N. and Matarazzo, J.D. (1978) *Nonverbal Communication*. New York: Wiley and Son.

Hartley, P. (1993) *Interpersonal Communication*. London: Routledge.

Hecht, L.M. and Ribeau, S. (1987) Afro-American identity labels and communicative effectiveness, *Journal of Language and Social Psychology*, 6: 319–26.

Hecht, L.M. and Ribeau, S. (1991) Sociocultural roots of ethnic identity: a look at black America, *Journal of Black Studies*, 21: 501–13.

Hecht, L.M., Ribeau, S. and Alberts, J.K. (1989) An Afro-American perspective on interethnic communication, *Communication Monographs*, 56: 385–410.

Heckmann, F. and Bosswick, W. (1995) *Migration Policies: A Comparative Perspective*. Stuttgart: Ferdinand, Enke Verlag.

Heinig, R.M. (1975) 'A descriptive study of teacher–pupil tactile communication in grades four through six'. Doctoral dissertation. Pittsburgh, PA: University of Pittsburgh.

Helms, J.E. (1984) Towards a theoretical explanation of the effects of race on counseling: a black and white model, *The Counseling Psychologist*, 12(4): 153–65.

Helms, J.E. (1986) Expanding racial identity theory to cover counseling process, *Journal of Counseling Psychology*, 33(1): 62–4.

Helms, J.E. (ed.) (1990a) *Black and White Racial Identity: Theory, Research, and Practice.* Westport, CT: Greenwood Press.

Helms, J.E. (1990b) Generalizing racial identity interaction theory to groups, in J.E. Helms (ed.) *Black and White Racial Identity: Theory, Research and Practice.* New York: Greenwood Press.

Helms, J.E. (1990c) Three perspectives on counseling visible racial/ethnic group clients, in F.C. Serafica, A.I. Schwebel, R.K. Russell, P.D. Isaac and L.B. Myers (eds) *Mental Health of Ethnic Minorities.* New York: Praeger.

Helms, J.E. (1992) *Race is a Nice Thing to Have.* Topeka, KS: Content Communications.

Helms, J.E. (1994) Racial identity and 'racial' constructs, in E.J. Trickett, R. Watts and D. Birman (eds) *Human Diversity.* San Francisco: Jossey-Bass.

Helms, J.E. (1995) An update of Helms's white and people of colour racial identity models, in J.G. Ponterotto, J.M. Casas, L.A. Suzuki and C.M. Alexander (eds) *Handbook of Multicultural Counseling.* London: Sage.

Helms, J.E. and Carter, R.T. (1986) Manual for the visible racial/ethnic identity attitude scale, in R.T. Carter, B.R. Fretz and J.R. Mahalik (eds) *An Exploratory Investigation into the Relationship between Career Maturity, Work Role Salience, Value-Orientation, and Racial Identity Attitudes.* Paper presented at the 94th annual convention of the American Psychological Association, Washington, DC.

Helms, J.E. and Carter, R.T. (1990) Development of the white racial identity attitude inventory, in J.E. Helms (ed.) *Black and White Racial Identity: Theory, Research and Practice.* New York: Greenwood Press.

Helms, J.E. and Carter, R.T. (1991) Relationships of white and black racial identity attitudes and demographic similarity to counselor preferences, *Journal of Counseling Psychology*, 38(4): 446–57.

Helms, J.E. and Cook, D.A. (1996) *An Introduction to Using Race and Culture in Counseling and Psychotherapy.* Fort Worth, TX: Harcourt, Brace, Jovanovich.

Helms, J.E. and Piper, R.E. (1994) Implications of racial identity theory for vocational psychology, *Journal of Vocational Behavior*, 44: 124–38.

Hemsley, G.D. and Doob, A.N. (1978) The effect of looking behaviour on perceptions of a communicator's credibility, *Journal of Applied Social Psychology*, 8(2): 136–44.

Henley, N.M. (1977) *Body Politics: Power, Sex, and Nonverbal Communication.* Englewood Cliffs, NJ: Prentice-Hall.

Henley, N.M. (1986) *Body Politics: Power, Sex, and Nonverbal Communication.* Englewood Cliffs, NJ: Prentice-Hall.

Hewitt, R. (1986) *White Talk Black Talk: Inter-Racial Friendship and Communication Among Adolescents.* Cambridge: Cambridge University Press.

Hewstone, M. and Giles, H. (1986) Stereotypes and intergroup communication, in W. Gudykunst (ed.) *Intergroup Communication.* London: Edward Arnold.

Hinton, P. (1993) *The Psychology of Interpersonal Perception.* London: Routledge.

Ho, Man-Keung (1976) Social work with Asian Americans, *Social Casework*, 57(3): 195–201.

Hofstede, G. (1980) *Culture's Consequences: International Differences in Work-related Values.* Beverly Hills, CA: Sage.

Hofstede, G. (1983) Dimensions of national cultures in fifty countries and three regions, in J.B. Deregowski, S. Dziurawiec and R.C. Annis (eds) *Explanations in Cross-cultural Psychology*. Lisse: Swets and Zeitlinger.

Hofstede, G. (1984) *Culture's Consequences: International Differences in Work-related Values*. Beverly Hills, CA: Sage.

Hofstede, G. and Bond, M. (1984) Hofstede's culture dimensions, *Journal of Cross-cultural Psychology*, 15: 417–33.

Howitt, D. and J. Owusu-Bempah (1994) *The Racism of Psychology. Time for Change*. Hemel Hempstead: Harvester Wheatsheaf.

Hui, H.C. and Triandis, H.C. (1986) Individualism–collectivism: a study of cross-cultural researchers, *Journal of Cross-cultural Psychology*, 17: 225–48.

Ickes, W. (1984) Composition in black and white: determinants of interaction in interracial dyads, *Journal of Personality and Social Psychology*, 47: 1206–17.

Jackson, A.M. (1983) A theoretical model for the practice of psychotherapy with black populations, *Journal of Black Psychology*, 10: 19–27.

Jackson, B. (1975) Black identity development, in L. Golubschick and B. Persky (eds) *Urban Social and Educational Issues*. Dubuque, IA: Kendall-Hall.

Jain, N.C. and Matukumalli, A. (1993) The functions of silence in India: implications for intercultural communication. Research paper presented at the Second International East Meets West Conference in 'Cross-cultural Communication, Comparative Philosophy, and Comparative Religion'. Long Beach, CA.

Jandt, F.E. (1995) *Intercultural Communication. An Introduction*. London: Sage.

Jenkins, A.H. (1982) *The Psychology of the Afro-American*. New York: Pergamon.

Jensen, J.V. (1973) Communicative functions of silence, *ECT: A Review of General Semantics*, 30: 249–57.

Johnson, F.L. and Buttny, R. (1982) White listeners' responses to 'sounding black' and 'sounding white': the effects of message content on judgements about language, *Communication Monographs*, 49: 33–49.

Johnson, K.R. (1971) Black kinesics: some nonverbal communication patterns in black culture, *Florida Foreign Language Reporter*, 9: 17–20.

Jones, D.L. (1979) African-American clients: clinical practice issues, *Social Work*, 24(2): 112–18.

Jones, B.E. and Gray, B.A. (1986) Problems in diagnosing schizophrenia and affective disorders among blacks, *Hospital and Community Psychiatry*, 37: 61–5.

Jones, E.E. (1985) Psychotherapy and counseling with black clients, in P. Pedersen (ed.) *Handbook of Cross-cultural Counseling and Therapy*. Westport, CT: Greenwood Press.

Jones, E.E. and Nisbett, R.E. (1971) The actor and the observer: divergent perceptions of the causes of behaviour, in E.E. Jones, D.E. Kanouse, H.H. Kelley, R.E. Nisbett, S. Valins and B. Weiner (eds) *Attribution: Perceiving the Causes of Behavior*. Morristown, NJ: General Learning Press.

Jones, J.M. (1972) *Prejudice and Racism*. Reading, MA: Addison Wesley.

Jones, J.M. (1981) The concept of racism and its changing reality, in B.J. Bowser and R.G. Hunt (eds) *Impacts of Racism on White Americans*. Beverly Hills, CA: Sage.

Justice, B. and Justice, R. (1990) *The Abusing Family*. New York: Plenum Press.

Kadushin, A. (1990) *The Social Work Interview*. Oxford: Columbia University Press.

Kakar, S. (1981) *The Inner World: A Psychoanalytic Study of Childhood and Society in India*. Delhi: Oxford University Press.

Kashima, Y. and Triandis, H.C. (1986) The self-serving bias in attributions as a coping strategy: a cross cultural study, *Journal of Cross-cultural Psychology*, 17: 83–97.

Katz, J.H. (1985) The sociopolitical nature of counseling, *The Counseling Psychologist*, 13: 615–24.

Katz, J.H. and Ivey, A. (1977) White awareness; the frontier of racism awareness training, *The Personnel and Guidance Journal*, 55: 485–9.

Katz, P.A. and Taylor, D.A. (eds) (1988) *Eliminating Racism: Profiles in Controversy*. New York: Plenum.

Keefe, F.E. and Padilla, A.M. (1987) *Chicano Ethnicity*. Albuquerque: University of New Mexico Press.

Keith, M. and Pile, S. (eds) (1993) *Place and the Politics of Identity*. London: Routledge.

Kendon, A. (1967) Some functions of gaze direction in social interaction, *Acta Psychologica*, 71: 359–72.

Kendon, A. (1987) On gesture: its complementary relationship with speech, in A.W. Siegman and S. Feldstein (eds) *Nonverbal Behaviour and Communication*. Hillsdale, NJ: Erlbaum.

Kim, J. (1981) 'Process of Asian-American identity development: a study of Japanese American women's perceptions of their struggle to achieve positive identities', unpublished doctoral dissertation. University of Massachusetts, Amherst.

Kleiner, R.J., Tuckman, J. and Lavell, M. (1960) Mental disorder and status based on race, *Psychiatry*, 23(3): 271–4.

Kloss, R.J. (1979) Psychodynamic speculations on derogatory names for blacks, *The Journal of Black Psychology*, 5(2): 85–97.

Kluckhohn, F. and Strodtbeck, F. (1961) *Variations in Value Orientations*. New York: Row, Peterson.

Knapp, M.L. (1978) *Nonverbal Communication in Human Interaction*. New York: Holt, Rinehart and Winston.

Knapp, M.L. (1980) *Essentials of Nonverbal Communication*. New York: Holt, Rinehart and Winston.

Kochman, T. (1981) *Black and White Styles in Conflict*. Chicago: University of Chicago Press.

Krogman, W.M. (1945) The concept of race, in R. Linton (ed.) *The Science of Man in World Crisis*. New York: Columbia University Press.

Kymlicka, W. (1995) *Multicultural Citizenship*. Oxford: Clarendon Press.

Labov, W.P. (1972) *Language in the Inner City*. Philadelphia: University of Pennsylvania Press.

Labov, W.P. (1982) Objectivity and commitment in linguistic science: the case of the black English trial in Ann Arbor, *Language in Society*, 11: 165–201.

LaFrance, M. (1981) Gender gestures: sex, sex role, and nonverbal communication, in C. Mayo and N.M. Henley (eds) *Gender and Nonverbal Behavior*. New York: Springer-Verlag.

LaFrance, M. and Mayo, C. (1976) Racial differences in gaze behaviour during conversations: two systematic observational studies, *Journal of Personality and Social Psychology*, 33: 547–52.

Lago, C. (1989) *Working with Overseas Students: A Staff Development Training Manual*. Huddersfield: Huddersfield University and British Council.

Lago, C. and Thompson, J. (1994) Counselling and race, in W. Dryden, D. Charles-Edwards and R. Woolfe (eds) *Handbook of Counselling in Britain*. London: Routledge.

Lago, C. and Thompson, J. (1996) *Race, Culture and Counselling*. Buckingham: Open University Press.

Langer, E. (1989) *Mindfulness*. Reading, MA: Addison-Wesley.

La Piere, R.T. (1934) Attitudes and actions, *Social Forces*, 13: 230–7.

Lau, A. (1988) Family therapy and ethnic minorities, in E. Street and W. Dryden (eds) *Family Therapy in Britain*. Milton Keynes: Open University Press.

Laval, R.A., Gomez, E.A. and Ruiz, P. (1983) A language minority: hispanics and mental health care, *The American Journal of Social Psychiatry*, 3: 42–9.

Leathers, D.G. (1986) *Successful Nonverbal Communication: Principles and Applications*. New York: Macmillan.

Lee, C. (1994) Introductory lecture to a conference on race, culture and counselling. (Unpublished) University of Sheffield, July.

Leong, F. (1992) Guidelines for minimizing premature termination among Asian American clients in group counseling, *The Journal for Specialists in Group Work*, 17(4): 218–28.

Levin, D. (1985) *The Flight from Ambiguity*. Chicago: University of Chicago Press.

Lippman, W. (1922) *Public Opinion*. New York: Harcourt Brace.

Lishman, J. (1994) *Communication in Social Work*. Basingstoke: Macmillan.

Littlewood, R. and Lipsedge, M. (1989) *Aliens and Alienists. Ethnic Minorities and Psychiatry*. London: Unwin Hyman.

Locke, D.C. (1992) *Increasing Multicultural Understanding: A Comprehensive Model*. Newbury Park, CA: Sage.

Lonner, W.J. (1994) Culture and human diversity, in E. Trickett, R. Watts and D. Birman (eds) *Human Diversity*. San Francisco: Jossey-Bass.

Lustig, M. and Koester, J. (1993) *Intercultural Competence*. New York: Harper-Collins.

Majors, R. (1991) Nonverbal behaviours and communication styles among African Americans, in R.L. Jones (ed.) *Black Psychology*. Berkeley, CA: Cobb and Henry.

Malandro, L.A. and Barker, L. (1983) *Nonverbal Communication*. Reading, MA: Addison-Wesley.

Mama, A. (1995) *Beyond the Masks: Race, Gender and Subjectivity*. London: Routledge.

Marcos, L.R. (1979) Effects of interpreters on the evaluation of psychopathology in non-English-speaking patients, *American Journal of Psychiatry*, 136(2).

Marcos, L.R. and Alpert, M. (1976) Strategies and risks in psychotherapy with bilingual patients: the phenomenon of language independence, *American Journal of Psychiatry*, 133: 1275–8.

Marcos, L.R. and Urcuyo, L. (1979) Dynamic psychotherapy with the bilingual patient, *American Journal of Psychotherapy*, 33: 331–8.

Marcos, L.R., Alpert, M., Urcuyo, L. and Kesselman, M. (1973) The effect of interview language in the evaluation of psychopathology in Spanish American schizophrenic patients, *American Journal of Psychiatry*, 130: 549–53.

Mares, P., Henley, A. and Baxter, C. (1985) *Health Care in Multiracial Britain*. Cambridge: Health Education Council/National Extension College.

Martinez, C. (1986) Hispanic psychiatric issues, in C. Wilkinson (ed.) *Ethnic Psychiatry*. New York: Plenum.

Maxime, J. (1986) Some psychological models of black self-concept, in S. Ahmed, J. Cheetham and J. Small (eds) *Social Work with Children and their Families*. London: Batsford.

Maxime, J. (1993) The therapeutic importance of racial identity in working with black children who hate, in V. Verma (ed.) *How and Why Children Hate*. London: Jessica Kingsley Publishers.

Mbiti, J.S. (1970) *African Religions and Philosophies*. Garden City, NY: Anchor Books.

McAvoy, B. and Sayeed, A. (1994) Communication, in B.R. McAvoy and L.J. Donaldson (eds) *Health Care for Asians*. Oxford: Oxford University Press.

McConahay, J.B. (1986) Modern racism, ambivalence, and the modern racism scale, in J.F. Dovidio and S.L. Gaertner (eds) *Prejudice, Discrimination, and Racism*. New York: Academic Press.

McConahay, J.B. and Hough, J.C. (1976) Symbolic racism, *Journal of Social Issues*, 32: 23–45.

Mehrabian, A. (1971) *Silent Messages*. Belmont, CA: Wadsworth.

Mehrabian, A. (1972) *Nonverbal Communication*. Chicago: Aldene-Atherton.

Mercer, K. (1993) Racism and transcultural psychiatry, in P. Clarke, M. Harrison, K. Patel, M. Shah, M. Varley and T. Zack-Williams (eds) *Improving Mental Health Practice*. Leeds: CCETSW.

Mercer, K. (1984) Black communities' experience of psychiatric services, *International Journal of Social Psychiatry*, 30: 22–7.

Miles, R. (1989) *Racism*. London: Routledge.

Milner, D. (1975) *Children and Race*. Harmondsworth: Penguin.

Milner, D. (1981) Racial prejudice, in J.C. Turner and H. Giles (eds) *Intergroup Behaviour*. Oxford: Basil Blackwell.

Mitchell, S.L. and Dell, D.M. (1992) The relationship between black students' racial identity attitudes and participation in campus organizations, *Journal of College Student Development*, 33: 39–43.

Modood, T. (1997) 'Difference', cultural racism and anti-racism, in P. Werbner and T. Modood *Debating Cultural Hybridity*. London: Zed Books.

Modood, T, Beishon, S. and Virdee, S. (1994) *Changing Ethnic Identities*. London: Policy Studies Institute.

Moghaddam, F.M., Ditto, B. and Taylor, D.M. (1990) Attitudes and attributions related to psychological symptomatology in Indian immigrant women, *Journal of Cross-cultural Psychology*, 21: 335–50.

Moyerman, D.R. and Forman, B.D. (1992) Acculturation and adjustment: a meta-analytic study, *Hispanic Journal of Behavioral Sciences*, 14: 163–200.

Munford, M.B. (1994) Relationship of gender, self-esteem, social class, and racial identity to depression in blacks, *Journal of Black Psychology*, 20: 143–56.

Nicolson, P. and Bayne, R. (1990) *Applied Psychology for Social Workers*, 2nd edn. London: Macmillan.

Nobles, W. (1976) Black people in white insanity: an issue for black community mental health, *Journal of Afro-American Issues*, 4: 21–7.

Oliver, R.T. (1971) *Communication and Culture in Ancient India and China*. Syracuse, NY: Syracuse University Press.

Olwig, K.F. and Hastrup, K. (1997) *Siting Culture*. London: Routledge.

Owusu-Bempah, J. (1994) Race, self-identity and social work, *British Journal of Social Work*, 24(20): 123–36.

Paniauga, F.A. (1994) *Assessing and Treating Culturally Diverse Clients*. London: Sage Publications.

Parham, T.A. (1989) Cycles of psychological nigrescence, *The Counseling Psychologist*, 17(2): 187–226.

Parham, T.A. and Helms, J.E. (1981) The influence of black students' racial identity attitudes on preference for counselor's race, *Journal of Counseling Psychology*, 28: 250–7.

Parham, T.A. and Helms, J.E. (1985a) Attitudes of racial identity and self-esteem in black students: an exploratory investigation, *Journal of College Student Personnel*, 26(2): 143–7.

Parham, T.A. and Helms, J.E. (1985b) Relation of racial identity to self-actualization and affective states of black students, *Journal of Counseling Psychiatry*, 28(3): 250–6.

Patterson, M.L. (1983) *Nonverbal Behavior: A Functional Perspective*. New York: Springer-Verlag.

Pearce, A. (1994) Investigating biases in trainee counsellors' attitudes to clients from different cultures, *British Journal of Guidance and Counselling*, 22(3): 4–28.

Pedersen, P.B. (1988) *A Handbook for Developing Multicultural Awareness*. Alexandria, VA: American Counseling Association.

Pedersen, P.B. (1991) Multiculturalism as a generic approach to counseling, *Journal of Counseling and Development*, 70: 6–12.

Pedersen, P.B. (1993) The culture-bound counselor as an unintentional racist, in J. Ponterotto and P.B. Pedersen *Preventing Prejudice*. London: Sage.

Pettigrew, T.F. (1979) The ultimate attribution error, *Personality and Social Psychology Bulletin*, 5: 461–76.

Pettigrew, T.F. (1981) The mental health impact, in B.P. Bowser and R.G. Hunt (eds) *Impacts of Racism on White Americans*. Beverly Hills, CA: Sage.

Philips, D. and Rathwell, T. (eds) (1986) *Health, Race and Ethnicity*. London: Croom Helm.

Phinney, (1990) Ethnic identity in adolescents and adults: review of research, *Psychological Bulletin*, 108: 499–514.

Phung, T. (1995) An experience of inter-cultural counselling: views from a black client, *Counselling*, February, 61–2.

Pinderhughes, E. (1989) *Understanding Race, Ethnicity, and Power: The Key to Efficacy in Clinical Practice*. New York: Free Press.

Politzer, R.L. and Hoover, M.R. (1976) *Teachers' and Pupils' Attitudes Toward Black English Speech Variables and Black Pupils' Achievement*. Stanford, CA: Stanford Center for Research and Development in Teaching.

Ponterotto, J.G. (1988) Racial consciousness development among white counselor trainees: a stage model, *Journal of Multicultural Counseling and Development*, 16: 146–56.

Ponterotto, J.G. (1991) The nature of prejudice revisited: implications for counseling intervention, *Journal of Counseling and Development*, 70: 216–24.

Ponterotto, J.G. and Casas, J.M. (1991) *Handbook of Racial/Ethnic Minority Counseling Research*. Springfield, IL: Charles C. Thomas.

Ponterotto, J.G. and Pedersen, P.B. (1993) *Preventing Prejudice: A Guide for Counselors and Educators*. London: Sage.

Ponterotto, J.G., Lewis, D.E. and Bullington, R. (1990) *Affirmative Action on Campus*. San Francisco, CA: Jossey-Bass.

Pope-Davis, D.B. and Ottavi, T.M. (1992) The influence of white racial identity attitudes on racism among faculty members: a preliminary examination, *Journal of College Student Development*, 33(5): 389–94.

Pope-Davis, D.B. and Ottavi, T.M. (1994) The relationship between racism and racial identity among white Americans: a replication and extension, *Journal of Counseling and Development*, 72: 293–7.

Porter, L.A. and Samovar, R.E. (1994) *Intercultural Communication*. Belmont, CA: Wadsworth.

Poston, W.S., Craine, M. and Atkinson, D.R. (1991) Counselor dissimilarity confrontation, client cultural mistrust, and willingness to self-disclose, *Journal of Multicultural Counseling and Development*, 19: 65–73.

Poyatos, F. (1992) *Paralanguage: Linguistic and Interdisciplinary Approach to Speech and Interactive Sounds*. Amsterdam/Philadelphia: John Benjamins.

Pyant, C.T. and Yanico, B.J. (1991) Relationships of racial identity and gender role attitudes to black women's psychological well-being, *Journal of Counseling Psychology*, 38: 315–22.

Rack, P. (1982) *Race, Culture and Mental Disorder*. London: Tavistock.

Ramsey, S. and Birk, J. (1983) Preparation of North Americans for interaction with Japanese: considerations of language and communication style, in D. Landis and R.W. Brislin (eds) *Handbook of Intercultural Training: Volume III*. New York: Pergamon.

Rattansi, A. and Westwood, S. (1994) *Racism, Modernity and Identity*. Cambridge: Polity Press.

Reeves, F. (1983) *British Racial Discourse*. Cambridge: Cambridge University Press.

Richardson, T. and Helms, J.E. (1994) The relation of racial identity attitudes of black men to perceptions of parallel counseling dyads, *Journal of Counseling and Development*, 73(2): 172–7.

Richmond, V.P. and McCroskey, J.C. (1988) *Communication: Apprehension, Avoidance and Effectiveness*. Scottsdale, AZ: Gorsuch Scarisbrick.

Ridley, C.R. (1984) Clinical treatment of the nondisclosing black client: a therapeutic paradox, *American Psychologist*, 39(11): 1234–44.

Ridley, C.R. (1989) Racism in counseling as an adversive behavioral process, in P.B. Pedersen, J.G. Draguns, W.J. Lonner and J.E. Trimble (eds) *Counseling Across Cultures*. Honolulu: University of Hawaii Press.

Ridley, C.R. (1995) *Overcoming Unintentional Racism in Counseling and Therapy*. London: Sage.

Robinson, L. (1995) *Psychology for Social Workers: Black Perspectives*. London: Routledge.

Robinson, L. (1997) Racial identity attitudes and self-esteem measures among African Caribbean children in residential care, unpublished report, CCETSW.

Rokeach, M. (1973) *The Nature of Human Values*. New York: The Free Press.

Rokeach, M. (1979) Value theory and communication research: review and commentary, in D. Nimmo (ed.) *Communication Yearbook 3*. New Brunswick, NJ: Transaction Books for the Intercultural Communication Association.

Romaine, S. (1995) *Bilingualism*. Oxford: Blackwell.

Rosaldo, R. (1989) *Culture and Truth; The Remaking of Social Analysis*. Boston, MA: Beacon.

Rosegrant, T.J. and McCroskey, J.C. (1975) The effects of race and sex on proxemic behaviour in an interview setting, *Southern Speech Communication Journal*, 40: 408–20.

Ruiz, R.A. (1981) Cultural and historical perspectives in counseling Hispanics, in D.W. Sue (ed.) *Counseling the Culturally Different: Theory and Practice*. New York: John Wiley.

Russell, D.M. (1988) Language and psychotherapy: the influence of nonstandard English in clinical practice, in L. Comas-Diaz and E.H. Griffith (eds) *Clinical Guidelines in Cross-cultural Mental Health*. New York: John Wiley.

Ryan, E., Giles, H. and Sebastian, R. (1982) An integrative perspective for the study of attitudes toward language, in E. Ryan and H. Giles (eds) *Attitudes Toward Language Variation*. London: Edward Arnold.

Sabnani, H.B., Ponterotto, J.G. and Borodovsky, L.G. (1991) White racial identity development and cross-cultural counselor training; a stage model, *The Counseling Psychologist*, 19: 76–102.

Samovar, L.A. and Porter, R.E. (1985) Nonverbal interaction, in L.A. Samovar and R.E. Porter (eds) *Intercultural Communication: A Reader*. Belmont, CA: Wadsworth.

Samovar, L.A. and Porter, R.E. (eds) (1994) *Intercultural Communication: A Reader*, 2nd edn. Belmont, CA: Wadsworth.

Samovar, L.A., Porter, R.E. and Jain, N.C. (1981) *Understanding Intercultural Communication*. Belmont, CA: Wadsworth.

Schneller, R. (1985) Changes in the understanding and use of culture-bound non-verbal messages, Paper presented at the 16th Israeli Sociological Conference, Tel-Aviv.

Scotton, C. (1993) *Social Motivations for Code-switching*. New York: Oxford University Press.

Sears, D. (1988) Symbolic racism, in P.A. Katz and D.A. Taylor (eds) *Eliminating Racism: Profiles in Controversy*. New York: Plenum.

Segal, U.A. (1988) Career choice correlates: an Indian perspective, *Indian Journal of Social Work*, 69: 338–48.

Segal, U.A. (1991) Cultural variables in Asian Indian families, *The Journal of Contemporary Human Services*, 11: 233–41.

Semaj, L.T. 1981 The black self, *Western Journal of Black Studies*, 5(3): 158–71.

Servaes, J. (1988) Cultural identity in East and West, *The Howard Journal of Communications*, 1: 58–71.

Seymour, H.N. and Seymour, C.M. (1979) The symbolism of ebonics: I'd rather switch than fight, *Journal of Black Studies*, 9: 397–410.

Shackman, J. (1985) *The Right to be Understood*. Cambridge: National Extension College.

Siegel, B. (1970) Counseling the color-conscious, *School Counselor*, 17: 168–70.

Singh, G. (1992) *Race and Social Work from 'Black Pathology' to 'Black Perspectives'*. Bradford: World View/Boulder, CO: Westview Press.

Sitaram, K.S. and Haapanen, L.W. (1979) The role of values in intercultural communication, in M.K. Asante, E. Newmark and C.A. Blake (eds) *Handbook of Intercultural Communication*. Beverly Hills, CA: Sage.

Smedley, A. (1993) *Race in North America: Origin and Evolution of a World View*. Boulder, CO: Westview Press.

Smith, A. (1983) Nonverbal communication among black female dyads: an assessment of intimacy, gender and race, *Journal of Social Issues*, 39: 55–67.

Smith, D.E., Willis, E.N. and Grier, J.A. (1980) Success and interpersonal touch in a competitive setting, *Journal of Nonverbal Behaviour*, 5: 26–34.

Smith, E. (1977) Counseling black individuals: some strategies, *Personnel and Guidance Journal*, 55: 390–6.

Smith, E.J. (1981) Cultural and historical perspectives in counseling blacks, in D.W. Sue (ed.) *Counselling the Culturally Different: Theory and Practice*. New York: John Wiley.

Smitherman, G. (1977) *Talkin' and Testifyin': The Language of Black America*. Boston, MA: Houghton Mifflin.

Smitherman, G. (1991) Talkin' and testifyin' black English and the black experience, in R. Jones (ed.) *Black Psychology*. Berkeley, CA: Cobb and Henry.

Smitherman-Donaldson, G. (1988) Discriminatory discourse on Afro-American speech, in G. Smitherman-Donaldson and T.A. van Dijk (eds) *Discourse and Discrimination*. Detroit, MI: Wayne State University Press.

Snyder, M., Campbell, B.H. and Preston, E. (1982) Testing hypotheses about human nature: assessing the accuracy of social stereotypes, *Social Cognition*, 1: 256–72.

Spiegel, J.P. (1982) An ecological model of ethnic families, in M. McGoldrick, J.K. Pearce and J. Giordano (eds) *Ethnicity and Family Therapy*, New York: Guildford Press.

Stanbeck, M. and Pearce, W.B. (1981) Talking to 'the man': some communication strategies used by subordinates and their implications for intergroup relations, *Quarterly Journal of Speech*, 67: 21–30.

Stern, F. (1991) Anti-Semitic and philosemitic discourse in postwar Germany, Paper presented at the Fourth International Conference on Language and Social Psychology, Santa Barbara, CA.

Stewart, W.A. (1970) Toward a history of American Negro dialect, in F. Williams (ed.) *Language and Poverty*. Chicago: Markham Publishing.

Stubbs, P. (1988) 'The reproduction of racism in state social work', unpublished PhD thesis. University of Bath.

Sue, D.W. (1981) Evaluating process variables in cross-cultural counseling and psychotherapy, in A.J. Marsell and P.B. Pedersen (eds) *Cross-cultural Counseling and Psychotherapy*. New York: Pergamon.

Sue, D.W. and Sue, D. (1990) *Counselling the Culturally Different*. New York: John Wiley and Sons.

Sue, D.W., Arrendondo, P. and McDavis, R.S. (1992) Multicultural competencies and standards: a call to the profession, *Journal of Multicultural Counselling and Development*, 20: 64–88.

Sutcliffe, D. (1986) British black English and West Indian creoles, in P. Trudgill (ed.) *Language in the British Isles*. Cambridge: Cambridge University Press.

Szapocznik, J., Scopetta, M.A., Kurtines, W. and Aranalde, M.A. (1978) Theory and measurement of acculturation, *International Journal of Psychology*, 12: 113–30.

Tajfel, H. (ed.) (1978) *Differentiation Between Social groups*. London: Academic Press.

Tajfel, H. (1982) Social psychology of inter-group relations, *Annual Review of Psychology*, 33: 1–39.

Taub, D.J. and McEwen, M.K. (1992) The relationship of racial identity attitudes to autonomy and mature interpersonal relationships in black and white undergraduate women, *Journal of College Student Development*, 33(5): 439–46.

Taylor, C. (1992) *Multiculturalism and 'The Politics of Recognition'*. Princeton, NJ: Princeton University Press.

Terrell, F. and Terrell, S.L. (1981) An inventory to measure cultural mistrust among blacks, *Western Journal of Black Studies*, 5: 180–4.

Terrell, F. and Terrell, S. (1984) Race of counselor, client sex, cultural mistrust level, and premature termination from counseling among black clients, *Journal of Counseling Psychology*, 31: 371–5.

Terrell, F., Terrell, S. and Miller, F.S. (1989) Cultural mistrust and its effects on expectational variables in black client–white counselor relationships, *Journal of Counseling Psychology*, 36(4): 447–50.

Thomas, A. and Sillen, S. (1972) *Racism and Psychiatry*. Secaucus, NJ: The Citadel Press.

Thomas, A. and Sillen, S. (1974) The significance of the e(thnocentrism) factor in mental health, *Journal of Social Issues*, 2: 60–9.

Thomas, C. (1971) *Boys No More*. Beverly Hills, CA: Glencoe Press.

Thomas, C. and Thomas, S.W. (1971) Blackness is a tonic, in C. Thomas (ed.) *Boys No More*. Beverly Hills, CA: Glencoe Press.

Thomas, L. (1995) Psychotherapy in the context of race and culture: an intercultural therapeutic approach, in S. Fernando (ed.) *Mental Health in a Multi-ethnic Society*. London: Routledge.

Thompson, C.E., Worthington, R. and Atkinson, D.R. (1994) Counselor content orientation, counselor race, and black women's cultural mistrust and self-disclosure, *Journal of Counseling Psychology*, 41(2): 155–61.

Thornton, B. (1984) Defensive attribution of responsibility: evidence for an arousal-based motivational bias, *Journal of Personality and Social Psychology*, 46: 721–34.

Tokar, D.M. and Swanson, J.L. (1991) An investigation of the validity of Helms' (1984) model of white racial identity development, *Journal of Counseling Psychology*, 38: 296–301.

Tom, D. and Cooper, H. (1986) The effect of student background on teacher performance attributions: evidence for counterdefensive patterns and low expectancy cycles, *Basic and Applied Psychology*, 7: 53–62.

Traugott, E.C. (1976) Pidgins, Creoles, and the origins of vernacular black English, in D.S. Harrison and T. Trabasso (eds) *Black English: A Seminar*. Hillsdale, NJ: Lawrence Erlbaum.

Triandis, H. (1986) Collectivism vs. individualism: a reconceptualization of a basic concept in cross-cultural psychology, in C. Bagley and G. Verma (eds) *Personality, Cognition, and Values: Cross-cultural Perspectives of Childhood and Adolescence*. London: Macmillan.

Triandis, H. (1990) Toward cross-cultural studies of individualism and collectivism in Latin America, *Interamerican Journal of Psychology*, 24: 199–210.

Triandis, H.C., Bontemo, R., Villareal, M.J., Asai, M. and Lucca, N. (1988) Individualism and collectivism: cross-cultural perspectives on self-ingroup relationships, *Journal of Personality and Social Psychology*, 19: 323–38.

Triandis, H.C., Brislin, R. and Hui, C.H. (1988) Cross-cultural training across the individualism–collectivism divide, *International Journal of Intercultural Relations*, 12: 269–89.

Turner, J.C. 1987 *Rediscovering the Social Group*. London: Basil Blackwell.

Valentine, C.A. (1971) Deficit, difference, and bicultural models of Afro-American behavior, *Harvard Educational Review*, 41(2): 137–57.

van Dijk, T.A. (1984) *Prejudice in Discourse*. Amsterdam: Benjamins.

van Dijk, T.A. (1987) *Communicating Racism: Ethnic Prejudice in Thought and Talk*. Newbury Park, CA: Sage.

van Dijk, T. (1993) Discourse, power and access, in C.R. Caldas (ed.) *Critical Discourse Analysis*. London: Hutchinson.

Vasquez, C.A. (1982) Research on the psychiatric evaluation of the bilingual patient: a methodological critique, *Hispanic Journal of Behavioral Sciences*, 4: 75–80.

Vontress, C. (1971) Racial differences: impediments to rapport, *Journal of Counseling Psychology*, 18: 7–13.

Vontress, C. (1981) Racial and ethnic barriers in counseling, in P. Pedersen, J.G. Draguns, W.J. Lonner and J.E. Trimble (eds) *Counseling Across Cultures*. Honolulu: University of Hawaii Press.

Wampold, B., Casas, J.M. and Atkinson, D.R. (1982) Ethnic bias in counseling: an information-processing approach, *Journal of Counseling Psychology*, 28: 489–503.

Wandsworth Council for Community Relations (1978) *Asians and the Health Service*. London: Wandsworth Council for Community Relations.

Watkins, C.E. and Terrell, F. (1988) Mistrust level and its effects on counseling expectations in black client–white counselor relationships: an analogue study, *Journal of Counseling Psychology*, 35: 194–7.

Watson, D. (1982) The actor and the observer: how are their perceptions of causality divergent? *Psychological Bulletin*, 92: 682–700.

Watson, O. (1970) *Proxemic Behavior: A Cross-cultural Study*. The Hague: Mouton.

Watts, A. (1966) *The Book: On the Taboo Against Knowing Who You Are*. New York: Pantheon.

Weber, S.N. (1991) The need to be: the socio-cultural significance of black language, in L.A. Samovar and R.E. Porter (eds) *Intercultural Communication: A Reader*, 6th edn. Belmont, CA: Wadsworth.

Wenger, J. (1993) Just part of the mix, *Focus*, 21(9): 3.

Werbner, P. and Modood, T. (1997) *Debating Cultural Hybridity*. London: Zed Books.

Wetherell, M. and Potter, J. (1992) *Mapping the Language of Racism*. Hemel Hempstead: Harvester Wheatsheaf.

Wheeler, L. and Reiss, H. (1988) On titles, citations and outlets. What do mainstreamers want? in M. Bond (ed.) *The Cross-cultural Challenge to Social Psychology*. London: Sage Publications.

White, J.L. (1972) Toward a black psychology, in R.L. Jones (ed.) *Black Psychology*, New York: Harper and Row.

White, J.L. (1984) *The Psychology of Blacks: An Afro-American Perspective*. Englewood Cliffs, NJ: Prentice-Hall.

Wilkinson, D. (1993) Family ethnicity in America, in H.P. McAdoo (ed.) *Family Ethnicity: Strength in Diversity*. Newbury Park, CA: Sage.

Williams, F. (1964) *Capitalism and Slavery*. London: Andre Deutsch.

Williams, I.J. (1975) 'An investigation of the developmental stages of black consciousness'. PhD thesis. University of Cincinnati. *Dissertation Abstracts International*, 36(5b): 2488–9.

Williams, W. (1982) Language consciousness and cultural liberation in black America. Paper delivered at the Sixth Annual Conference of the National Council for Black Studies, Chicago.

Willis, F.N. and Hoffman, G.E. (1975) Development of tactile patterns in relationships to age, sex and race, *Developmental Psychology*, 11: 866.

Willis, F.N., Reeves, D.L. and Buchanan, D.R. (1976) Interpersonal touch in high school relative to sex and race, *Perceptual and Motor Skills*, 43: 843–7.

Wilson, M. (1993) *Mental Health and Britain's Black Communities*. London: Kings Fund.

Witte, K. and Morrison, K. (1995) Intercultural and cross-cultural health communication, in R.L. Wiseman (ed.) *Intercultural Communication Theory*. London: Sage.

Wodak, R. (1991) Black–white speech differences revisited, in W. Wolfram and N.H. Clark (eds) *Black–White Speech Relationships*. Washington, DC: Center for Applied Linguistics.

Wolfgang, A. (ed.) (1984) *Nonverbal Behavior: Perspectives, Application, and Intercultural Insights*. Toronto: C.J. Hogrefe.

Wong, A. (1986) Creole as a language of power and solidarity, in D. Sutcliffe and A. Wong (eds) *The Language of the Black Experience*. Oxford: Basil Blackwell.

Word, C.O., Zanna, M.P. and Cooper, J. (1974) The non-verbal mediation of self-fulfilling prophecies in interracial interaction, *Journal of Experimental Social Psychology*, 10: 109–20.

Wrench, W. and Solomos, J. (1993) *Racism and Migration in Western Europe*. Oxford: Berg.

Wrenn, C.G. (1985) Afterward: the culturally encapsulated counselor revisited, in P.B. Pedersen (ed.) *Handbook of Cross-cultural Counseling and Therapy*. Westport, CT: Greenwood Press.

Yates, A. (1972) *Current Problems of Teacher Education*. Oxford: Basil Blackwell.

Yazdani, L. and Anjum, A. (1994) Report of the Brighton, Hove and Lewes District Ethnic Minorities Council Health Needs Project. Brighton: Council Voluntary Service.

Yee, A.H., Fairchild, H., Weizmann, F. and Wyatt, G.E. (1993) Addressing psychology's problem with race, *American Psychologist*, 48(11): 1132–40.

Yinger, J.M. (1976) Ethnicity in complex societies, in L. Coser and O. Larsen (eds) *The Uses of Controversy in Sociology*. New York: Free Press.

Zerubavel, E. (1991) *The Fine Line*. New York: Free Press.

Index

accents, 79–80, 112
  see also language
acceptance, 49
acculturation, 55, 72–3
achievement, 43–4
activity orientation, 45–6
adaptation, 42–3, 49
African Caribbeans, language, 86–9
African languages, 81
African worldview, 45, 64
age, 74, 111–12
alien identity, 47
Anjum, A., 75, 92, 93–4
anxiety, 94, 138
articulation, synergetic, 18
Asians, 93
  cultural values, 63–4, 68–9
  stereotypes, 136, 137
assimilation, 58
Atkinson, D.R., 17–18
attitudes, 34–53, 75
  definition, 35–6
  and interethnic communication, 38–42
  transmission through discourse, 98
  see also racism; values
attribution theory, 129–32
authority, 73, 74, 105, 117
autonomy, 23, 48
awareness, 18, 48
  integrative, 19

behavioural expressiveness, 67–8
'being' cultures, 45–6
beliefs, 34–53
  definition, 34–5
  and interethnic communication, 37
  see also values

Bennett, M., 34, 49–50, 51, 52
bias
  attributional, 130–1
  ethnocentric, 43–4
  in interpretation, 95
  perception and, 127–8
bilingual issues, 89–98
  interpreters, 93–6, 99
  racist language, 96–8
'black'
  definition, 3–4
  language usage, 96–7
Black English (BE), 79, 80–6, 143
  African Caribbean experience, 86–9
black perspective, 2–3, 59
black racial identity development, 9–19
  Atkinson, Morten and Sue's model,
    17–18
  Cross's model, 8–9, 11–15
  Helms's people of colour model, 18–19
  Parham's model, 16–17
  and prejudice, 125
body language, 104–7, 113–14

Carter, R., 50, 124
categorization, 128
channels of communication, 2
checking, understanding, 93
child development, 83
code switching, 84–5
collective identity, 47
  see also group identity
collectivism–individualism dimension,
    43–4, 62–4, 111, 113
colour blindness, 21, 139
confidentiality, 93–4

confluent paranoics, 71
conformity, 17, 18, 47
contact, 21, 48, 124–5
contact cultures, 67, 107–8, 111
context, level of, 65–6, 103–4, 117
control, of prejudice, 133–4
'cool pose', 116
cooperation, 43–4
core beliefs, 37
counselling, 116
   attitudes and, 40, 41
   bilingual issues, 90
   culture and, 57, 63, 68–9
   mistrust, 41
   racial identity development and, 24–6
   racism and, 40–1
   values and, 44, 48–9
Coupland, N., 78
covert racism, 40
credibility, 106
credibility-enhancing strategies, 98
Creole, 81, 83, 86–9
Cross, W.E., 8–9, 11–15
crossed relationships, 29, 31
cultural deprivation, 56
cultural encapsulation, 57
cultural identity, see racial identity
cultural paranoia, 70–1
cultural racism, 39–40, 55–6
culture, 2, 54–76, 142
   attribution theory, 130–1
   cultural values, see values
   definitions, 54–9
   hierarchy of cultures, 55–6
   implications for practitioners, 73–6
   intracultural differences and interethnic
      communication, 72–3
   and nonverbal communication, 74,
      103–14

Dalphinis, M., 89
D'Ardenne, P., 79
deception, 41–2
decreolization, 81
defence, 49–50
defence mechanisms, 41
defensive attributions, 130
defensive behaviour, 138
deficit/deficiency model, 56–8
denial, 49–50, 69–70
depression, 136–7
developmental model, 49–50, 51, 52
dialects, 79–80, 112
   see also language

diffused identity, 47
Dijk, T.A. van, 98, 126
Dillard, J.L., 81
discrimination, 114–16, 123
discursive deracialization, 126–7
disintegration, 21–2, 48, 125
dissonance, 17, 18, 47
distress, 94
district health authorities (DHAs), 93–4
distrust, 41–2, 70, 119
Dodd, C.H., 140
'doing' cultures, 45–6
dominant culture-identity development
      model, 48, 52
Doss, R.C., 85
dyadic interactions, 27–30

Ebonics, see Black English
ego statuses, 18–19
Eleftheriadou, Z., 74–5, 75–6
embarrassment, 93–4
emotional expressiveness, 67–8
encounter, 12, 25, 26–7
English as a Second Language (ESL), 89
ethnicity, 5
ethnocentric bias, 43–4
ethnolinguistic identity theory, 77–8
Euro-American worldview, 45–6
Eurocentric perspective, 1, 43–4, 56–8
expectations, stereotypes and, 132, 134
expressiveness, 67–8
external attributions, 129–30
eye contact, 74, 104–7

facial expressions, 104
faculty mentors, 42
family, 91–2
   Asian values, 63–4
   as interpreters, 94–5
first impressions, 128–9
fixation, 15
flexible categories, 128
functional paranoia, 70–1
fundamental attribution error, 130

'games' model of social interaction, 118
gender, 75
   nonverbal communication, 106–7, 108,
      111
   and racist attitudes, 124
gesture, 114
Giles, H., 77, 78
Gross, A.M., 85
group identity, 82–3, 87

group process, 31–2
group work, 69
groupness, 43–4, 64
Gushue, G.V., 47–9, 52, 74

Hall, E.T., 65–6, 110–11
harmony, 64
healthy cultural paranoiacs, 71
Helms, J.E., 9, 50
    interaction theory, 27–32
    people of colour racial identity
        development, 18–19
    white identity development, 19–23
hierarchy of cultures, 55–6
high contact cultures, 67, 107–8, 111
high context cultures, 65–6, 103–4, 117
Hofstede, G., 60, 61, 62, 73
human nature, 44–6

identity
    collective, 47
    group, 82–3, 87
    language and ethnic, 77–86
    racial, see racial identity development
immediacy, 67
immersion, 17–18
immersion–emersion, 12–13, 15, 18–19,
        23, 25–6, 48
impression management, 114–16
impressions, first, 128–9
indirect stereotyping, 135
individual racism, 38–41
individualism–collectivism dimension,
        43–4, 62–4, 111, 113
information processing
    and stereotyping, 134, 135–6
    strategies (IPS), 18–19
institutional racism, 39–41
integration, 49
integrative awareness, 19
intentional racism, 40–1
interaction theory, 27–30
    group process, 31–2
intercultural communication, 6
intercultural nonparanoic disclosers, 71
interdependence, 43–4
interethnic communication, definition, 6
internal attributions, 129–30
internalization, 13–14, 19, 26
internalization-commitment, 14
interpreters, 93–6, 99
interviewees, job, 84–5
intracultural differences, 60, 72–3
introspection, 18, 47

job interviewees, 84–5

kinesics, 104–7
Kluckhohn, F., 34, 36, 44–6, 51, 53
Kochman, T., 67–8

La Piere, R.T., 36
Lago, C., 40, 95
language, 77–100, 143
    African Caribbean experience, 86–9
    bilingual issues, 89–98
    Black English, 79, 80–6, 143
    and ethnic identity, 77–86
    racist language, 87, 96–8, 99
    use of interpreters, 93–6, 99
lifespan nigrescence model, 16–17
Lishman, J., 1
low contact cultures, 67, 107–8, 111
low context cultures, 65–6, 103–4, 117

Mahtani, A., 79
Majors, R., 116
Mares, P., 93
masculinity, 64–5
Maxime, J., 24–5
Mehrabian, A., 113–14
mental health, 26
    culture and, 57, 75
    language and, 91, 95–6
    stereotypes, 136–9
mentors, 42
mindfulness, 140
minimization, 49–50
minority-identity development (MID)
        model, 17–18
miscommunication, 115
mistrust, 41–2, 70, 119
modern racism, see cultural racism
Modood, T., 64, 87–8
monochronic time, 109–10
Morten, G., 17–18
multicultural perspective, 58–9

nature, people's relationship to, 45–6
negative other-presentation, 98
negative stereotyping, see stereotypes
'Negromachy', 11
noncontact cultures, 67, 107–8, 111
nondominant culture identity model,
        47–8, 52
nonprejudiced responses, 133–4
nonverbal communication, 2, 101–20,
        142–3
    and attitudes, 38

culture and, 74, 103–14
gesture, 114
high and low context, 103–4
impact of racism on self-presentation
    and impression management, 114–16
implications for practitioners, 116–20
kinesics, 104–7
nonverbal behaviours, 102–14
paralanguage, 112
posture, 113–14
proxemics, 110–12, 117–18
silence, 112–13
time, 109–10, 117
touching, 107–8, 111, 118
normative values, 37

Oakland Unified School District,
    California, 83, 85
overt racism, 40, 55

paralanguage, 112
    see also language
parallel relationships, 28, 31
paranoia, 138
    functional and cultural, 70–1
Parham, T.A., 16–17
Patois, 86–9
people of colour racial identity
    development, 18–19
people–nature relationship, 45–6
perception, 121–40
    attribution theory, 129–32
    and communication, 127–39
    definition, 121–2
    first impressions and persistence of
        perceptions, 128–9
    stereotypes and interethnic
        communication, 132–9
    see also prejudice
personal space, 110–12, 117–18
pidginization, 81
police questioning, 106, 118
polychronic time, 109–10
Porter, L.A., 36–7
positive self-presentation, 98, 126
posture, 113–14
power
    and language, 79
    and racism, 38, 142
    social and prejudice, 48
power–distance (PD), 60–1, 73
power metaphor, 113
pre-encounter, 11–12, 24–5, 26
prejudice, 36

and communication, 126–7
definition, 123
racial identity models and, 123–5
    see also racism; stereotypes
progressive relationships, 29–30, 31
proxemics, 110–12, 117–18
proxy self, 71–2
pseudo-independence, 22–3, 48
psychiatry, 136–9
    assessment, 136–7
    treatment, 137–8
    see also mental health

'race', definition of, 4–5
racial identity development, 8–33, 141
    attitudes and communication patterns,
        24–7
    group process, 31–2
    Helms's interaction theory, 27–30
    and language, 99
    models of black racial identity, 9–19
    models and cultural values, 47–9,
        49–50, 53
    models and prejudice, 123–5
    models of white racial identity, 19–23
racism
    communication of attitudes, 36
    cultural, 39–40, 55–6
    impact on self-presentation and
        impression management, 114–16
    and interethnic communication, 38–42
    and language, 81, 87
    need for practitioners to address own,
        119–20, 141–2
    self-disclosure and, 69
    and white racial identity attitudes,
        124–5
    see also prejudice
racist language, 87, 96–8, 99
rage, 138–9
rationalization, 123
recycling, 16–17
regression, 15
regressive relationships, 30, 32
reintegration, 22, 48, 124–5
relationship-oriented people, 109–10
relationships, interpersonal, 45–6
resistance, 17–18, 47–8
Ridley, C.R., 40, 70–1
Rokeach, M., 34–5
role exchange, 95
'rolling the eyes', 105

Samovar, R.E., 36–7

schizophrenia, 71, 137
schools, 83, 88–9
Segal, U.A., 68–9
selective perception, 127–8, 132, 133
self-disclosure, 68–72
self-expression, 45–6
self-fulfilling stereotypes, 134
self-presentation
    impact of racism and discrimination,
        114–16
    positive, 98, 126
self-serving bias, 130
Semaj, L.T., 47
semantics, 81
sentence structures, 81
Shackman, J., 96
silence, 112–13
simplification of language, 93
slaves, 81, 82
Smitherman, G., 81
social attribution, 131–2
social identity theory, 77–8
social power, 48
social relations, 45–6
social services departments (SSDs), 93–4
somatization, 137
space, personal, 110–12, 117–18
speech
    accents/dialects, 79–80, 112
    paralanguage, 112
    style, 84
    see also language
stage-wise linear progression, 16
stagnation, 15, 16
Standard English, 79, 83
    bilingual issues, 90, 91
    Black English as a dialect of, 80
    rejection of, 82, 83, 87
    switching between Black English and,
        84–5
    see also language
stereotypes, 39
    definition, 122–3
    and interethnic communication, 132–9
    multicultural perspective, 59
    vocal, 79–80, 112
strengths-coping perspective, 142
stress, reducing, 93
Strodtbeck, F., 34, 36, 44–6, 51, 53
style switching, 84–5
Sue, D.W., 17–18
suspicion, 41–2, 70–1, 138
switching, code/style, 84–5
synergetic articulation and awareness, 18

task-oriented people, 109–10
teachers, 88–9, 130–1
teenagers, 83, 87
Thompson, J., 40, 95
time orientation
    culture and, 45–6
    and nonverbal communication, 109–10,
        117
touching, 67, 107–8, 111, 118
training, 118
    need to include black perspective, 59
Triandis, H., 62
trust
    mistrust, 41–2, 70, 119
    need to establish, 42, 119, 142–3
    'trying too hard', 135

uncertainty avoidance (UA), 61
unintentional racism, 40–1
United States, 68, 83
university faculty mentors, 42

value orientations model, 44–6, 50, 51, 53
values, 34–53, 142
    cultural, 37, 59–72, 142
    definition, 36–7
    developmental model, 49–50, 51, 52
    emotional and behavioural
        expressiveness, 67–8
    immediacy and expressiveness, 67
    individualism–collectivism dimension,
        43–4, 62–4, 111, 113
    and interethnic communication, 42–52
    level of context, 65–6, 103–4, 117
    masculinity, 64–5
    power–distance, 60–1, 73
    racial identity models and cultural,
        47–9, 49–50, 53
    racist language and, 97
    self-disclosure, 68–72
    uncertainty avoidance, 61
verbal communication, see language
'vibes', 115
visual behaviour, 74, 104–7

'white', language usage, 96–7
white racial identity development model,
    19–23
    and prejudice, 123–5

Yazdani, L., 75, 92, 93–4